SAN FRANCISCO

Architecture of the San Francisco Bay Area: A History & Guide

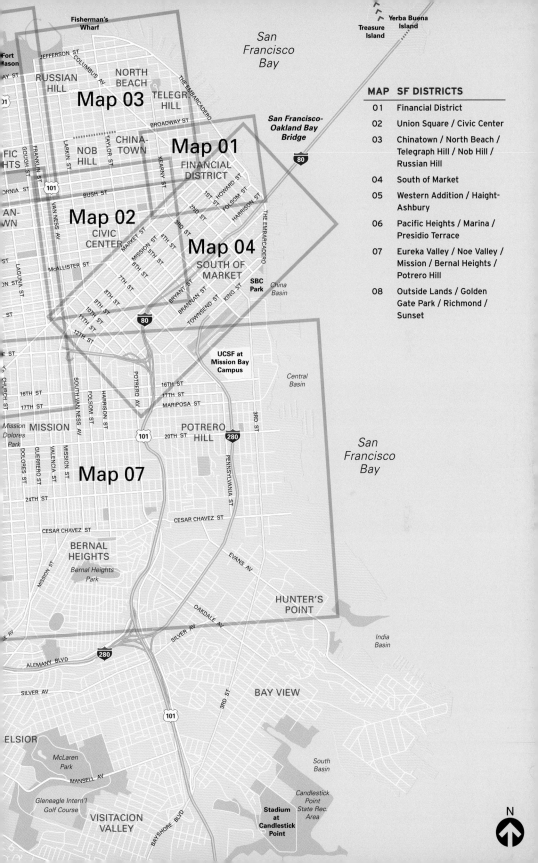

Mitchell Schwarzer is professor of art and architectural history at California College of the Arts, where he is also chair of the Department of Visual Studies. His previous books include *Zoomscape: Architecture in Motion and Media(2004)* and *German Architectural Theory and the Search for Modern Identity* (1995). He has written extensively for architectural magazines, academic journals,and edited books on architecture and the built environment. He lives in Oakland.

SAN FRANCISCO

Architecture of the San Francisco Bay Area: A History & Guide

Mitchell Schwarzer

William Stout Publishers
530 Greenwich Street
San Francisco, CA 94133

Author
Mitchell Schwarzer

Editor
Anthony Watts

Graphic Designer/ Cartographer
Betty Ho

Indexer
Ken DellaPenta

Architectural Illustrator
John G. Ellis

Thank you to the CED Environmental Design
Archives

ISBN: 0-9746214-5-5
LCCN: 2006928044

Cataloguing-in-Publication Data available from
the Library of Congress

Printed in China by Overseas Printing.

Acknowledgments

I want to begin by thanking my wife Marjorie Schwarzer for her ongoing encouragement and careful and repeated editing of this book. The book would not have been possible without the inspiration of my publisher Bill Stout. Likewise, its superb visual quality is largely the result of his efforts, alongside those of the cartographer and book designer, Betty Ho; the two principal photographers, Pad McLaughlin and John Santoro; and the creator of the drawings, John Ellis.

Many individuals have provided me with insights into the specific instances of Bay Area architecture. Among them, Pierluigi Serraino was extraordinarily generous with his research materials and contacts. I have also to thank Michael Lordi, the architecture librarian at California College of the Arts, and Elizabeth Byrne and the research librarians and archivists at the Environmental Design Library at the University of California, Berkeley. Several other writers and historians provided me with insights and feedback, and include Jim Chappell, Michael Corbett, J. Philip Gruen, Scott Hassler, William Littmann, Mabel Wilson, and Mary Wilson.

I would like to acknowledge the conversations I had with a great many architects and their provision of imagery of their works: Philip Banta, Cary Bernstein, Obie Bowman, Will Bruder, Douglas Burnham, Pierre de Meuron, Charles Dilworth, Steven Ehrlich, Laura Hartman, Anne Fougeron, Gensler, Craig Hartman, Richard Fernau, Jim Jennings, Owen Kennerly, Rem Koolhaas, Byron Kuth, Kava Massih, McCue Boone & Tomsick, Luke Ogrydziak, Peter Pfau, Stanley Saitowitz, Neil Schwartz, Cathy Simon, Richard Stacy, Craig Steely, Beverly Thorne, Bruce Tomb, and Todd Williams.

Finally, I would like to thank Mark Johnson, who published my book *Architecture and Design: SF* (San Francisco: The Understanding Business, 1998), upon which parts of the San Francisco listings are based.

Contents

HISTORY ~ Introduction

COLONIZATION

On the western edge of the North American continent, the San Francisco Bay Area was one of the last places of the New World to be discovered, conquered, and settled by Europeans. Although Spanish and British explorers—from Juan Rodriguez Cabrillo to Sebastián Vizcaino to James Cook—had charted the Pacific littoral for centuries, none mention the Bay, even though it is the finest natural harbor along California's 1264-mile coastline. Legend has it that the region's famous fogs prevented navigators from sighting the inland estuary. The first record of the Bay was made in 1769 by Gaspar de Portola, the newly appointed Spanish Governor of Baja California, but not from the vantage point of the Golden Gate. Portola and his men hiked from the San Mateo County coast in Pacifica to the top of Sweeny Ridge. From a promontory now known as the Discovery Spot, they saw to their astonishment a great expanse of water enclosed by mountains.

Over the subsequent 240 years, the lands surrounding the Bay have become the second largest metropolis on the Pacific Coast of North America. Yet the Bay Area wasn't built overnight. The first century of settlement proceeded in fits and starts. California was difficult to reach from Europe as well as the East Coast of the United States. One either took an eight-month sea voyage around Cape Horn (which could be slightly shortened by adding a land journey through the Panama Isthmus), or an equally lengthy and arduous land crossing over the great plains, the sage-brush deserts of the Great Basin and the formidable snow wall of the Sierra Nevada Mountains. In 1869, the completion of the transcontinental railway ended California's isolation. One could now reach it from the East in a little over a week's time. Later, with the advent of the Lincoln Highway in 1919, the Interstate Highway system in the 1950s, and jet airplanes in the 1960s, California became a central part of global routes of trade, tourism, and migration.

Initially, architectural development reflected the region's dependence on its distant centers of control: the Spanish Empire and then Mexico; Great Britain and its American colonial offspring. In 1776, Juan Bautista de Anza, a Franciscan priest, established the Spanish Presidio at the Golden Gate and Mission San Francisco de Assisi a few miles inland. In 1848, California became part of the United States and later that year the San Francisco Bay estuary leading up to Sacramento became the nexus for the Anglo-led Gold Rush. In each phase of development, from feudal agricultural settlement to entrepreneurial boomtown, important works of architecture were designed as imitations of monuments in the motherland—be it Mexico City or Boston. The preferred materials were adobe, for the Spanish-Mexican era, and wood, during Anglo-American times. Since knowledge of architectural theory and design was in short supply, compositions and decorations took on a loose and improvised appearance. Both Mission and Victorian design simplified and distorted the academic traditions of European classicism and to some extent, medievalism.

During the twentieth century, the earlier Spanish and Anglo architectural languages persisted. First, the Mission heritage bloomed into a broad Spanish-Italian Mediterranean revival, which crested in the 1920s, but has flowered once more since the 1980s. Then, beginning in the 1960s, San Francisco rekindled its love affair with Victorians. Other architectural languages have also taken root in the region's multi-ethnic soil. Most notably, after the Great Earthquake of 1906, Chinese architectural elements were affixed to commercial buildings in San Francisco's Chinatown in order to stimulate tourism. The result was one of

Alta Plaza in Pacific Heights

and thrown up by market forces. Much architecture has a Potemkin-like quality, where loud or restrained veneers conceal utilitarian boxes. The history of the urbanized landscape is one of sprawl, blanketing the flatlands along the Bay, marching up hillsides, snaking through canyons, and powdering interior valleys. While dense San Francisco is the center of gravity, the Bay Area has many centers that include: Oakland, Berkeley, San Jose, Palo Alto, Walnut Creek, Dublin-Pleasanton, San Rafael and Santa Rosa. The region has experienced incredible, ongoing growth to the point where the seven million residents of the nine Bay Area counties—San Francisco, Marin, Sonoma, Napa, Solano, Contra Costa, Alameda, San Mateo, Santa Clara—live in a megalopolis that unfolds into Sacramento, Stockton, Modesto and Monterey.

The frenzy to build brings up the irony of paving paradise in order to live in it. A spectacular climate and environment have long been the reasons for the Bay Area's real estate mania. It should be no wonder, then, that ruthless domination of the land has been tempered by a deep devotion to that "flashing and golden pageant of California" Walt Whitman celebrated. On one hand, the bounty of the land allowed a series of economic booms—mining, agriculture, transportation, finance, tourism, industry, high technology, lifestyle, and, most importantly, real estate. On the other hand, the fertile and glorious landscape inspired the nation's environmental movement. John Muir became the first president of the Sierra Club in 1892; the club henceforth put forth a radical agenda to conserve and preserve natural resources. In 1961, three East Bay women founded Save the Bay, in an effort to stop development on bay waters, leading to a 1965 referendum prohibiting new landfill. Today, the Bay Area boasts one of the largest acreages of parkland for a metropolitan area in the world. The East Bay Regional Park system, launched in 1934 with one property on 2100 acres, has grown to encompass almost 70 parks on almost 100,000 acres.

the world's first themed districts—the city created as much from ideas of fantasy as those of function.

TRANSFORMATION

In order to build their city, the new settlers remade the environment. European grasses suited to the tastes of Spanish cattle replaced native grasses. The golden hills of summertime came into existence; beforehand, native bunch grasses and shrubs kept their gray-green color year round. Waterways were polluted with effluent runoff from mining, and swathes of Bay were filled with leveled hills for portside development—since the late nineteenth century, the Bay has shrunk from an original 700 square miles to just over 400 square miles.[1] The region's magnificent forests, especially the lofty Redwood Groves, were chopped down to satisfy demand for quality lumber.

Construction, in the mild atmospheric climate and ferocious economic climate, has been quick, cheap, and temporary. From false-front main streets to tilt-up office parks, from row houses to ranch houses, buildings have been speculative

MODERNIZATION

From the Arts and Crafts Movement through Modernism, responding to nature has been one of the distinguishing themes of significant Bay Area architecture. The design of indoor/outdoor relationships has been a priority and architects have crafted innovative intermediate spaces that utilize glass, skylights, trellises, eaves, and cantilevers.

Landscape design that connects building and site has been influential around the world. All the while, the absorption with nature has been deeply mediated by technology. The influential photographs of Ansel Adams and Edward Weston recast nature's diversity as emblematic shapes and textures, setting a stage for abstract design. Likewise, the depiction of Northern California's cities, coast and forests, as seen in the films of Alfred Hitchcock and Clint Eastwood, elevated the region's landscape and cityscape into the realm of legend. Over the past couple of decades, scores of car commercials have highlighted the allure of driving the sinuous curves of Marin and Sonoma County's coastal ranges. Through photography, film, and television, Northern Californians have come to see their region as often and as profoundly as through direct exposure. How else can one explain the creation of the world's most sophisticated platform of indoor reality–the personal computer and Internet–in the stunningly beautiful Bay Area? A technological lens on landscape has long been part and parcel of the way people experience the region.

Cliff House in Ocean Beach

Another seeming incongruity of the Bay Area has been that in a place developed by large-scale forces, a culture of small-scale values has taken root. For a long time big projects were the norm. The few passes over the coastal ranges and the expanse of the Bay concentrated transportation projects—from nineteenth-century railroads to twentieth-century bridges and freeways and BART system. The annual six-month summer drought forced government to set aside great watersheds, and later dam and canal projects that brought water (into local reservoirs) from distances as far as the Sierra Nevada. Worries about attack from foreign powers, from the Spanish to the Japanese to the Soviets, led to the construction of a network of military bases. Perhaps most of all, the region's bounty and laissez-faire capitalism contributed to the emergence of spectacularly wealthy businessmen, who threw their money and power into mega-projects like hotels, skyscrapers, subdivisions, universities, museums, and a considerable number of hair-brain schemes that never came to pass–like damming much of San Francisco Bay or lopping off the top of San Bruno Mountain.

Over time these large-scale projects shifted from private initiative to government control. By the middle of the twentieth century, architects, landscape architects, and city planners became the expediters of a vast and rationalized development process. Great leaps were made locally in housing, school, and

Downtown Oakland

office design as well as regional planning. Manifold ideas and approaches were imported from the East Coast and abroad, especially Europe. California became a design laboratory for the future. On the hem of the Pacific, on lands that had not witnessed recorded cycles of conquest and ruin, radical solutions to old problems could be explored. At mid century, California architectural modernism seemed to have only the sky as it's ceiling.

Alas, the region's youthfulness could lead to insecurity as much as exuberance. As some citizens started to realize, modernist architectural projects were neither rational nor free from business interests. Beginning with the freeway revolt in 1959, and continuing through resistance to urban renewal and skyscrapers, neighborhood groups turned against mega-projects. In the home of the Free Speech Movement and Black Panther Party, protesting was second nature. The citizenry turned government around. City planning departments changed from instigators of development to gatekeepers. By the 1980s, the citizen reaction to large-scale modernism spilled over to distaste for avant-garde art and architecture. Paradoxically, politically progressive cities like Berkeley and San Francisco became hotbeds of traditionalist aesthetics. Human scale and fine-grain detail became the new buzzwords. Outrage at the ravages of capitalism led many residents to adopt a provincial urban outlook, premised less on the reality of the global

metropolis that they lived in than on a romance with a village community that they yearned for.

A COMPLEX METROPOLIS

As the above examples suggest, the history of Bay Area architecture cannot be described through simple, linear development. Rather, a back and forth movement between seemingly opposed poles–Anglo and Spanish, Boom and Conservation, Nature and Technology, Large and Small, Concentrated and Sprawling, Planned and Speculative, Cosmopolitan and Provincial, High Art and Vernacular–marks the region's architectural past. Out here on the perimeter, the elusive search for new beginnings has yielded a succession of entrepreneurial, radical, and reactionary impulses. The San Francisco Bay Area has always had an ephemeral quality that expresses the fact that this was an instant metropolis whose development has been fueled by constant demographic migration and economic innovation. It is a place of composites, of individualists and seekers of collective solutions, of capitalists and activists, of traditional and alternative families, and of a diverse ethnic intermixture from Europe, Asia, Africa, and Latin America. Not surprisingly, the construction of the region's physical identity has been a source of great creativity and conflict. Whether Gold Mountain to the Chinese or the new Pacific civilization to Europeans, whether labor capital of the Pacific or Summer of Love, whether a networked digital colossus or an organic gourmet utopia, the social dynamics of the San Francisco Bay Area have always uplifted and unsettled its architecture.

The Environment

OF FAULTS AND WATERS

Midway in the long Coastal Range of California, the mountains exhaust themselves and plunge to the sea. The breach was named the Golden Gate, no doubt to connect the Imperial ambitions of Anglo settlers with the Golden Horn at Roman

San Francisco Bay

View of Golden Gate Bridge from Marin

Constantinople. The topography of the region is even more precipitous than the meeting point of Europe and Asia, and is the most seismically active metropolitan area in the United States. The Bay Area rests astride a transform plate boundary, a junction between the crushing embrace of the North American and Pacific geological plates. While other segments of this boundary, north and south, generally contain a unified fault (the San Andreas), here the fault fractures into at least five fissures (including the Hayward and Calaveras faults). The pushing together and pulling apart of these faults over millions of years erected the geography of hills, valleys, and bay, all following a generally northwest/southeast direction.

Arrayed around the Bay are several mountain ranges, consisting largely of chunks of rock that once made up the ocean floor and were thrust skyward by plate tectonics. These oceanic crust rocks are known as the Franciscan complex. Atop this complex formation are thin sedimentary layers. Local bedrock consists of crumbly and thin-layered rocks not suit-

able for building; combined with steep slopes and winter storms, the geology makes a wonderful recipe for mudslides.

The Bay was formed by the action of these seismic faults, which pulled apart and depressed the land between them into a low valley. It is likely that an ancient river carried the waters from the Sierra Nevada through to the ocean in the general trajectory taken by today's Delta, Straights of Carquinez, San Francisco Bay, and Golden Gate. The saline quality of the Bay's waters results from the ongoing rise of ocean levels since the last retreat of glaciers that began over 10,000 years ago; at that time, there was no bay since the coastline was over 20 miles west of the Golden Gate.[2]

MEDITERRANEAN ON THE PACIFIC
At 37.5 degrees north latitude on the western side of a continent, the Bay Area is dominated by a Mediterranean climate and ocean winds. In wintertime, storms typically originating in the Gulf of Alaska pound the area. From roughly April until October, the Pacific High deflects storms

to the north, casting the region into drought. Powerful Pacific currents create pronounced maritime conditions for all coastal or bayside areas. In summertime, the region's infamous fog is pushed from the Pacific High and pulled in by the inland Central Valley heat. Mudflats, marshes and scrub vegetation—Lupine, Coyote Brush, Monkey Flower—once blanketed coastal areas. The reason for the dominance by soft chaparral was the constant presence of wind, fog, and sand. Most people have forgotten about the sand. At one time, as environmental writer Harold Gilliam explained, "the sand was borne by the wind eastward over the peninsula, encountered obstacles in the form of rocky ridges and outcrops, piled into drifts, swirled into eddies, rose up the seaward side of the higher hills, flowed profusely through gaps and passes."[3]

Behind the coastal ranges, the climate is far more equable—one of the most pleasant in North America. The mountain foothills boast grasslands and dense hard chaparral communities—Ceanothus, Manzanita, Toyon—on their south faces. Forests of Madrone, Laurel and Oak took root on the north faces and as well in sheltered canyons on the south slopes. Some of the tallest redwoods in California grew nearby the Bay's waters in riparian valleys benefiting in summertime from the dripping moisture of the Pacific fog.

Indian and Hispanic Period (Before 1848)

THE OHLONE AND COAST MIWOK

Prior to the arrival of the Spanish, the lands surrounding the Bay had close to 25,000 California Indian inhabitants who lived in close harmony with the land and waters, and had an intricate knowledge of local plants and animals with which to construct a culture. Ohlone tribelets extended south from San Francisco, and, in the East Bay, reached up to the Carquinez Strait and Delta. Coast Miwok

tribelets inhabited present-day Marin and Sonoma counties. The California Indians did not practice domesticated agriculture, either of plants or animals. Their technologies were rudimentary and resulted in temporary, or seasonal dwellings.

Between thirty and forty Ohlone villages once ringed the Bay, and hundreds more shell mounds, the nuclei of past settlements, have been found. Built over hundreds of years, Ohlone shell mounds could attain the height of a six-story building. The sites reveal a miscellany of cultural artifacts–tools, religious objects– and were commonly located at the foot of creeks as they emptied into the Bay. Writer Malcolm Margolin has reflected on what an Ohlone village might have looked like: "an immense, sprawling pile of shells, earth and ashes elevates the site above the surrounding marshland. On top of this mound stand some fifteen dome-shaped tule houses arranged around a plaza-like clearing. Scattered among them are smaller structures that look like huge baskets on stilts–granaries in which this year's supply of acorns are stored."[4] The Ohlone built both their boats and houses out of bent willow poles and tule reeds. The small houses were used only for sleeping and storage. A larger house, the sweat-house (or Temescal in Spanish) was the ceremonial center. Historical Ohlone petroglyphs and grinding rocks are preserved at the Chitactac-Adams County Park in Gilroy. A small Ohlone village has been reconstructed at the Coyote Hills Regional Park in Fremont.

Coast Miwok villages were strung along the Bay, inland waterways, and inlets of the Pacific Ocean. Their conical houses (kotkas) were built over a circular depression in the ground. In addition to tule reeds, redwood bark slabs were also fastened to the branched frame. A hole in the top would act as an outlet for smoke. Larger roundhouses were used for community assembly and ceremony, and sweatlodges (or lammas) accommodated spiritual and physical cleansing. Coast Miwok used kitchen rocks, a boulder full of little holes or pockets, to pound acorns, their basic food source. Two facsimiles of Miwok villages have been constructed in Marin: one at Kule Loklo in the Point Reyes National Seashore; the other at Olompali State Historic Park in Novato.

FURTHEST REACHES OF THE SPANISH EMPIRE

Spanish settlement of Alta (or upper) California proceeded from south to north, extending the Royal Road, El Camino Real, which links the 17 Missions established earlier by the Dominicans and Jesuits in Baja (or lower) California. All in all, from 1769 to 1823, 21 missions were built from San Diego to Sonoma; three presidios and three pueblos were also founded. The five northernmost missions were: Mission Santa Clara de Asis (1777); Mission San Jose de Guadalupe (1797); Mission San Francisco de Asis (1776); Mission San Rafael Archangel (1817); and Mission San Francisco Solano in Sonoma (1823). Additionally, in 1776, a presidio, or military fort, was set up at the southern side of the Golden Gate. San Jose was the first pueblo, or civilian town, of Alta California, founded in 1777 as a farming community. During this period, productive lands were divided up into scores of vast grazing tracts, or ranchos.

The Spanish brought a feudal system of agriculture and light industry to the lands of the Ohlone and Coast Miwok. They also considered it their duty to bring Catholicism to the heathen Indians. The harsh new order brought widespread disease and death to the Indian communities, resulting in the catastrophic decline of their population and culture. The condition of California Indians only worsened after the Gold Rush.

Adobe bricks were the basis of construction for Spanish buildings.[5] Adobe bricks are made from heavy, wet clay bonded by an admixture of straw, manure, and occasional fragments of tile or brick. They are sun dried within wooden molds. Adobe construction had long suited building needs in the arid Southwest. Even in the forested Bay Area, adobe was favored due to the lack of

Peralta Adobe in San Jose

adequate tools and technology for timber construction. Un-reinforced adobe buildings mandate extra-thick walls–often between three and eight feet–that provide excellent insulation. Window openings were kept to a minimum and rooms were rather narrow. The low-strength nature of adobe construction meant that walls rarely exceeded two stories. For taller buildings, buttresses were added for stability.

The architecture of Franciscan missions and settlements followed Spanish traditions. A residence was grouped around a small patio or courtyard, part of which was often enclosed by a veranda that served as the center of family life. For two-story buildings, a covered porch was extended along at least one side. Roofs were kept lightweight, thatched from tree branches or tule reeds, or built out of wooden supports and planks. On the better residences, walls were covered by mud plaster and whitewashed. Extant adobe houses provide clues as to the centers of Spanish-Mexican culture, and are located in: Concord, El Cerrito, Orinda, Martinez, Novato, Petaluma, Pleasanton, Pacifica, San Pablo, San Jose, Santa Clara, and Sonoma.

For important public buildings, such as the Missions, all aspects of construction were elaborated. Courtyards grew into large quadrangles, graced by fountains and fruit trees, and framed by massive arcades. From the outside, high walls and occasional towers called attention to the religious centers. Another feature was the customary pediment raised over the entrance and supported by real or painted columns. Inside, naves were narrow and plain; decorations were painted atop the plaster walls. The magnificent Spanish ornamental traditions of the churrigueresque or plateresque never made it to California, and with the exception of Mission Dolores in San Francisco, the northern missions are far less elaborate than those further to the south. Still, the missions' distinctive features—broad, unrelieved walls, arcades, bell towers, low-sheltering roofs covered in heavy tile–formed the basis for an enduring (and unchanging) building tradition. The buildings sheltered their inhabitants from more than just cold, wind, and rain. They demonstrated Catholic Spain's permanence in the American wilderness. The predictable missions, presidios, and pueblos were a bulwark against the encroachments of Northern European capitalism, science and settlers.

MEXICAN INTERLUDE
In Alta California the Spanish order did not last long. Mexico won its independence from Spain in 1821. In order to secure sparsely settled Alta California, Anglo settlers were permitted residence. In the 1830s, these Anglo-Americans founded the future commercial center of San Francisco alongside Yerba Buena Cove (between Rincon and Clark points), the closest sheltered anchorage to the Golden Gate. The small town had a smattering of adobe and frame buildings, and was dominated by the wrap-around porches and Monterey-style pyramidal roof of merchant William Leidesdorff's cottage.[6] Alas, this Mexican-Anglo town did not last long either.

The Victorian Era (1848-1900)

THE GOLD RUSH
"San Francisco is eastern, a creation of the Gold Rush, colonized by sea, Yankee architecture and Yankee attitudes boated around the Horn and grafted onto the

Bay,"[7] wrote novelist John Gregory Dunne. The announcement that gold had been discovered in the Sierra foothills in 1848 abruptly ended California's provincialism and hastened its integration into the American and world economies. Overnight the sleepy village alongside Yerba Buena Cove blasted off into one of history's greatest boomtowns. The population soared from 450 in 1847 to 40,000 in 1850. By 1865, well over 100,000 persons from every corner of the earth lived in the fledgling city. Since most people and supplies arrived by sea, San Francisco became the crucial junction between the Mother Lode and a world ravenous for gold.

San Francisco's action was the waterfront. From Black Point (now Fort Mason) to Hunter's Point, the shoreline was devoted to the maritime trade of clipper ships and then steamships, threaded with railways, piers, and public warehouses. The harbor functioned as the root system for the developing branches of urban land, and horse-drawn streetcars began operating on the Market Street Railroad. Oakland and Berkeley similarly developed from the shoreline inland. In 1853, a grid was laid out for Oakland, centered on a line pointing inland–Broadway–from the estuary. Berkeley's earliest settlement was Jacob's landing, near the present-day junction of Delaware Street and San Pablo Avenue. From these and other points ferries circumnavigated the Bay and ran to Sacramento and the

Dolores Street Cottages

nearby Mother Lode. The early water links became the basis for a transportation structure lasting well into the twentieth century.

When the transcontinental railroad was completed in 1869, it terminated in Oakland and ferries were needed to complete the trip to San Francisco. Over the years a number of ferry slips were extended deep into the Bay from Oakland, Alameda, and Berkeley. The largest was the Oakland Mole, built in 1879, and stretching one and a quarter miles into the Bay. It boasted an impressive wood, steel and glass shed with twelve tracks connecting to the ferry slip.

Gold Rush San Franciscans threw up ramshackle architecture. Hordes of fortune hunters made do with wooden shanties, lean-tos, and canvas tents. Abandoned ships were salvaged for building. To alleviate the housing shortage, some ships came loaded with prefabricated dwellings, no-frills wooden structures that were called Boston Houses to indicate their origin. A few corrugated iron buildings were imported, although they proved to have horrible climate control. Gradually permanent frame buildings, copies of architecture back east, were erected, as attested by the rapid establishment of sawmills and widespread logging. Northern California was blessed with immense redwood, fir, cedar and pine forests. There weren't nearby deposits of hardy stone, such as limestone and granite. Given the actuality of earthquakes, such as the large trembler of 1868, wooden construction made sense anyhow. Over time, the lumber industry unleashed an eerie landscape of bald hillsides where redwood forests once stood. Below arose grid cities constructed of redwood boards.[8] As if by divine retribution, this "urban forest" burned several times.

"San Francisco," architect William Wurster once commented, "is a city that has vertical chaos and horizontal order." Because of the steep hills, buildings "tumbled raggedly down to meet the Bay in a confused vague mass of roofs,

Victorian Row

cornices, cupolas, and chimneys."[9] Yet unlike other cities that must navigate mountains, San Francisco's streets did not follow topographical contours. Instead, gridiron platting imposed an exacting order on the peninsula's rugged landscape. In 1836, the first ordering of land had taken place.[10] Drawn by Jean Vioget, a Swiss engineer, it consisted of nine blocks centered on a plaza (Portsmouth Square)—planning regulations deriving from the Spanish *Law of the Indies*. Vioget's survey called for blocks to measure 275 feet by 412 feet; most street widths were 69 feet. The survey became the basis for several extensions that by 1855 reached all the way to what is now First Avenue in the Richmond District. In 1847, Jasper O'Farrell's survey platted streets south of Market Street at a 45 degree angle from those north of Market, and adopted outrageously large blocks: 550 feet by 825 feet. O'Farrell based the orientation of the South of Market survey on the route of the Plank Road between Yerba Buena Cove and the Mission. It is likely that he envisioned these large blocks for agriculture. O'Farrell also laid out a 125-foot wide street (Market) that separated the two grids and stretched from the mid-point of Yerba Buena Cove to a point below Twin Peaks. While the triangular and trapezoidal blocks along Market Street's northern edge have encouraged innovative architecture, the lack of provision for north-south streets has led to lingering transportation problems.

DISPLAYING NEW WEALTH

In part because of the runaway, topsy-turvy economy, few substantial public buildings were built at first. Granted, the gold-rush economy required a stock exchange, banks, insurance agencies, commercial businesses, and other industries. Yet these needs were met with cheap wood-frame structures. In 1853, Gordon Cummings erected the four-story Montgomery Block, supported by two-foot thick brick walls. For a time, San Francisco's first substantial edifice operated as its commercial heart. Hotels were the next major building endeavor. In 1875, not long after the Comstock silver strike in Nevada, William Ralston built the grandest–the seven-story, 755-room Palace Hotel. Although the city could barely support such a lavish enterprise, baronial architecture was the order of the day. San Francisco's instant millionaires wanted everything money could buy. They measured the importance of their buildings in room counts, sugary decorations, and daring technologies.

One technological invention, developed from prototypes in the mines, was the cable car. In 1874, Andrew Hallidie invented a form of transit for hills too steep for horse-drawn omnibuses. Atop Nob Hill, the millionaires built their Valhalla. The Big Four of railroad fame–Charles Crocker, Mark Hopkins, Leland Stanford, Collis Huntington—erected highly-visible wooden mansions, each trying to outdo the other in grandiosity,

each crowding the sky with turrets and towers. These mansions were temples to individual gain as well as the protocols of power. Architecture transformed from a marker of collective stability, as in Spanish America, into a sign of personal advancement and success.

In the years that followed, other millionaires tossed up other mansions festooned with other trophies. They blanketed hallways and rooms with "Europe's finest," the trappings worthy of royalty. Shielded by fences, walls, drapes, and servants, the business elite carried out parlor rituals and stilted exercises in social hierarchy. "That Victorian hearths and ornamentals took on something of the appearance of altars does not seem accidental," wrote architectural historian Randolph Delhanty.[11]

Outside, estate gardeners cultivated broad lawns and necklaces of exotic plant species. Alongside palms, the genus Araucaria was especially favored. Originating in Australia and South America, the Bunya Bunya and Monkey-Puzzle trees brought a startling, almost Jurassic look to an estate. The trees, which had to be transported by sea in special containers, were as much a sign of wealth as any carved marble fireplace or tall tower. Especially in the East Bay, the locations of estates, both extant and extinct, can still be discerned by the sighting of a spiky Araucaria tree on the horizon.

The great civic and arboreal endeavor of the times was Golden Gate Park. In the 1860s, Frederick Law Olmsted was asked to present a plan for a large city park in San Francisco. His recommendation for planting the park with drought-tolerant Mediterranean plants and placing it in the valley presently occupied by Van Ness Avenue was not followed. The city fathers, accustomed to grand and imprudent schemes, wanted to attract development to the barren Outside Lands in the western part of the city. William Hammond Hall, an engineer, was given the seemingly impossible task of creating a lush, English-style park atop the sand

Mountain View Cemetery in Oakland

Golden Gate Park

dunes. During the 1870s, through an ingenious series of successive plantings, Hall
and his assistant John McLaren were able
to hold back the wind, stabilize the dunes,
and establish tall trees and verdant meadows. An Old England by the Pacific arose,
strangely done up in Monterey Pine,
Monterey Cypress, and Eucalyptus trees.

Perhaps the most noteworthy architectural attraction of the nineteenth century was the burgeoning city itself, its
wooden buildings rising up from sand and
bare rock, marching in close ranks with
the grids up and down the hills. This phenomenon was captured in a remarkable
panorama photographed by Eadweard
Muybridge in 1878. From the unfinished
site of the Mark Hopkins Mansion atop
Nob Hill, Muybridge took a 360-degree
view of the emerging city in thirteen
continuous panels. Looking at the panorama, it is easy to notice that forbidding
mountains and open sea surrounded San
Francisco. This was truly a city rising out
of the wilderness. Muybridge's panorama
also shows that urban development was
dense, especially by the standards of
Western America. Most buildings were
small—the standard lot being 25 by 100
feet. Row houses occupied the full width
of the narrow parcels, and front-yard
setbacks were negligible. Balloon-frame
construction methods–replacing mortised
beams and fittings with lightweight two
by four inch studs placed close together—
were favored by builders like William
Hollis or Fernando Nelson because of

the abundance of lumber and the lack of
skilled craftsmen. Inside, plans were just
as standardized as construction. Rooms
were strung one after the other, either in
single- or double-loaded corridors.

A FRENZY OF ORNAMENT

Initially, wood-frame buildings of the
Classic Revival Period (1848 – 1865) were
noted for their simplicity of ornament
and severity of line. A gabled roof, sometimes hidden by a false front, topped the
one or two-story boxes. Windows and
doors were detailed with hood moldings, floral carvings, and dentils. Eaves
were underlain with brackets. There were
occasional Gothic Revival buildings as
well, used mainly for churches and synagogues.

During the post-Civil War boom and
Comstock Silver Rush, everyday architecture turned up the decorative heat,
resulting in the region's most famous
residential type, the Victorian. Not just
on Nob Hill, but throughout the urbanized core a fantastical cityscape cropped
up. Collectively, Bay Area Victorians
are among the most richly ornamented
buildings of nineteenth-century America.
Ornament substituted for aesthetic
sophistication in the fast-growing, frontier metropolis. In remote California, new
architectural ideas came from books,
especially the hundreds of pattern books
that arrived on the ships. The populist
pattern books tried to accomplish two
contradictory goals. First, building upon
classical treatises, they attempted to
codify architectural knowledge by illus-
trating the lasting masterworks of the
past. California architecture thus sought
to measure up to the standards of Europe
and the East Coast. Even more importantly, though, the pattern books, like
modern magazines, published the newest
styles. After all, they were aimed not only
at builders but also at homebuyers. Their
drawings, like those in fashion magazines,
brought the latest trends to consumers.
The firm of Samuel and Joseph Newsom
epitomized this attitude in architectural
imaging. Designers of the famed Carson

Edwardian Row

Mansion in Eureka, they worked first from Oakland and then San Francisco, designing opulent, picturesque Victorians. Over the years, their works could be read like annual fashion trends, the latest and quickly dated efforts to capture a client's social aspirations of living life on the design forefront.[12]

The Victorian fondness for ornament was also a reaction to the sculptural possibilities of wooden construction. Inexpensive pre-sawn Redwood and Douglas Fir construction was conducive to complex massing (with gables or turrets) while wooden sheathing allowed for proliferating surface patterns. Wooden decoration often simulated stone or masonry detailing, entangling the classical orders in yet another play of illusions. Softwood corner quoins became imitations of masonry reinforcements; wooden columns, pilasters and other embellishments were carved in the shape and proportions of stone originals. The most conspicuous act of imitation was the widespread painting of wooden row houses in shades of gray reminiscent of limestone or granite. In the space of a couple of generations, San Franciscans cut down one of the greatest forests on earth, rapidly built a wooden city, and tried to pass that city off as a lasting work of stone.

Many Victorian styles were popular between 1865 and 1900. The earliest of these were the Italianates (1865–1880), whose three-windowed flat fronts featured hooded and bracketed doors and windows. Later Italianates were noted for their slanted and projecting stack of tall arched windows—the onset of the bay window. "Because the bay window admirably met the demands of light, convenience, space, and sanitation," wrote architectural historian Harold Kirker, "every architectural style domesticated on the West Coast was altered to accommodate it."[13]

From the late 1870s to 1890, the Stick Eastlake style transformed the rounded Italianate massing into a composition of right-angles, taller proportions, and, of course, diagonal "stickwork," flat narrow boards nailed to the clapboard skin. Less self-effacing than their predecessors, Stick houses were ornamented with spindles, curved brackets, grooved moldings and incised sunrays and starbursts. False fronts extend the desired vertical proportions.

The culmination of the Victorian era was the Queen Anne, which propered during the late 1880s and 1890s. A vibrantly picturesque composition, Queen Annes returned to curvilinear form but through asymmetry and complex massing. Round corner towers with peaked witch's caps intersect steep gables, recessed upper balconies replete with balustrades tower over front porches trimmed with arched latticework. In addition to the customary Victorian use of horizontal lap siding, shaped shingles, foliated plasterwork, fish-scale shingle patterns, paneled friezes, and stained glass gave this style an extravagance of erratic desires.

The 1890s also ushered in a Georgian or Colonial Revival, and a turn to more restrained decoration. Likewise, between 1906 and 1915, the Edwardian style brought with it a calmer use of ornament, even though corner buildings often have lavish curvilinear windows. Wooden Edwardians, whether on single lots or on larger double-and-triple lots, are the most representative house type of San Francisco, and are also found throughout Oakland.

Industrial Landscape

REINFORCED CONCRETE

The most important architectural development of the Victorian era wasn't in the field of design, but in engineering. Beginning with San Francisco's Arctic Oil Works Building of 1884, engineer Ernest Ransome developed a groundbreaking building method—reinforced concrete technology. Ransome added twisted, square iron rods to poured concrete floors, walls or other building members, greatly strengthening their capacity to carry loads. Henceforth, architects would be able to design buildings and bridges of far greater heights and spans. Ransome went on to refine the new technology at San Francisco's Alvord Lake Bridge (1889) and the Junior Museum at Stanford University (1894) as well as for industrial buildings in San Francisco, Alameda and Port Costa.[14] His pioneering efforts with reinforced concrete count as one of the milestones of American building practice.

Eclecticism (1890–1935)

BEAUX ARTS AND THE CITY BEAUTIFUL

In 1893, the World's Columbian Exposition opened in Chicago. The white city on the shores of Lake Michigan showed the sumptuous possibilities of French Beaux Arts composition and decoration. The nation was enthralled, and the City Beautiful Era began. In San Francisco, businessmen looked to Chicago and began to argue for substantial civic monuments. Michael de Young, publisher of the *San Francisco Chronicle,* salvaged parts of the Chicago Fair and erected them in Golden Gate Park. The ensuing 1894 California Midwinter International Exposition was a design smorgasbord. Among the famous structures were a 260-foot Electric Tower—a very loose recreation of the Eiffel Tower—and the Fine Arts Building, which afterward became the first version of the de Young Museum. As described by architectural historian David Gebhard, for the Fine Arts Building "a pyramid or at least something approaching it has been plopped down on a pylon, and the pylon has been disconcertedly broken by strange stubby columns. Simply put, the building was an abridged encyclopedia of all the motifs which in the popular mind were thought to typify the ancient mysterious architecture of Egypt."[15] San Franciscans wanted its architecture to measure up with the great world cities. But as of yet it did not.

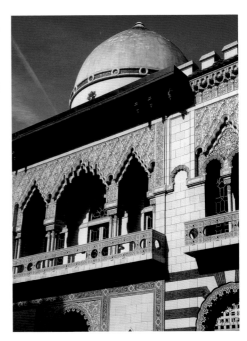

Alcazar Theater

Ferry Terminal Proposal (Polk)

The Chicago and San Francisco fairs did help launch the Mission Revival: the first stylistic revival linked to California's past. Instigated by the writings of Helen Hunt Jackson, especially the 1884 novel *Ramona*, interest had been brewing for some time in the forgotten, rumpled Spanish missions of California. An older and mysterious California beckoned the state's growing population. A. Page Brown's California State Building at the Chicago fair, a mixture of Richardsonian Romanesque and Mission Revival, rekindled that interest in a palpable, architectural direction. Locally, a Mission Revival vocabulary of stucco walls, round arches, red tile roofs, and parapets with scalloped arches became popular, especially for train stations. In 1894, the Southern Pacific Railroad unveiled a Mission Revival station in Burlingame. Depots in Berkeley and Petaluma followed.

A more important work catalyzed in part by the Mission Revival was Leland Stanford's grand scheme for a college in Palo Alto. It would become Stanford University. In the late 1880s, Olmsted was hired to plan a long entrance drive from downtown Palo Alto that would bore through a lush arboretum and culminate at the heart of the future campus. Within a few years, Palm Drive terminated in a weighty Romanesque Quadrangle, built during the 1890s to the designs of Boston architects Shepley, Rutan, & Coolidge. California received its first major work of architecture designed by a prominent East Coast firm. Toward the end of the century, in 1898, an international competition was held, at the behest of Phoebe Hearst and Bernard Maybeck, to design a similarly monumental core for the University of California campus in Berkeley. The plan was eventually awarded to John Galen Howard, who created, over the next twenty years, a great axis from the hillside campus toward the Golden Gate. By the early twentieth century interest in the Mission Revival and Richardsonian Romanesque had waned, and Howard ended up lining his axis with weighty Beaux-Arts buildings clad in light-gray granite and topped by red tiles.

Grandiose schemes for San Francisco were harder to realize. In 1897, Willis Polk proposed a colonnade and triumphal arch that would create a hemispherical plaza in front of San Francisco's Ferry Building. It never got built. Practical transportation concerns trumped the static set piece. The boldest proposal of them all was unveiled in 1905 when Chicago architect Daniel Burnham envisioned an Imperial city plan for San Francisco. Inspired by Baron Georges Haussmann's recent remaking of Paris, Burnham grafted numerous diagonal boulevards, ring roads, public squares, and large parks onto the city's grids.

A year later, in 1906, an 8.1 earthquake centered in Tomales Bay rocked the entire Bay Area. During the ensuing three days of fire, over four square miles of inner San Francisco burned, some 512 blocks. Burnham came immediately to San Francisco. Expectations for implementing his plan of monumental axes were initially high. But property owners clamored to rebuild as quickly as possible. Pragmatic interests prevailed, and the grids were rebuilt where they had been. The year of the earthquake, Charles Mulford Robinson, one of the principal exponents of the City Beautiful Movement, proposed a comprehensive plan for parks and park drives in the foothills of Oakland.[16] Again, hardly any of the ambitious recommendations were acted upon.

The great exception to the prevailing business climate was the development of a Beaux-Arts Civic Center for San Francisco a few years later. Beginning in 1913, gray-granite buildings with classical details began to rise around a formal plaza. Bakewell & Brown's City Hall, finished in 1915, was the tallest and most impressive building west of the Mississippi. Its towering dome could have housed a state (or even national) capitol. Not coincidentally, that same year, the Panama-Pacific International Exhibition was held along the shores of the Bay in what later became the Marina district. Unlike Civic Center's monochrome formality, designer Jules Guerin's palette of Mediterranean colors emanating from the arid California landscape adorned a make-believe city of fabulous towers and courts. Celebrating the opening of the Panama Canal, the fair sought to impress the world with the myths of California. The most extraordinary attractions were the 435-foot Tower of Jewels, the Court of the Universe, and the Arch of the Nations.

Although the fair was up for less than a year, its vision of Mediterranean classicism was captivating for the increasingly sophisticated city. The Great Seawall, completed in the 1920s, was the offspring of both Civic Center and the P.P.I.E. fair. The most far-reaching of the city's landfill operations, the Great Seawall featured 46 new piers and terminals as well as a belt railroad. It replaced a serrated edge of wharves and piers with a smooth curve and a 200-foot wide harbor side boulevard, the Embarcadero. Its pier bulkheads formed a rhythmic sequence of immense arches and pediments; the design, stretching almost two miles, was classical north of Market Street and scalloped Mediterranean to the south. San Francisco finally had its grand boulevard, just not within the city, but along the working waterfront.

The succession of public projects was spurred by the development of architectural journalism and education. There had been architectural publishing in San Francisco since the start of *California Architect and Building News* in 1880. In 1905, one of the most important architectural magazines in California's history was launched. Based in San Francisco, the *Architect and Engineer,* long edited by B.J. Cahill, would comprehensively cover the State until 1961.[17]

Architectural education also made great strides. Throughout the nineteenth century most local architects were trained in the apprenticeship method. With the passage of time, however, increasing numbers of Americans began to study at architecture schools, either the Paris Ecole des Beaux Arts, the London Royal Academy, or East Coast schools like MIT and Columbia University. Formal architectural education began at the University of California, Berkeley in 1903. The architecture school at Berkeley was headed by John Galen Howard until 1927, and followed a Beaux Arts model of education based on copying classical exemplars–from antiquity, Early Modern Europe, and the recent classicist past, and composing modern functions within their framework. French Beaux-Arts pedagogy continued under Warren Perry, Howard's protégé, until 1950.

THE ARTS AND CRAFTS MOVEMENT

Not all architects followed the Beaux Art model at the turn of the century. In the late 1890s, a group of Berkeley women founded the Hillside Club with the express purpose of protecting their north side neighborhood from rampant and unsightly development. Men were allowed to join a few years later, and several prominent architects–among them Bernard Maybeck and Howard–became members. As exemplified by the Hillside Club building, designed by Maybeck in 1906, this Northern California offshoot of the English Arts and Crafts Movement promoted the values of rusticity, simplicity, and fidelity to local materials and lifestyle. English Arts and Crafts ideology borrowed much more strongly from the Middle Ages than from Classical Antiquity. Instead of symmetry, designers favored informality. Instead of geometric severity, picturesque silhouettes were commonplace. The making of a building became an important ingredient in its visual presentation; structure must not be hidden.

Architects associated with the Arts and Crafts Movement were critical of Victorian design. In the essay "The Western Addition" (1893), Willis Polk lambasted that district's rampant mass-produced, crazy visual effects as an "architectural nightmare conceived in a religion of terror and produced by the artistic anarchists who are continually seeking to do something great, without any previous experience or preparation for their work. The real estate speculators, speculative contractors, and disappointed carpenters who have passed themselves off on an indulgent public as architects

all over the country, seem to have found their last refuge in San Francisco."[18]

The publication of Charles Keeler's *The Simple Home* in 1904 lent theoretical sophistication to the nascent artistic movement. Keeler was a naturalist with a keen interest in coming up with a way of designing buildings in harmony with the California landscape. Like Polk and other followers of the Arts and Crafts Movement, he disdained the placeless products of Victorian architecture. Keeler recommended the liberation of buildings from arbitrary and superficial ornaments, the panoply of imitative turrets, spires and corbels, the wallpapered walls, and the cracking veneer. He wrote: "In the simple home all is quiet in effect, restrained in tone, yet natural and joyous in its frank use of unadorned material. Harmony of line and balance of proportion is not obscured by meaningless ornamentation; harmony of color is not marred by violent contrasts. Much of the construction shows, and therefore good workmanship is required and the craft of the carpenter is restored to its old-time dignity."[19]

Already during the 1890s, architects like Maybeck, Polk, and Ernest Coxhead had begun to look to their own surroundings for a naturalistic alternative. Northern California's climate demanded a certain type of building. The roofs must shed rain, but not snow; windows must let in all the sunlight possible. Over the course of many decades, local architects would experiment with unpainted exterior redwood shingles and interior paneling, dramatic roof gables extending as wide eaves, exposed ceiling rafters, crafted wooden joinery, and extensions of interior space through wooden trellises and patios. An architecture was created that would embody the Bay Area's informality, its indoor-outdoor lifestyle, and its ties to the panorama of nature.

These architects did not abandon, however, the historic styles. America's succession of styles–from Greek to Gothic to Romanesque, and so on–had turned into an eclectic carnival by the 1880s. Led by the firm of McKim, Mead and White, this free wheeling method of composition married the two great European traditions, rule-bound classicism and the medieval picturesque. While historicist in surface ornament, East Coast academic eclecticism also merged tradition with contemporary needs and building methods as well as individual taste. "The Arts and Crafts Movement was more a complement than a counterforce to academic eclecticism," wrote architectural historian Richard Longstreth. "Both movements were reform efforts, calling for a return to simplicity in expression, honesty in materials, beauty that was an outgrowth of practical needs, unity between architecture and the allied arts, and a harmonious order in the environment."[20]

Northern California architects were more catholic in their choices and more radical in their inventions than their East Coast counterparts. Theoretical rules and standards of propriety didn't mean as much. Nor did the gulf of culture or time that separated the different styles. Within a classical plan, Japanese carpentry could turn up next to Romanesque carving. Architects raided the storerooms of history. Indeed, "with their synthesis of historic fragments from a wide variety of times and places, with their manipulation of expected scale, their elaborately sculptural spatial concepts, their frequent experiments (both esthetic and structural), and their use of seemingly contradictory formal elements, they are not simple productions in any way," wrote the architect John Beach about the local architectural scene.[21]

In 1894, Arthur Page Brown produced the singular Church of the New Jerusalem in San Francisco, a simple chapel to complement Keeler's *The Simple House*. The small sanctuary is dramatically Californian. Unfinished madrone logs, their redness and peels still evident, form the roof beams. A red tile roof signals the Mission past. By contrast, Coxhead's numerous houses and churches are deeply indebted to the Shingle Style as well as English church design. But if they seem as if they could be located elsewhere, local building materials and a particularly free play with ornament cement them to the region. Polk too used shingles, dormers, and other Arts and Crafts insignia for many of his early works. Later, though, he also designed in the classical style and his

Julia Morgan Theater in Berkeley

Claremont Hotel in Berkeley

THE AGE OF INDUSTRY AND MECHANIZED TRANSPORT

From the 1890s to the 1920s, transportation innovations opened considerable lands for development, shifted the geography of land uses, and influenced the creation of new building types. Until this point, inner San Francisco and Oakland had contained a rich mix of warehouses, industry, high-end retail establishments, and residences. An expanded railroad network and new port facilities now shifted industry away from the downtowns toward undeveloped land. In San Francisco, heavy industry relocated along the bay front south of China Basin. More heavy industry moved to the shores of the East Bay.

Suburbanization affected commerce and residences too. Around 1890, trolleys with electric traction motors replaced horses, and streetcars and cable cars radiated out from the waterfront's ferry and steamship slips. (At its peak, 43 boats crossed the Bay daily, carrying 60,000 passengers). End stations and transfer points along the trolley lines became important retail and apartment districts. High-end residential development moved uphill–to Pacific Heights in San Francisco, to Piedmont and the Claremont district in the East Bay–while the flatlands become working class–the Mission, North Oakland. Marin County developed through ferry service with San Francisco, and the Northwestern Pacific Railroad that began in Sausalito and ran

most important building is proto modern. For the Hallidie Building in San Francisco, Polk designed what may be the world's first glass curtain wall. Julia Morgan too designed in many stylistic modes and occasionally saw no problem in mixing them together, as in the 1930s castle she built for William Randolph Hearst at San Simeon.

Maybeck was a sculptor of form who freely took from history to shape the present and from the ends of the earth to shape the region. "His plans broke with precedent to create a background for what we now consider modern living," said architectural critic Esther McCoy. "He was ingenious in solving the problems of bringing light into his buildings. He linked living areas to gardens. He used materials directly and with craftsmanship, while taking full advantage of technology. He created new and personal forms that arose naturally out of plan."[22] Maybeck's early masterpiece on the Berkeley campus, Hearst Hall (1899), which burned down in 1922, illustrated eclectic massing and ornament alongside innovative structure. The massive edifice consisted of an entry topped by a pediment, a lancet-arched hall with six bays, and a pair of square pavilions with hipped roofs. If its composition was bizarre, its construction via sections of movable, easily reassembled units was pioneering.[23]

Retail street in Oakland

Spanish style home

Magellan stairs

up to Humboldt County. The peninsula's development was catalyzed by the double tracking of the Southern Pacific line between San Francisco and San Jose in 1900.

In San Francisco, the Outside Lands became accessible to streetcar development with the opening of the Twin Peaks tunnel in 1917 and the Sunset tunnel in 1928. Row-house developers quickly filled the desolate sands. Between 1920 and 1945, the Gellert Brothers development company constructed close to 20,000 houses. Those same years, Henry Doelger built over 25,000 small homes in the Sunset District. The streets of the district have since been called the "White Cliffs of Doelger." In the East Bay, the Oakland Transit Company, later known as the Key System, ran its streetcars from the Oakland Mole through the flatlands and up into the hills. Housing tracts sprouted like wildfires.

STYLES OF THE RUSTIC SUBURB

Early twentieth-century tastes in housing were toned down as compared to their Victorian predecessors. As architectural historian Gwendolyn Wright noted, builders around the nation now opted for practicality. Houses changed "from an exuberant, highly personalized display of irregular shapes, picturesque contrasts and varieties of ornament, supposedly symbolizing the uniqueness of the family, to a restrained and simple dwelling, with interest focused on the scientifically arranged kitchen."[24] Given California's

mild winters, such houses could be built inexpensively in order to attract more homebuyers.[25] The most widespread of the new practical house types was called the bungalow. These single-family houses, composed by builders like Ida McCain in San Francisco and Leola Hall in Berkeley, were one story in elevation. They were covered by a shallow gable roof, and featured a large front porch covered by a smaller gable supported by extra-wide, tapered columns. Initially, bungalows were clad with brown shingles or dark-stained clapboard. Later, stucco became the preferred surface material and the range of colors lightened considerably.

Prairie-style house tracts were less common than bungalows, but also widespread within the Bay Area. Inspired by Frank Lloyd Wright's homes in the Chicago area as well as the European art nouveau, vernacular prairie-style houses have predominantly horizontal lines, flat roofs, and overhanging eaves. Some of them also feature details—especially leaded-glass decorations—inspired by European Moderne or Jugendstil architects. A fine collection of two-story Prairie-style houses lines Lakeshore Avenue in Oakland as it winds up the foothills toward Piedmont.

After 1920, builders turned to Spanish Colonial design. To many architects (from E.R. Swain to the Reid Brothers), the low-slung masses, sumptuous courtyards, thick plaster surfaces, and undulating red-tile roofs seemed a logical source of ideas for contemporary design in a Mediterranean climate. But as any walk through one of the 1920s and 1930s residential districts will show, there was no preferred architectural style. Built by architects like Albert Farr and John Hudson Thomas, the references ranged across the globe, from Spanish Colonial Revival to French Chateau, English Tudor, Italian Renaissance palace, and even a style called Medieval dollhouse.

The mish-mash fit the mix of trees and shrubbery, urns and benches that were massed along the serpentine streets of new rustic subdivisions. No longer would new Bay Area communities ignore topography. Duncan McDuffie's St. Francis Woods in San Francisco was a regional trendsetter. Platted by Frederick Law Olmsted Jr. and John Galen Howard, the neighborhood was entered through stone portals and organized around loping boulevards. From this point on, wealthier subdivisions readily followed land contours and preserved creeks and impressive landforms, resulting in the irregular blocks and curving streets of McDuffie's Northbrae in Berkeley, John Leonard's Ingleside Terraces in San Francisco, and Frank Newlands's Burlingame Park. On an even grander scale, the same aesthetic notions of picturesque rusticity were applied to wealthy towns, like Hillsborough. Already during the late nineteenth century, San Francisco's business elite had chosen these fog-sheltered hills as a country refuge. Between 1910 and 1938, most of Hillsborough's great estates were subdivided into mini-estates, usually leaving the main house and several acres intact. Around them were built some of the largest houses in the region, all on at least one-half acre of land; most on quite a bit more.

SKYSCRAPER DOWNTOWN
Lateral expansion of the urbanized Bay Area impacted the verticality of historic downtowns. Oakland, and especially San Francisco developed a tight core of high-rise office buildings and nearby hotels.

The concentration of transportation lines encouraged San Francisco's dense downtown. Yet the Financial District did not grow skyward because of a lack of space on its periphery. Rather, the growth of large railroad, shipping, mining, timber, agriculture and newspaper companies warranted a new geographical conquest: vertically-stacked floors of flexible office space from which to rule business empires; commercial buildings closely grouped together for purposes of communication and prestige. The golden triangle—marked by Market, Montgomery, and California streets–was born.

Until around 1890, with the exception of the tallish Palace and Baldwin Hotels, San Francisco's downtown had topped off at about five stories. For a time, Temple Emanuel's twin pomegranate-shaped cupolas on Sutter Street, erected in 1866 and reaching 165 feet in height, formed the tallest structure in the city.[26] Testimony to San Francisco's tolerance, it was perhaps the first time in the history of a Christian city that a Jewish synagogue towered over all churches.

450 Sutter Street (Pflueger)

Building heights soon rose. Only three years after the first steel-frame skyscraper debuted in Chicago, the Chicago firm of Burnham & Root designed one for San Francisco.[27] The Chronicle Building opened in 1889, and was followed two years later by the Mills Building, also by Burnham & Root. The two ten-story buildings dominated the skyline. Subsequently, as in most large American cities, the heights of San Francisco skyscrapers continued to get higher and higher: the twelve-story Call Building (1898) by Albert Roller; Willis Polk's 21-story Hobart Building (1914); and George Kelham's 31-story Russ Building (1927), which remained the tallest building in the city until the 1960s.

Although built with steel frames and equipped with elevators, skyscraper facades looked back in time. Most of them were clad with Beaux-Arts decoration owing to the City Beautiful Movement, but some were done up in Romanesque or Gothic. The mass of the tall buildings was often visually divided into three parts, like a classical column—base, shaft, and capital. The bottom parts were outlined by belt courses while a cornice, underlain with moldings, capped the structure. Several buildings culminated in towers or domes, and from the 1920s setbacks sculpted the mass of the tall buildings into a tapered, vertical silhouette–a dreamy commercial counterpart to the romantic suburbs business leaders favored for their residences. Although most of these skyscraper attributes were common to other American cities, architects tended to use light-colored brick or stone cladding as well as ample terra cotta ornamentation.

ART DECO

By the late 1920s, Art Deco began to influence design. Inspired by the 1925 World Exposition in Paris, the Art Deco era moved toward an ornamental vocabulary derived from the age of industrial transportation and, occasionally, remote eras of the past. In the works of architects like George Kelham and Timothy Pflueger,

Grand Lake Theater in Oakland

motifs like zigzags and chevrons were combined with simplified and overlapping forms to create an architectural language of speed and exoticism. For instance, on Pflueger's 450 Sutter Street Building the customary division of a tower into three parts was dropped, allowing the slab skyscraper to rise over 400 feet without any horizontal divisions or setbacks. Nonetheless, ornament was not banished; Pflueger used Mayan motifs on his trend-setting building. This mixing of past and future, while puzzling at first, actually makes sense within California's anxious grappling for identity. As California came of age as an industrial power, its leaders sought to associate the state's progress with borrowed, bygone monuments— despite the fact that the state's architectural roots were humble. In the case of buildings, new engineering technologies or massing solutions came wrapped in the latest historicist ornaments. Apparently, few people in the building industry believed that the public could be engaged by an architecture shorn of symbol and fantasy.

Movie theater buildings, in particular, explored how to attract the public's attention with architectural whimsy. At first, their designs borrowed from established European styles. But, as time went on, the need to present the public with decorative systems that could match the escapist fantasy of the motion pictures grew. Architects turned to the less-known Egyptian, Islamic or Mayan styles, and, finally to the transportation-inspired Art Deco. Pflueger's theaters illustrate this progression: from San Francisco's Spanish-Baroque Castro (1922) to its Islamic Alhambra (1930) and later to Oakland's Art Deco Paramount (1931).

In the years leading up to the Second World War, Bay Area architecture continued a fascination with escapism that dates back to the Victorian era. Despite the local importance of both the Beaux Arts and Arts and Crafts Movements, fanciful styles kept interceding. Despite new steel and reinforced concrete technologies, architects and their clients kept covering structure with ornaments. Indeed, in 1939, architects went on to use plaster forms in order to create yet more exotic references at the Golden Gate International Exposition, located on a new 400-acre, artificial island named Treasure Island. Held to celebrate the completion of the city's great new bridges—the San Francisco-Oakland Bay Bridge in 1936 and the Golden Gate Bridge in 1937—, the G.G.I.E. went all out to link California's material progress to the diverse cultures of the Pacific Basin. California's architects, as they had done so many times before, once more reached out to the far points of the globe and assembled their elements into a striking, if short-lived design vocabulary.

Modern apartment

Modernism (1930-1970)

THE IMPACT OF EUROPEAN DESIGN
All through the 1930s and early 1940s students dissatisfied with Beaux Arts architectural instruction at the University of California demanded recognition of the architectural advances that had just taken place in Europe. Embodied in movements like De Stijl, schools like the Bauhaus, and architects like Le Corbusier and Mies van der Rohe, European architects had cast off the conventions of the past. Building materials like stone and wood gave way to glass, steel and concrete. Frames and columnar grids replaced load-bearing walls. Interiors were turned from boxy

rooms and narrow passages into open, flowing spaces. Ornament, symmetry, and complex roof profiles were banished. Building shape became an experimental geometry of intersecting line, plane, and volume. It was the most thoroughgoing architectural revolution since the High Gothic, but the leadership of the School of Architecture at Berkeley hardly seemed to notice.

Many Berkeley students gravitated to the office of William Wurster, who would eventually, in 1950, take over the reigns of the school.[28] Wurster was by no means a machine-age modernist, working from a tabula rasa like the Europeans to erect a pristine white city of towers on stilts. But he was no traditionalist either, at least if that meant adherence to academic rules of composition. Looking to rural ranches, Wurster designed a series of modest houses that appear, at first glance, as if a carpenter built them. For the Gregory Farmhouse and Pasatiempo development, both in Santa Cruz County, and a large number of houses, he used unadorned shapes set in close proximity to the ground–one of the influential precedents for the suburban ranch house. Wurster paid greater attention than most of his peers to site, local building materials and methods, as well as client desires. He opened his homes to the outdoors, employing over time kitchen caves, screened verandas, or glazed sun porches. Most of his work was carried out in wood, both for framing and cladding and he especially liked redwood. There

Modern house

were notable exceptions. In 1937, for the McIntosh House in Los Altos, Wurster expressed the concrete-block structure on the house's exterior and interior. The 1940 Pope House in Orinda, a concrete block and corrugated-sheet metal structure, arrayed its rooms around a central courtyard that communed with the sky through a giant circular cutout.

Wurster greatly influenced the development of modern architecture in the Bay Area. Many important architects were associated with him, and these include John Dinwiddie, Henry Hill, and John Funk. In their work, features like smooth redwood siding, interior plywood paneling, and large walls of glass became standard practice. Wood lattices and slats were used to filter light and extend the space of a house into the outdoors. One important contemporary, Gardner Dailey, built some of the first large plate-glass walls, and especially favored exposed structural framing. Dailey was known as well for inventive planning solutions, crafting compact houses without long halls.

At the same time, Richard Neutra, although based in Southern California, built a number of houses around the Bay whose glass walls merged indoors with outdoors. Some of these buildings were sheathed in redwood, while others were closer to the pulse of the modern movement, and featured white walls and horizontal bands of windows. Neutra also experimented with new materials. His Sciobereti House (1939) in Berkeley

had an unusual cladding of cement celetex panels framed by galvanized aluminum. Another pivotal LA modernist, Rudolf Schindler, built a small redwood house in Richmond in 1935 that is memorable for its functional division of the residential volume into separate living and garage/studio quarters. Many architects took up this approach in subsequent decades.

Modern Bay Area architecture soon caught the nation's eye. In 1944, the Museum of Modern Art in New York held an exhibition on the development of modernism in the United States in the twelve years following its epochal International Style exhibition of 1932. The 1944 catalogue lists 46 buildings around the country, many of which were in California, and six in the Bay Area: Dailey's Owens House (1939) in Sausalito as well as his U.S. Merchant Marine Cadet School (1942) in San Mateo; Henry A. Thomsen Jr. and William Wurster's Valencia Gardens (1943) housing project in San Francisco as well as Wurster's Schuckl Canning Company (1942) in Sunnyvale; Ernest Kump's Acalanes High School (1941) in Lafayette; and Raphael Soriano's Hallawell Seed Company (1942) in San Francisco. The cover of this important catalogue had a photograph of John Funk's 1939 Heckendorf House in Modesto.[29] It was praised for its sleek rectangular shape and horizontal glazing opening onto a composed landscape.

Former V.C. Morris Store (Wright)

In 1952, MOMA followed up with another canon-making show. This time, four Bay Area buildings were included: Kump's San Jose High School (1952); and three San Francisco structures, Dailey's Red Cross Headquarters (1948); Erich Mendelsohn's Maimonidies Hospital (1950); and Frank Lloyd Wright's V.C. Morris Store (1949).[30] The works cited in both MOMA shows illustrated the exploratory nature of modernism in its early American phase. They employed a variety of cladding solutions, including redwood, stucco, and concrete as well as copious glass walls. Some of them were quietly rectilinear while others made bold, plastic statements. All utilized the latest innovations in constructional methods.

THE BAY REGION IDEA

In between these shows, architectural critic Lewis Mumford penned an article for *The New Yorker,* appearing in 1947, in which he identified a Bay Region manner of design. In large part, Mumford was searching for an alternative to the white-skinned, flat-roofed hegemony of Henry-Russell Hitchcock and Phillip Johnson's International Style. Mumford hungered for an American modernism more independent of Europe. His idea was given weight in an exhibition entitled "Domestic Architecture of the Bay Region," held at the San Francisco Museum of Modern Art in 1949. In the catalogue, Mumford complained how the area's architecture had been unfairly ignored until now: "Here the architects have absorbed the universal lessons of science and the machine, and have reconciled them with human wants and human desires, with full regard for the setting of nature, the climate and topography and vegetation, with all those regional qualities whose importance Frederick Law Olmsted wisely stressed two generations ago in his exemplary program for the development of Stanford University."[31] The idea of a Bay Region approach to architecture was born.

While useful at the time for advertising the Bay Area to the wider world, in hindsight the idea must be questioned.

Did the label of "Bay Region" hinder the exploration of region? Did it, likewise, limit future architectural creativity? The problem begins with the fact that "Bay Region" did not just refer to mid-century design. Mumford (and later historians) extended the idea to other periods of Bay Area architecture. Attempting to cast much of the history of local architecture within the parameters of a specific method, the Bay Region idea was extended back in time to encompass Maybeck and his contemporaries–what became known as the first Bay Region. It was also later extended forward in time by David Gebhard to include developments in the 1960s. This making of linear history makes little sense. Maybeck or Polk would have rejected such an idea as far too narrow and anti-cosmopolitan to encompass their own work, which veered from Arts and Crafts to classicism to idiosyncratic modernism. Likewise, most mid-century architects included in the canon, such as Wurster, Hill and Dinwiddie disavowed a Bay Region style.[32] The Bay Region canon also omitted numerous important architects because their work did not conform to its narrow stylistic parameters. This despite the fact that other than wood cladding and frameworks, the principle characteristics of the Bay Region–natural light as a molder of space and enhancer of texture, the outdoors as an extension of the house, eschewal of ornament–were common to so-called internationalists.[33] As the *Built in U.S.A.* catalogues from the Museum of Modern Art in New York show, Bay Area architecture of all stripes actually received significant public attention, something lost on the promoters of the Bay Region.

LANDSCAPE ARCHITECTURE

One development of true significance at the time was modernist landscape architecture. Because of the region's breathtaking natural beauty and pacific climate, the desirability of an architecture intertwined with nature and the outdoors was more pronounced here than anywhere else in the United States—with the possible exception of Los Angeles. Close attention to landscaping had been a feature of Bay Area architecture since the construction of the great estates of the nineteenth century. The details of California nature were lost on architects and businessmen of that era, however. To them, California was a Garden of Eden far more beautiful but also far wilder than anything they had ever encountered. Their response, as illustrated by the design for and most estates, was to obliterate California nature, replacing native plant species with exotics, and creating a botanical fantasyland to go along with their architectural fantasyland.

Modern landscape architects, beginning with Thomas D. Church and Garrett Eckbo, took design beyond English meadows and French parterre boxwood into an increasingly close dialogue with the local environment. They faced two different challenges. First, in the expanding suburbs, Church and Eckbo borrowed compositional techniques from modern art to craft settings and vistas that were not only sublime but also beautiful—that

Donnell Garden (Church) in Sonoma

is to say, not just overwhelming but also intimate and approachable. For not only did the region's climate allow a cornucopia of plants to be grown, the awe-inspiring views of hills, canyons, and bays demanded a sophisticated design lens by which to be apprehended. Second, in developed urban quarters, they struggled to impart the grandeur of the region to cramped spaces. How could a small backyard or space between large buildings become a refreshing natural experience? How could landscapes tie buildings together?

In 1937, Eckbo published work he had done for a thesis at the University of California. The article "Small Gardens in the City," presented 26 experimental gardens for small city lots. Instead of axes, Eckbo thought in areas. Instead of static forms, he thought of circulation. And instead of planes, he conceived the garden in volumes. Under the influence of abstract painting, from Cubism to De Stijl and Surrealism, Eckbo created patterns in wood, brick and planting, warping space to break up the feeling of enclosure, and screening portions of the garden to suggest additional space.[34] The firm of Eckbo, Royston & Williams went on to design some of the most rigorous modern gardens in the United States. Among them is the 1941 garden for John Dinwiddie's Frazier Cole House in Oakland, where wrinkled planes define the lawn and patio, and curved, wooden screens create wave-like spaces. Unfortunately for the Bay Area, the bulk of the Eckbo's work

Alcoa Forecast Garden (Eckbo)

shifted to Los Angeles after the Second World War. Robert Royston later completed many Bay Area parks with the firm Royston, Hanamoto & Mayes.

Thomas Church dominated the landscape architecture scene from the 1930s to the 1950s. His trademarks were curving paths, patios, and pools, influenced by the paintings of Jean Arp and Jean Miro as well as the built work of Alvar Aalto. Church favored circular or rectangular boxes to formalize plantings, screens to separate areas, and small hills to introduce surface movement. He envisioned the garden as an extension of architecture and frequently laid down hard surfaces or ground covers to continue interior floor planes. Like Eckbo, Church saw the garden as offering multiple, even random perspectives—not a dominating axial sequence. Lines were his forte. Church would use strong curving lines to set apart areas of the garden and indicate that some spaces were for visual enjoyment alone.[35] For the Martin Garden in Aptos, completed in 1949, he cast a zigzag bench alongside a wooden deck as a counterpoint to a biomorphic enclosure of sand. The Dewey Donnell Garden (1947) in Sonoma was his masterpiece. Photographs typically show the same vantage point. The view begins across the blue waters of the biomorphic pool, at whose center rests Adaline Kent's surrealist sculpture. One's eyes then rise to take in a large oak tree at the left corner of the frame and the straight line of the horizon holding the blue heavens. Church understood that the secret of great landscape architecture, like great architecture, is to open a limited view onto a world and in so doing indicate an entire set of relationships not visible, not knowable, and yet compelling.

WORLD WAR II AND THE RATIONALIZATION OF DESIGN

The great event of mid-century was the Second World War. In the space of one year, 1942, the San Francisco Bay Area became the arsenal of the Pacific struggle with Japan. Building com-

Dirigible Hanger in Mountain View

menced first on military bases and then in the industrializing cities. Existing bases expanded and new facilities, like Alameda Naval Air Station, were built. Fourteen shipyards, from Alameda to Vallejo, employed thousands of workers, over 90,000 alone at the Kaiser yards in Richmond. The Bay Area experienced its most dramatic migration since the Gold Rush. Half a million new residents arrived between 1940 and 1945.[36] Many of them were African Americans from Louisiana and Texas.

The chief building characteristics of the war boom, as compared to the Gold Rush boom, were its rational planning, inventive development of prototypes, and sophisticated management of resources. These efforts extended architecture and planning into sectors of the building economy that had previously been dominated by speculators. In the post-war era, regional planning was inaugurated. Housing, schools, shopping, workplaces, and transportation would be thoroughly investigated and modernized. Architectural design became something of a scientific process.

In 1939, the G.G.I.E. at Treasure Island had contained a futuristic vision of San Francisco, exhibited at the U.S. Steel pavilion. Walter Dorwin Teague's "San Francisco in 1999" envisioned the entire city rebuilt along Corbusian principles–downtown turned into a grid of 30 cruciform skyscrapers, with elevated parkways running along the waterfront.[37] Although far too brash to be taken seriously, the visionary aspects of the plan struck a nerve.

That same year, six architects, landscape architects, and city planners founded a utopian organization called Telesis. The name of the group was taken from Webster's Dictionary for new words, and means progress intelligently planned. It included Garrett Eckbo, Vernon DeMars, Henry Hill, Frances McCarthy, and Burton Cairns. The founders saw the group as an outgrowth of the Fifth Conference of the C.I.A.M. (International Congress of Modern Architecture) held in 1937 in Paris. The chief concern of Telesis, like the C.I.A.M., was the growing confusion and irrationality of urban development. At an exhibition held at the San Francisco Museum of Art in 1940, "Space for Living," four areas were identified: Man Works, advocating decentralization and the creation of an agricultural greenbelt; Man Lives, with its emphasis on combating congested slums through functional and well sited dwellings; Man Plays, recommending more open space and recreational facilities; and Man is Served, with its call for new transportation systems as well as energy sources. The conference received a great deal of publicity, but the war cut off its momentum. After the war, in 1950, Telesis put on a second exhibition at the museum entitled "The Next Million People," advocating for comprehensive metropolitan planning.

Although Telesis disbanded in 1953, its influence is felt to this day in the statewide adoption of master planning, drafted and administered by large city planning departments. At Berkeley, in 1959, the departments of Architecture, Landscape Architecture and City Planning were grouped together in the new College of Environmental Design, a pedagogical move that had ripples throughout the world. In 1961, the Association of Bay Area Governments (ABAG) was founded as the regional planning arm of 101 cities and towns. It produced a regional plan for the area in 1970, on issues ranging from water policy to waste management to seismic hazards. All told, Telesis, the

College of Environmental Design, and various city and regional planners set into motion a rethinking and retooling of every aspect of the built environment.

MASS HOUSING

One longstanding issue in regional planning was mass housing. The Bay Area's dramatic growth during the Second World War greatly exacerbated its housing crisis. Already in 1940, the Federal Works Agency (FWA) had authorized construction of large numbers of housing units at military bases. These projects were influenced by both international trends, particularly the C.I.A.M., and California efforts to house migrant farm workers. The production of mass housing transformed from a private, speculative venture into a planned, governmental mandate.

In 1942, Wurster was selected as architect for the Carquinez Heights housing section of the Mare Island Navy Base in Vallejo. At what became known as Chabot Terrace he experimented with materials and structure, efforts that would influence the post-war housing boom. According to architectural historian Greg Hise, "Wurster found value in blending standardized production and construction practices with local knowledge concerning site conditions and patterns of behavior or cultural preferences."[38] On the one hand, the inexpensive wood-frame buildings were in-filled with homosote panels and topped by flat roofs. On the other hand, Wurster paid attention to the site. Rows of buildings stepped along slopes to afford views; houses were sited as windbreaks for each other.

Nearby, in Marin County a city of 6,000 inhabitants was constructed in five months during 1943. The architect, Carl Grammé, placed most houses on easterly slopes for wind protection. Again, the house designs for Marin City weren't all that different from military bases: utilitarian, horizontal wood-frame structures with flat roofs. The formula was repeated—barrack-like buildings arranged on a hill with respect to sun angles, winds, views, and topography.

A new housing prototype–buildings rationally placed on large sites and threaded by open space, roads and parking—was unveiled. In the years to come it would play an increasingly large role in both urban and suburban housing development.

After the war, many of these "temporary" complexes were converted to public housing and several are still used in this capacity. New public housing complexes adopted many of the lessons of wartime housing, albeit at much greater densities and on sites that demanded the demolition of older city fabric. By and large, they followed national trends of single-use high-rise development on superblocks–towers arranged on large swathes of land with hardly any commerce. For instance, in 1964, Aaron Green and John Carl Warnecke re-designed part of Marin City. This time many of the buildings were built of reinforced concrete and reached five-stories in elevation. The public housing authority cut corners, however, and no elevators were provided. In San Francisco and Oakland, likewise, campaigns were underway to replace the narrow-lot development of old districts with superblock complexes, replete with open space, and affording excellent light and air circulation to occupants. Redevelopment agencies declared certain "slum" districts "blighted" and thereby subject to eminent domain seizure of land and urban renewal. The Western Addition Master Plan of 1952 by Vernon DeMars and Albert Roller, proposed the replacement of much of the Victorian row-house district with low-and high-rise housing. By the mid-1950s, several high-rise towers were underway there: Yerba Buena Plaza East and West, and Yerba Buena Plaza Annex. The neighborhood was torn apart in the process.

Upon completion, the new housing projects were lauded for their social and architectural qualities. With the passage of years, approval turned to dismay. Impoverished projects became centers of drugs, gangs and crime, poorly served by commerce and isolated from their sur-roundings. One seeming exception was Vernon DeMars's Easter Hill Village in Richmond, opened in 1954. Ahead of its time, the 300-unit complex was strictly lowrise. It consisted of one- and two-story buildings arrayed around parking courts and open spaces landscaped by Lawrence Halprin. Halprin preserved the strewn boulders on the site in order to avoid the typical scorched earth appearance of new housing projects. Similarly, DeMars sought to avoid numbing homogeneity in building by coming up with different design treatments and providing each unit with an individual front porch. Alas, this architectural/landscape masterwork could not solve the social ills of the community, especially as it grew increasingly poor over the years and maintenance funds dried up. By the 1970s, Easter Hill Village was labeled a fiasco, and the entire complex was demolished in 2003.

Marquis & Stoller's St. Francis Square project in San Francisco's Western Addition has proven more successful than most large public housing projects. Built in 1962, its buildings hugged the street, like older row-house development, preventing the grounds of the complex from becoming a zone of circulation and other less desirable activities. The buildings were then arranged around open courts with small fenced backyards that provided residents with what came to be known as "defensible spaces." Public housing henceforth would have to pay much greater attention to occupant safety.

THE FLEXIBLE SCHOOL

The rationalization of building was nowhere more inventive than in the realm of school design. In the 1920s, German architects, like Ernst May in Frankfurt, had inaugurated pavilion school design–one or two story wings dispersed over a large site. The first American iteration of this idea occurred in Winnetka, Illinois in 1940–the Crow Island Elementary School by Perkins, Wheeler and Will. That same year the larger Acalanes High School in Lafayette opened.

Acalanes High School in Lafayette

Designed by Ernest Kump, Acalanes High School revamped the spatial planning of a public school building, and in so doing, revolutionized the American school campus. Until then, schools had been multiple-story blocks, connected by laborious staircases, and beset with differently sized rooms and poorly lit and ventilated spaces. They were designed more from the standpoint of symmetry than flexibility. The fixed plans of older schools, while spatially varied, actually hindered the implementation of new school activities and pedagogies. Kump's innovation became known as the finger plan. Canopied, exterior courtyards connected separate, one-story building volumes. Windows surrounded classroom buildings. In California it made sense to situate circulation outdoors, under the covered walkways. Another benefit of the finger plan was its ability to be changed according to new circumstances. New buildings could be added on as needed. Certain sectors could be closed off. Different functions of the school could be linked or separated.

Another local architect, John Lyon Reid, was also active in school design. Reid reacted to wartime shortages and new demands for adult education. Like his counterparts in the mass housing sector, he favored buildings with ample light and air as well as quick construction timelines and economical construction costs. His insight was to design from the standpoint of a rational unit system of structural parts, standardizing equipment and furniture as much as possible. "Prefabrication," he wrote, "may afford a means of achieving a fluidity in building which is capable of meeting the needs of the constantly changing fabric of community and regional life. The schools of the future must be a flexible organism capable of developing with our growing concept of education."[39] During the 1950s, Reid came up with a plan for total flexibility, in which all rooms and corridors could be changed with respect to both size and shape.[40] With the enlightened leadership of the San Mateo Union School District, he built four high schools where every aspect of the plan could be altered—Hillsdale High School in San Mateo (1955), Mills High School (1958) in Millbrae, Aragon High School (1961) in San Mateo, and Crestmoor High School (1962) in San Bruno.

Kump soon approached flexibility from another angle, the module concept. He first chose a standard set of spatial dimensions. Then he devised a way to span that space in order to leave it open and changeable. The formula could be repeated or multiplied as often as needed. These spatial modules accommodated classrooms, offices, the cafeteria, library, and even bathrooms; some uses occupied one module while others as many as ten. Next, Kump aligned the modules in rows or clusters, depending upon functional needs and topographic conditions. From school to school, the modules' dimensions, framing and materials could vary, and the architect likened the idea to Pullman cars. Important examples of modular Kump schools are White Oaks Elementary School (1945, 1948) in San Carlos, Woodside High School (1957), and Mountain View High School (1961) as well as Foothill College (1962) in Los Altos. In the work of both Reid and Kump, standardization allowed for ease of changes over time.

University planning took a giant step forward during the late 1950s and 1960s. Energized by a federal mandate to expand secondary education, the state built scores of new community colleges, four-year colleges, and branches of the University of California system. The California State University launched new campuses in Hayward, beginning in 1957, and Sonoma, starting in 1960. Many of their buildings, however, especially those executed by the State Division of Architects, sacrificed design inventiveness to bureaucratic planning. By far, the most architecturally adventurous campus was the nearby new University of California at Santa Cruz, which opened in 1965 and soon included important buildings by Moore, Lyndon, Turnbull & Whittaker, Anshen & Allen, Campbell & Wong, Ernest Kump, McCue Boone & Tomsick, Hugh Stubbins Jr., and John Carl Warnecke. Existing university campuses were also dramatically enlarged, although this process damaged the fine campus plans of both the University of California at Berkeley and Stanford University. At the two venerable institutions, scores of new academic buildings, vehicular drives, and parking lots blocked historic axial corridors, towered over older buildings, and ate up precious green space. The bedlam of city redevelopment had intruded into the ivory tower.

SHOPPING AT THE MALL

Until the post-war era, retail buildings had received little attention as regards their functional and constructional logic. Most stores, like schools, were multi-story structures (with offices or apartments on upper floors). Inside, they contained diverse and often cramped spaces. More problematic, stores were located on city streets with minimal off-street parking. Retail space was generally a speculative venture that responded to transportation extensions and housing developments. Planned shopping centers, like the groundbreaking Country Club Plaza in Kansas City, were not built in the Bay Area before the war. In 1948, though, a small shopping center opened in Corte Madera that grouped several stores around a pedestrian walkway, placing parking and travel lanes on the

Shopping Mall in Hayward

periphery. Residences and other uses were not included. Other parking friendly, single-use shopping complexes quickly followed.

Retail now tended toward huge building sites accessed by automobiles. The first regional shopping malls were built locally in 1952, two years after the pioneering Northgate Mall in Seattle. Designed by Welton Becket, Stonestown Shopping Center in San Francisco and Hillsdale Shopping Center in San Mateo were situated on large, previously undeveloped parcels. They included an anchor department store, specialty shops as well as office and medical buildings. Building volumes were grouped around a central mall, separating pedestrians from cars. Up to 3,000 parking spaces surrounded the complexes. Signage and landscaping enlivened parts of the exteriors' vast, blank walls. At Stonestown, the Emporium department store sign was a wedge-shaped tower faced with white-porcelain enamel and set off by a trio of angled palm trees.

The master of malls, Victor Gruen, designed two early shopping centers locally. Gruen had just pioneered enclosed malls of clustered stores in Minneapolis and Detroit. In the Bay Area, he took a different tact. Bay Fair in San Leandro (1956) and Valley Fair (1957) in San Jose featured a similar cluster arrangement of two levels of stores within open-air concourses. Both were anchored by Macy's and were landscaped by Eckbo, Royston, and Williams. Bay

Fair's 47-acre site had room for 650,000 square feet of retail space and parking for 3,600 cars. At Valley Fair, the chief visual symbol was a boiler chimney faced with colorful tiles. Gruen's malls were paradoxical undertakings. Although they produced urbane places graced by shops, restaurants, public art, and quality architecture and landscaping, their existence depended upon a considerable infrastructure of parking, roads and automobiles. In effect, the urban downtown was sacrificed for the urbane mall.

By the 1970s, shopping centers and malls had been built throughout the nine counties, and contributed to the economic deterioration of old city downtowns like Richmond and Pittsburg. Oakland too gradually lost the substance of its once-vital retail core, as department store after department store moved to the suburbs. Malls were simply too convenient for driving, parking, and then walking. In 1969, Welton Becket's Serramonte Center, in Daly City, employed a pinwheel plan to minimize walking. What's more, the malls kept growing. Among the biggest was the enclosed Eastridge Shopping Center (1971) in San Jose; it contained 150 stores and 1.7 million square feet of retail space. Downtown San Jose lost its retail vitality soon afterward.

Not all retail development deserted the older city. The seminal innovation of Bay Area shopping design was the renovation of the Ghirardelli chocolate factory in San Francisco into an urban specialty mall. When the chocolate factory moved to San Mateo in the early 1960s, citizens feared the choice bayside site would be developed as an apartment tower. William Matson Roth, the site's owner, hired Wurster, Bernardi & Emmons to renovate it (and design other buildings) for tourist shops and restaurants. The redesign was completed in 1967 and the large precincts of the former factory provided space to create an interior landscaped plaza as well as a network of shopping paths. The formula of shopping amongst old bricks and stones proved successful and in 1968 Joseph Esherick remodeled the nearby

Del Monte Cannery into three maze-like levels of commercial space for tourists. These projects became the prototype for later festival marketplaces planned in old city cores, such as the Rouse Company's Faneuil Hall project in Boston. Unlike regional malls, erected with modernist design principles and located on previously unbuilt land, specialty shopping centers recognized the appealing equation of old city architecture, tourism, and niche retail. In time, retail conversions of industrial buildings became popular in other parts of the region. Specialty-shopping districts, like Oakland's Jack London Square, became an economic development strategy for older cities.

GLASS OFFICES AND OFFICE PARKS

Hardly any commercial office space was constructed between the Great Depression and late 1950s. When business got going again, two developments stood out. First, downtown design shed its ties to the punched-window wall historicism of the early twentieth century.

Kaiser Building in Oakland

Buildings would henceforth rise without setbacks, feature glass curtain walls, and end in flat roofs (frequently containing a mechanical penthouse). 1959 was the year two of the best skyscrapers ever to be built in the Bay Area were completed: in Oakland, Welton Becket's Kaiser Building; in San Francisco, Skidmore Owings & Merrill's Crown Zellerbach Building. Each embodied the superb qualities of modern office design. The steel frame was expressed in visible supports. Hung from the frame, glass curtain walls alternated with contrasting metal or porcelain-metal spandrels. The functional nature of a highrise was expressed by setting the mass of the circulation tower apart from the office floors. Each zone was given its own aesthetic treatment—often, an opaque shaft for circulation and bands of horizontal windows for the office floors. The tall buildings showed the potential of a curtain wall to function as a canvas in the sky. High above the sidewalk, abstract rectilinear compositions reflected the changing positions and intensities of the sun. Indoors, attention was commonly paid to the lobby, where staircases (and occasionally fountains) became sculptural works in their own right.

Second, developers began to build office space in the suburbs. Before the war, office buildings outside of downtowns were usually tied directly to a manufacturing plant. Such was the case with Wurster's celebrated and since-demolished 1942 office structure for the

Schuckl Canning Company in Sunnyvale. According to architectural historian John Jacobus, "the characteristics of the International Style—thin, smooth walls, strip windows, and flat roof terraces—are translated from the earlier media of steel, concrete, and stucco to an expression in wood with a display of elegance and sensitivity."[41]

The Stanford Research Park, begun in 1951, was the first industrial park in the world to be devoted to high technology companies. Instead of gas-enshrouded smokestacks and oil-slicked back alleys, the Research Park boasted grassy setbacks from the street, abundant foliage, large patios, concealed services, and low-hung buildings along Page Mill Road in Palo Alto. This blending of imagery from the residential suburb and university campus was to prove irresistible in the years to come. Over time, the Palo Alto site grew from one building on 35 acres to over 160 buildings on 700 acres. Almost all the companies along Page Mill Road and its neighboring streets responded to the horizontal nature of California living, and the desire to place office space in close proximity to the outdoors, and parking. The office-campus concept soon spread across the nation.

SUBDIVIDING THE RANCH

Construction of single-family housing exploded during the post-war years. For the first time, developers began to build on land far beyond the lines of commuter rail trains and trolley cars. The new suburbs were distinguished from their predecessors by their dependence on the automobile, their larger lots and their signature housing type, the ranch house. The plainness and simplicity of the ranch house fit perfectly with the informal and practical lifestyle emerging in American suburbia. But romance was also a factor. Print and screen media capitalized on the origins of this house type on the working ranch.[42] Here, then, was a house, so the ads promised tongue-in-cheek, that would be appropriate for the rugged, individualistic life at the city's

Alcoa Building (Skidmore, Owings & Merrill)

edge. In 1932, Cliff May had built the first suburban ranch house in San Diego. His designs influenced post-war production of one-story ranch houses that employed rambling L- or U- or H-shaped plans, and opened to their surroundings through covered porches and eventually sliding-glass doors. Variations of this simple idea were built throughout California, and usually without a great deal of detailing. A ring of suburbs around San Francisco and Oakland became ranch-house communities.

House (Corbett) in Sausalito

The informality of the ranch house and its architectural features—low-pitched gable roofs, deep-set eaves, asymmetrical windows—accorded well, of course, with Wurster's design philosophy. It was followed as well by Joseph Esherick, who designed understated houses with shingled exterior walls. Their intricacy emerged from the way their multiple levels engaged the frequently steep sites. Esherick built up Gardner Dailey's modular system—the idea of volumetric planning—and extended these ideas through innovative fenestration, trellises, and balconies. As Esherick saw the matter, a house was a box with holes torn into it for enclosure, views, privacy, and climate control. Fenestration responded to the site-specific nuances of view and lighting. He also believed in what he called fuzzy exteriors, non-suggestive masses that disappeared into the landscape. A building should be "like a forest, where you can stand outside and sense the nature of the spaces inside without actually seeing them."[43]

HIGH MODERN

Architectural understatement was not in vogue with most modern architects of the post-war decades. In 1947, a local architect, Mario Corbett, unveiled a project for a radical steel-frame house whose infill would have been almost completely glazed. The crisp box had no overhangs and would have appeared as a perfect, transparent geometry. Although never built, Corbett's vision paralleled Philip Johnson's famous Glass House in New Canaan, Connecticut. Subsequently, two renowned architects designed buildings of striking and singular form in the Bay Area. Eric Mendelsohn's 1952 Russell House in San Francisco placed its best views in a cantilevered round corner pavilion. At the Marin Civic Center (1959) Frank Lloyd Wright designed his last major project. Although not residential, it was a miniature vision of what his unrealized urban plan, Broadacre City, might have looked like.

In Los Angeles, John Entenza sponsored the Case Study House program, the most influential forum for domestic modern design in American history. Between 1945 and 1966, 36 prototype houses were illustrated in his magazine *Arts and Architecture*. Almost all of the designs—by architects like Neutra, Craig Ellwood, Gregory Ain, Pierre Koenig, and Charles and Ray Eames—were built in the Los Angeles area. The houses gloriously exhibited their basic attributes—a steel frame, an open plan, and glass walls opening out onto long views of cityscape and nature. A couple of projects were intended for Northern California. One by Don Knorr was planned for Atherton, but never built. (Knorr later erected a steel-frame house with adobe-brick infill on the site). Beverly Thorne built the sole Bay Area Case Study House, #26, in San Rafael in the late 1950s. Here and elsewhere Thorne cast dramatic cantilevers off rectilinear volumes, which allowed his homes to appear as jet-age ranches.

Exemplified in houses by Dailey and Neutra, architects had long experimented with transparency. Now, in the works of Donald Olsen, glazing was set within a framework of white walls. The references to Le Corbusier couldn't be clearer. Olsen's 1968 Ruth House in Berkeley consists of two white cubic masses, one oriented vertically and the other horizontally, held together by a paper-thin glazed passageway. Large asymmetrical windows further shape the pristine volumes.

While Olsen might have been looking to the early work of Le Corbusier, Mario Ciampi and Paffard Clay played off the Swiss architect's late career. Ciampi's museums, schools, churches and plazas fit their functions into scabbards of raw reinforced concrete. The Berkeley Art Museum and nearby Newman Center highlight the heaviness of the material—respectively, hovering above the ground and protruding up into walls that look like battlements. Others, particularly the Daly City schools, display concrete's states of delirious thinness—the shells that undulate as curves, scallops or acute butterfly angles. Paffard Clay produced muscle-bound concrete structures that culminate, as witnessed in two San Francisco academic buildings, in spiky, steep-pitched slopes. The most plastic of building materials, concrete is architecture at its most melodic, and in Clay's hands the formal melodies are so varied as to cross over into the realm of sculpture. Although these and other architects embraced the bold possibilities of concrete form-making, some members of the general public were turned off, seeing the design approach as nothing more than its colloquial name–brutalism.

Like Thorne, a number of local architects built primarily in wood, but used (and expressed) steel beams to achieve dramatic cantilevers and wide spaces. The use of steel for residential construction was unprecedented. Steel allowed for daring shapes. For his houses, Jack Hillmer inserted skylights into the wide bays between the steel I-beams, opening up horizontal planes to the penetration and effects of light. On other fine houses of the era by George Rockrise, Henrik Bull, Campbell and Wong, and Charles Warren Callister, the material dominance of redwood frames and cladding was tempered by steel I-beams, cement foundations, concrete walls and piers and floors, as well as infills of brick, stone, stucco, metal, or homosote. Callister's counterpoint of concrete and redwood tracked the chiaroscuro spectrum and grainy rivulets of texture. Generally, flat roofs were less common than in Southern California, as the longer rainy season encouraged steeper pitches. But, all through this period, sharp prows and hovering cantilevers added to the complexity of building shape. Modernist architects were responding to surrounding nature. Their cantilevered rooms and terraces took inspiration from the region's ridges and rocky outcrops and remade them in sharp shapes on a linear horizon. Their skylights and cut-outs mimicked the open-work nature of the Oak and Laurel forests. Architects designed the modern house as a supple enclosure. Its walls could be opaque, translucent or transparent. They could open or close. Foremost, they could respond to client- and site-specific paths of movement, sight, and illumination.

It is worth emphasizing that these pivotal Northern California modernists were neither dry functionalists nor spacey utopians. Architectural writer Pierluigi Serraino has made a convincing case for understanding their work as a forward-looking, yet tradition-bound response to changing times: "Beverly Thorne yearns for a return to Egyptian endurance through steel. Jack Hillmer creates environments in which the sheen of the redwood he saw at the 1933 Century of Progress Fair (in Chicago) could be expressed by designing masterpieces in lumber. Donald Knorr focuses on a principle he accidentally encountered in his youth, "Simplicity has genius, power, and magic in it.'"[44]

Eichler Home in Terra Linda

THE EICHLER PHENOMENON

Northern California modernism did not just appear on a select number of elite houses. All through the early twentieth century, developers had dreamed up ways to mass-produce homes in the manner of other commercial products like automobiles. After the war, William Levitt perfected the rationalization of factory construction of home parts in New York. Joseph Eichler applied some of Levitt's ideas to the Bay Area. From the late 1940s to 1960s, his firm constructed approximately 11,000 modern homes (and several apartment buildings). Eichler was noted for not permitting discrimination against blacks and other minorities. He also hired superb architects like A. Quincy Jones and Claude Oakland. Five subdivisions were built from prototypes by Anshen and Allen: El Centro Gardens, Green Gables and Greer Park in Palo Alto, Sunnyvale Manor in Sunnyvale, and Atherwood in Redwood City. Other Eichler neighborhoods appeared in Terra Linda and Lucas Valley in Marin County; the San Mateo Highlands; and Rancho San Miguel in Walnut Creek.

Eichler homes present an opaque face to the street. Instead of picture windows, which most people covered up with drapes, they used clerestory and slit windows. Instead of a basement, construction was slab on grade; radiant heating was installed in the floor slabs. Instead of a garage, a carport was the central feature in the front of the home. Inside, Eichler standardized modernist ideas on housing. Post and beam construction was left visible. Materials (like wood veneer for partition walls) were similarly kept natural. One of Claude Oakland's innovations was the central glazed atrium, around which were arranged the rooms of the house. The demand for privacy was acknowledged by the placement of living and dining areas to the rear of the house; floor-to-ceiling picture windows opened onto the back garden.

Freeway Interchange in Oakland

THE FABULOUS AND FRIGHTENING FREEWAY

One last factor shaped the post-war city, automobile parking and roads. In the affluent California society, driving had become a necessity, not a luxury. Automobiles were a key ingredient in the development of the new malls, schools, subdivisions, and office parks. Downtown, buildings were torn down for parking lots and multi-level parking structures. In the neighborhoods, parking garages were gored into hillsides and carports were fitted atop residences. Multi-family residential developments even balanced designs atop narrow piers that pointedly displayed the lair of the automobile.

Cars were especially leading San Francisco, the dense core of the region, into unexplored frontiers, some of which would have drastic consequences. After the construction of the city's two bridges, motorists could easily move between the city and its surrounding counties. The result was a massive increase of traffic congestion. For highway engineers, the solution was the limited-access freeway. In 1937, Miller McClintock's *Limited Way Plan for San Francisco* had envisioned 65 miles of elevated and depressed superhighways.[45] The audacious plan was ahead of its time and was never realized. But by the 1950s, the nation's thirst for high-speed automotive movement had grown dramatically. The region's

first freeway was a redesign of the old Bayshore Highway. The new Bayshore freeway, Highway 101, connected the city and its peninsula suburbs and airport.

In 1956, President Eisenhower signed the Federal Aid Highway Act into law. The Interstate Highway System was born. About the same time, California's State Department of Transportation proposed ten freeways connecting all points in San Francisco, running them through Golden Gate Park and the Panhandle, all along the waterfront, over Marina Green, and on top of Mission Street. Freeways would not only get people around the suburbs, they could ease movement within the city and facilitate the high-speed movement to and from downtown. In San Francisco, however, the freeway plan ran into opposition from the start. It was far too sweeping.

The birth of neighborhood organizing can be traced to the city's freeway revolt. In 1959, in response to citizen protests, the Board of Supervisors cancelled seven of the proposed freeways. The Embarcadero Freeway also stopped dead in its construction tracks at Broadway in North Beach. In 1966, the Park-Panhandle freeway was reduced to the rump Central Freeway. The only new freeway completed, besides Highway 101, was the Southern/Junipero Serra Freeway (today's Interstate 280). Another bridge across the Bay, the Southern Crossing, would have linked up to the freeway network. It too was cancelled. Plans for the densest freeway net in the world led the populace to reject the inevitability of technological progress and urban development. For the first time citizens saw the historic city fabric as an environment worth fighting for.

Throughout the Bay Area freeway plans were scaled back. In Berkeley, a citizen's revolt stopped Highway 13 from boring down Ashby Avenue to connect with I-80. In Contra Costa County, the extension of Highway 24 through Walnut Creek toward Clayton was dropped. In Marin, conservationists defeated Gulf Oil Corporation's plan–which included a new 30,000-person community called

Marincello—to build a freeway over the Headlands to the West County.

Elsewhere, though, a host of freeways were built. In the East Bay, for example, Interstate 580 was rammed through Oakland's foothills during the 1960s. The growth of San Jose from a small city in 1950 to the state's third largest city today was abetted by the construction of a massive freeway net over the entire Santa Clara Valley. New bridges were also built, such as the cantilever-truss Richmond-San Rafael Bridge (1956) and a replacement for the Hayward-San Mateo Bridge (1967).

BART station in Oakland

IMPROVING THE INFRASTRUCTURE

Upon its completion, the Hayward-San Mateo Bridge was the longest in the world. It was designed in part by the structural engineer and University of California professor T. Y. Lin. He opened the seven-mile span to the sky by setting it upon a concrete trestle for the lowrise section and an arching higher span supported by steel-box girders. Lin was pivotal in the international development of prestressed concrete, where, during construction, concrete is put into a state of stress—often using tensioned steel cables—so that during the subsequent carrying of real loads it remains in a stable state of compression. The most important local example of Lin's work in prestressed concrete is the Moscone Convention Center in San Francisco. Completed in 1981, the 260,000 square-foot hall was the world's largest continuous space ever built underground.

In 1962, voters in San Francisco, Alameda, and Contra Costa counties approved another massive engineering project, Bay Area Rapid Transit (BART). Construction on the initial 75-mile system began in 1964, travel in the East Bay started in 1972, and the subway line through San Francisco opened in 1974. The eight stations in the city are linked to the East Bay by a 3.6 mile-long tube. Fifteen different architectural firms were chosen to design stations (with certain standardized elements such as graph-

ics and fare machines). Fittingly, skyscraper architects Skidmore, Owings & Merrill designed the Embarcadero and Montgomery stations in downtown San Francisco, with stainless steel columns and hung luminous ceilings. For the Glen Park and Balboa Park stations, Ernest Born crafted above ground edifices of bold concrete forms that support glass and steel roofs. The MacArthur and Rockridge stations in Oakland, by Maher & Martens, were situated in the middle of Highway 24, and covered by a forthright skeleton of steel I-beams and corrugated metal. Maher & Martens also covered the downtown Berkeley station with a dome.

While BART has provided an alternative to vehicular travel, initial hopes for densification around the stations were not realized. According to historian Robert Self, BART set "off a two-decade boom in downtown San Francisco that produced thirty-four new high-rises and sixteen million square feet of office and retail space. BART did less for downtown Oakland, which now suffered from even greater comparative disadvantage; high-end shoppers could by-pass the city altogether in favor of San Francisco, an eight-minute train ride away, and San Francisco had more high-quality office space than Oakland. It did nothing to assist in the structural rehabilitation of West Oakland, now a throughway for transportation lines that carried people other places."[46]

BART did not reverse the spiraling disinvestment of inner-city, working-class neighborhoods. Post-war suburbanization had brought both white flight and capital flight. A host of neighborhoods–much of Richmond, West and East Oakland, Southwest Berkeley, Bayview-Hunters Point in San Francisco, East Palo Alto— became largely African-American and increasingly bereft of basic commercial and municipal services. Because of their residents' lack of economic and political power, these neighborhoods became the sites for unwanted land uses, including: freeways, incinerators, power plants, light industry, and the bulk of the region's low-income housing projects. Unlike the East Coast or Midwest, however, housing abandonment was not widespread in these districts. Because of the need for more housing in growing California, another destabilizing condition emerged. Throughout older working-class neighborhoods, multiple-unit apartment complexes were slotted onto small lots, replacing single-family or duplex housing. The community fabric of small-scale houses was torn apart. Block after block in the Eastlake district of Oakland, for example, reveals substantial Victorian or craftsman houses hemmed in by slab apartments held up on stilts over parking.

The Contemporary (1965–Present)

INKLINGS OF THE POSTMODERN

San Francisco was one of the birthplaces of architectural postmodernism. In 1962, Charles Moore designed an addition to the turn-of-the-century Citizens Savings Bank on Market Street that matched many aspects of the older building's form–overall height and width, tripartite division, Mansard roof. Moore, who the same year quoted from numerous historical sources for his own house in Orinda, was dissatisfied with the severe structural rationalism popular in the nation. His idea was to create connections between a current design project and its historical, geographic and typological context. A new building's form, in other words, might respond to a set of conditions–both on- and off-site—reaching far beyond basic structure, materials, and function. For instance, in his Orinda home he referred to Mycenean fire sanctuaries, baroque church baldachins, and traditional American house roofs. Anything and everything was possible in postmodernism.

A couple of years later, Moore, along with Donlyn Lyndon, William Turnbull, and Richard Whitaker (MLTW) went on to design one of the epochal buildings of California history, Condominium 1 at Sea Ranch–what has come to be known as the wooden rock by the sea.[47] The compound responded to the angular modernism of Alvar Aalto while paying close attention to its craggy site above the Pacific Ocean that had been used for grazing sheep and still contained wooden barns. Unlike the ranch houses of mid-century, Condominium 1 rose to the sky in sharp and slanting vertical planes whose wood weathered into a cool gray color over time. The bunched massing and sloping roofs without over-

Condominium I in Sea Ranch (Moore, Lyndon, Turnbull, Whitaker)

hangs were an example of site-specific architecture packed with the energy of action painting. Many other architects, including Joseph Esherick, designed more sedate buildings for the large Sea Ranch project, but the shed roofs and fractured geometries in redwood and glass of Condominium 1 grabbed the nation's attention and went on to became a vernacular style. In the wake of wartime and post-war housing experiments, the complex also sparked the popularity of cluster housing—multiple unit complexes organized around common grounds and parking areas.

Lawrence Halprin crafted the landscape plan for Sea Ranch. It minimized development impacts to the site and maximized architectural responses to it. Rather than hugging the shoreline, as most beach communities had done in the past, the coastal bluffs were kept open, and houses were tucked into bunches on the folds of inland meadows. Following agricultural traditions, hedgerows were planted perpendicular to the shore to shelter house groupings from the relentless winds. Likewise, the landscape plan encouraged building shapes that would play off the silhouettes and materials of weathered barns on the site and vicinity.

In a long career, Halprin expanded the concerns of landscape architecture beyond the contemplative visual perception of shape and space. A product of the 1960s, he was driven to liberate people's kinetic sense as well, and saw landscape design as the choreography of human activity. As artist Jim Burns wrote: "Halprin contrasted the classic garden with its carefully balanced vistas and artfully arranged focal points with contemporary, more free-form gardens that encourage vigorous participation in a wider range of activities."[48] His parks and landscaped gardens around complexes featured fountains shaped by jutting and jagged concrete forms that invited exploration and illustrated the playful possibilities of both natural and human processes. To Halprin, modern landscape design was open to all sorts of

Sea Ranch (Moore, Lyndon, Turnbull, Whitaker)

arrangements and motions; it was modern dance and not ballet.

CAPITAL OF THE COUNTERCULTURE
In 1968 in San Francisco Halprin led a workshop, "Experiments in Environment" that allowed people to discover themselves within their surroundings. This landscape "happening" followed the raucous contours of San Francisco's blossoming counterculture, and momentous occasions such as the earlier Gathering of the Tribes in Golden Gate Park and Summer of Love in the Haight-Ashbury. The hippie counterculture brought about a rediscovery of the city's long-neglected Victorian legacy. For the first time, the formerly white and gray wooden buildings were painted vivid colors, an architectural counterpart to the paisley-print fabrics, tie-dye shirts, sinuous rock posters and psychedelic light shows popular at concerts.[49] At 710 Ashbury Street, the Grateful Dead tinted their house in a variety of colors best described as purple haze.

By the 1970s, rural Northern California was dotted with back-to-the-land communes. Many of their makeshift dwellings were simple A-frame or post-and-beam constructions, whose surfaces were left purposefully rustic.[50] Popularized by Stewart Brand in his 1968 *Whole Earth Catalog,* geodesic domes became another key architectural statement of the hippie era. Geodesic domes had been developed by Buckminster Fuller as lightweight structures held together by triangles in tension. Never adopted for the mass-housing market, their unusual appearance proved irresistible to the communes. Domes, as architectural historian Margaret Crawford wrote, introduced a new kind of space: "their circularity, frame-and-skin construction, and portability linked them with nomadic dwellings such as North American teepees or Mongolian Yurts."[51] While domes also became popular in architecture schools, over time their difficulty of construction and awkward spaces limited their use.

Among the more striking countercultural buildings were those executed by students of Bruce Goff and Herb Greene, who, during the 1960s, led the school of architecture at the University of Oklahoma.[52] These designs were guided by close attention to the local terrain and palette of materials. Influenced by artistic happenings and performance art, designers purposefully incorporated both lasting site characteristics and circumstantial/happenstance events. For example, Robert Overstreet's Oyama Houseboat, from 1978, relates both to the neighboring houseboat community of Sausalito and the temple complexes of Japan, its owner's homeland. The copper roof is shaped both like an inverted ship's hull and a Shinto shrine. Valentin Agnoli's houses, primarily in Stinson Beach, embody the notion of analogical architecture—where the form of a building produces associations with other worldly morphologies. His 1968 house boasts a sinuously curving gable roof that reflects the half-moon shape of the beach as well as the body of a whale. Agnoli's 1970 house consists of an oval cylinder that splays outward at its third story like the cap of a mushroom. The tectonic exploration includes an exposed framework of Douglas-Fir wooden posts and beams that refers to the nearby forest.

When it came to hiring established architects, some of the larger countercultural complexes looked to recent architectural prototypes like Sea Ranch. In 1958, Chuck Dederich founded the Synanon Church to rehabilitate drug addicts. By the late 1960s, Synanon was growing rapidly and Dederich commissioned Ellis Kaplan (of Kaplan, McLaughlin, Diaz) to design a center for the community on Tomales Bay. "Synanon City," noted urban critic Roger Montgomery, promised "a fundamental alternative to the life-style of the suburban subdivision with its nuclear families, detached houses and commercial exploitation of the land."[53] The most innovative part of the complex was the dwelling caves, wood-frame cells providing units for sleep, lovemaking or just hanging out. The caves and community building adapted the Sea Ranch shed-roof and redwood vernacular.

The connection with Sea Ranch was not accidental. The countercultural rejection of mainstream culture dovetailed with a mounting critique of mainstream architectural culture. Since the publication of Jane Jacobs' The Death and Life of American Cities in 1960, architects and critics began to question fundamental elements of modernist city design–the skyscraper, the expressway, the parking garage, and the superblock. But, at least initially, these critiques were uncoordinated. So was design, as illustrated by the diverse mix of offerings at an exhibition of California architecture at the San Francisco Museum of Modern Art in 1976.[54]

THE REACTION AGAINST MODERNISM

In 1960, a few months after the first freeway revolt architectural critic Allan Temko came out against freeways and underground parking garages–the complete ones at Union Square and St. Mary's Park and a proposed one for Portsmouth Square–that destroyed city parks. At the same time, though, he lauded Justin Herman's urban renewal plans, which proposed to demolish the old produce district to construct Embarcadero Center and Golden Gateway, and similarly tear down much of the Western Addition. Temko also encouraged tall buildings for Civic Center and along the waterfront, districts that, in his opinion, had become abjectly tawdry.[55]

Asian-style House in Daly City

By contrast, in 1965, Charles Moore criticized the newest additions to the San Francisco skyline, and especially high-rise buildings, like the Fontana Apartments by Hammerberg and Herman, which blocked the view of the Bay. Moore wasn't opposed to skyscrapers; he just wanted them to be in the right place. He stressed the importance of situating a building, and wrote that "the sensible and thrilling cityscape of Russian Hill, whose crest is studded with free-standing skyscrapers, dazzled with panorama, and whose flanks allow low buildings to participate as well in the city's great game (if you take the picture from just the right angle)."[56] Moore's writing on California during the 1960s approached architecture in a cinematic mode, and understood built form and space as narratives the public might follow and enjoy. Instead of quoting buildings by Walter Gropius or Eero Saarinen, his articles are filled with references to kitschy roadside attractions like the Madonna Inn in San Luis Obispo and the Nut Tree restaurant and rest stop in Vacaville. Pop architecture had become the vogue. Halprin too was preoccupied with new modes of mobile perception. In 1966, he published one of the most insightful aesthetics of the freeway, writing that while freeways were destroyers of the urban fabric, in less developed areas they could positively engender "a series of constantly changing impressions which move by like the frames in a motion picture."[57]

These nascent critiques of varied aspects of modernism were to congeal into a comprehensive reaction by the early 1970s. To many citizens and city planners, San Francisco seemed under assault by a hurricane of development. Large-scale public and private housing projects broke apart the city's fine-grain fabric. New apartments reached higher and higher into the sky, blocking cherished views. The thorniest development turned out to be the South of Market Redevelopment scheme, among the flop-houses and bars for seamen and working-men. Beginning in the late 1950s, a succession of developers and city officials produced a succession of plans for convention centers, hotels, and sports stadiums. An ambitious 1969 urban design by Japanese architect Kenzo Tange never got off the drawing board.[58] Still, by 1980, the Redevelopment Agency had demolished much of the area and a new convention center was under construction.

In the expanding Financial District, a boom in high-rise construction created a skyscraper hill dominated, as of 1972, by the dark Bank of America Headquarters and the light Transamerica Pyramid. Preservationists coined the term Manhattanization to describe the soaring and undesired skyline. A couple of mega-projects broke the camel's back. In 1970, Skidmore, Owings & Merrill proposed a skyscraper called Ferry Port Plaza next to the Ferry Building, and more audaciously, a massive U.S. Steel Building (with a 550-foot tower) on land-fill alongside the old piers north of the Bay Bridge. Both projects were voted down, and in 1971 the city adopted the Urban Design Element of its Master Plan. For the first time in American history, urban design was put on an equal footing with zoning. In 1972, allowable building heights were lowered everywhere, and especially along the waterfront. The Urban Design Element discouraged site planning that didn't enhance the city's steep topography.[59] Provisions called for low-rise buildings at the waterfront and on the slopes of hills with higher densities permitted at the summits. Urban design guidelines also encouraged new construction to relate visually to the pre-modernist cityscape.

Ongoing real-estate pressures led, though, to more skyscrapers and more demolitions of historic buildings. Back in 1959, the Montgomery Block, the most important building from the days of the Mother Lode, had been demolished for a parking lot that eventually became the Transamerica Building. In 1968, the Crocker Building by A. Page Brown, one of the downtown's first skyscrapers when it was built in 1890, was torn down. In 1975, the Alaska Commercial Building in the Financial District met the wrecking ball. In 1980, Philip Johnson's Neiman-Marcus Building replaced the beloved City of Paris Building on Union Square. While several citizens' referenda to restrict downtown development failed, the die was cast. The city adopted the *Downtown Plan* in 1985, which further lowered heights and densities. This time, an ambitious preservation component enacted controls to save over 500 of the most significant older downtown buildings. The plan also mandated urban design controls that would force architects to design nostalgic towers with distinctive tops. Architectural postmodernism was now legally enforced.

POSTMODERN HEYDAY

Throughout the country, postmodern design was the rage during the 1980s. Classical elements returned in pastel colors, inflated sizes, and incongruous places. For several suburban houses in the East Bay, Thomas Gordon Smith imported the spatial planning and ornamental vocabulary of the Roman villa. Andrew Batey and Mark Mack built private homes in Marin, Napa, and Sonoma counties, drawing on the geometric severity and axial orientation of Aldo Rossi's neo-rationalism. Michael Graves designed the Clos Pegase Winery in Calistoga, and helped set off a Tuscan-design frenzy. Dan Solomon's

residential works fused the Anglo and Spanish past, developing a row-house manner of composition around a central courtyard–alas, at a scale of development that dwarfs any historical prototypes. The range of formal references in these architects' works far exceeded the modest vernacular models that had been popular from the 1930s to the 1970s: principally cottages, ranches, and barns. It was as if Bay Area architectural culture had returned to the heady days of stylistic eclecticism, albeit with a strong dose of irony and theory.

Postmodernism, while advertised as contextual, was often anything but. Mark Mack's use of elementary forms leapt beyond place into elementary Platonic forms. Michael Graves and Dan Solomons' works took great liberties with history, mixing up styles separated by continents and centuries. Fundamentally reactive to the pace of social change, postmodernism retreated from the concrete, everyday building life of the metropolis. It wrenched architecture from its ties to new structural, material, and functional developments, and set the building art within a separate, abstract realm.

Locally, the turn to history and theory was supported by several intellectual endeavors. William Stout, an inveterate bibliophile, opened an architectural bookstore in North Beach, William Stout Architectural Books in 1975. A couple of years later, Stout and Steven Holl began *Pamphlet Architecture* as an alternative to mainstream architectural publishing. The goal of the occasional journal was to disseminate the work and ideas of young architects. Mark Mack, along with Diane Ghirardo and Kurt Foster, edited *Archetype* from 1979 to 1983. Unlike most magazines on architecture in California, *Archetype* did not focus on local work. At the time, it was felt that California needed a version of New York's *Oppositions*, an intellectual forum that would connect design with history and theory, and California with international currents.

All through those years, however, the overall architectural culture in Northern California was getting more provincial. In 1989, San Francisco adopted *Residential Design Guidelines* that forced architects to include a host of features on new buildings that conform to the pre-1930s cityscape–bay windows and punched windows, belt courses and cornices, materials like wood or stucco. Guidelines similarly encouraged breaking down the massing of larger buildings into smaller pieces. Similar statutes were enacted in other Bay Area cities.

Von Stein House in Sonoma County (Fernau & Hartman)

COLLAGE AESTHETIC

Since then, several architects have taken the contextual spirit into a collage aesthetic. David Baker crafts housing complexes that gather the varied visual moments of their locale. Different colors, façade materials and textures, bays or gables, are researched and then assembled atop the frame of a single building. Because the parts stand out more than the whole, the buildings break apart in a temporal sense. They appear to have been built, like the larger city around them, piecemeal over time, rather than, as is actually the case, in a single stroke of design. One building looks as if it is a series of different buildings. Large-scale development, therefore, yields small-scale visual appearance. Similarly, Fernau & Hartman have built a number of commodious residences as well as commercial and institutional buildings that feature different materials—clapboard, wooden battens, concrete block, metal sun shades–to cause a building to appear older than it actually is. For the Von Stein House (1993) in Sonoma County, the architects cast a single residence in the visual role of a village of structures climbing a hill. Several outdoor terraces (including an observation tower) intertwine with three detached masses of house.

Public housing too began to go the way of tradition. In West Oakland, Michael Pyatok employed gable roofs, projecting bracketed bays, and clapboard siding

for a 1992 grouping of two- and three-story townhouses, the Marcus Garvey Commons. The details reduce the scale of the project and blend in with the older nineteenth-century cityscape. Later in the 1990s, many cities, especially San Francisco and Oakland, began tearing down their highrise and crime-ridden public housing projects and replacing them with lowrises. Again, the concentration of low-income residents and poor maintenance were not the only culprits. Modernist design was unfairly blamed for the social failures. Thus, in cases like Backen, Arrigoni & Ross's Hayes Valley Dwellings (1999), gables replaced flat roofs. Even lowrise complexes—like William Wurster's Valencia Gardens and Ernest Born's North Beach Housing—fell to the wrecking ball because they were modernist and had flat roofs. The postmodern fervor didn't bode well, in fact, for other modernist masterpieces. The list of demolished buildings includes: Gardner Dailey's Red Cross Building, Raphael Soriano's Hollawell Seed Company, and Jones & Emmons' Daphne Funeral Home, all in San Francisco, as well as Robert Mittelstadt's City Hall in Fremont.

ENVIRONMENTAL EVENTS AND EFFORTS

In 1989, the Loma Prieta Earthquake destroyed numerous buildings and collapsed a section of the Bay Bridge and the double-decker Cypress Freeway in West Oakland. That double-decker structure and the similar Embarcadero Freeway in San Francisco were torn down. While the Oakland freeway was rebuilt nearby, in San Francisco no replacement was made. The Embarcadero was suddenly open again, and re-designed into a boulevard replete with Canary Island Palms and a trolley line. San Francisco's Central Freeway was also gradually reduced to the point where, in 2005, it ended at Market Street. New boulevards have been built on the vacated land, Mandela Parkway in Oakland, and Octavia Boulevard in San Francisco. Additionally, the Loma Prieta quake left a long trail of seismic retrofitting projects, and resulted in the current one to replace the eastern span of the Bay Bridge.

Another disaster struck a couple of years after Loma Prieta, the Oakland Hills Fire of 1991. Close to 3,000 houses burned. Among them were a couple of Maybecks, Julia Morgan's Redgate (1911), and MLTW's Talbert House (1965). Rebuilding has dramatically changed the character of the neighborhood, giving architects a license to experiment. Given today's preferences, new homes are roughly twice as large as their predecessors and quite boxy. On the steep slopes, complex sectional compositions have emerged; some buildings step down from one-story entry facades as many as four levels. Landscaping guidelines advise against dense plantings of flammable exotics, especially Eucalyptus trees.

Not surprisingly, green architecture has drawn a large local following, stressing recycled content, salvaged materials, passive solar panels on roofs for hot water, cisterns to collect rainwater, and radiant floor slabs. In 1977, Sim van der Ryn, then professor at Berkeley's School of Architecture, completed the Bateson Building in Sacramento, which pioneered low-energy heating, cooling, and day-lighting strategies.[60] In recent years, both straw-bale and rammed-earth building techniques have received a lot of attention, principally due to their ability, like stucco, to provide excellent insulation with inexpensive, easy-to-construct methods. At Hopland, in southern Mendocino County, the Real Goods Solar Living Institute exhibits a 5,000 square foot straw-bale dwelling. The two-foot thick walls of straw-bale—held together by rebar, then covered with chicken wire and stucco—provide buildings that are self-heating and self-cooling. In Napa, since the early 1980s David Easton's Rammed Earthworks has built a number of houses that exemplify the energy-reducing qualities of rammed-earth thermal mass.

Co-housing is another partially green idea where units are grouped to save space and reduce consumption. The first American experiment with co-housing, which originated in Denmark, took place at the Muir Commons in Davis, where every aspect of design was geared to encourage social interaction. In 1992, Doyle Street Co-housing opened in Emeryville, the first urban iteration of the idea. An existing brick and steel warehouse was renovated and enlarged to create space for twelve loft units and 2,200 square feet of common area. Here, as elsewhere, the design focus was spatial: how to construct circulation routes that weave between private and communal areas.

Peter Calthorpe, one of the founders of the school of New Urbanism, has maintained a local practice since 1983.[61] New Urbanism rejects the low-density vehicular suburb and replaces it with dense, public transit-oriented communities modeled after the commuter rail suburb of the early twentieth century. Calthorpe's largest Bay Area project is "The Crossings" in Mountain View, completed in 2000, and built on the 18-acre site of the Old Mill Mall. This medium-density community of 400 single-family homes is walking distance from stores and a planned Caltrain commuter station. Architecturally, Calthorpe is less overly historicist than his Florida counterparts, Duany/Plater Zyberg, but this abstracted traditionalism does include gables, front porches, and plenty of trim.

Urban sprawl in the East Bay

SPRAWL, SILICON AND YET MORE STYLES

The anti-growth, New Urbanist, and environmental movements have not greatly hindered overall development. The Bay Area added over two million residents between 1970 and 2000. Vehicular-focused industrial parks, office parks, malls, power centers, and subdivisions of condominiums and single-family homes have proliferated. The route of Interstate 80 heading toward Sacramento is almost completely urbanized, and residents of the Central Valley towns of Modesto, Manteca, and Tracy now commute to the Bay Area.

Along the freeways and their nearby arterials, a patently-vehicular landscape has emerged. Signs, as Robert Venturi and Denise Scott-Brown prophesized in 1971's *Learning from Las Vegas,* have become the dominant visual cues for drivers and passengers. For a range of building types, from motels to big-box stores, design is economical and temporary—blank walls of concrete block or dry-vit that can be replaced in 10-year cycles. But nowadays, it is not just signs that matter. Signs are all the more valued and prominent if they carry a brand name.

Sometimes, as in the case of Best Buy or Target, branded signage overwhelms much of the building. The roadside landscape here, like in much of America, has become a corollary of television advertising, an alluring stage-set for consumption glimpsed at considerable speed and distraction.

As arterials blazed with stores, signs and parking lots, the design of residential subdivisions retreated from the street. Cluster housing, inaugurated at Sea Ranch, became a widespread phenomenon. Beginning in the late 1970s, at Orindawoods, attached townhouses were grouped around cul-de-sacs and oriented to the steep topography. As compared to earlier subdivisions, cluster developments preserved a far greater share of land for common open space. This idea found an unappealing iteration in the gated community, a housing development that restricts public access to its site. In 1979, the first homes of Blackhawk opened in the San Ramon valley west of Mount Diablo. Developed by Ken Behring, the 2,400-residence elite community, completed by the early 1990s, surrounds two eighteen-hole golf courses and other sports complexes.

Those same years witnessed the rise of Silicon Valley, a massive agglomeration sprawling from Fremont to San Jose to Redwood City. Santa Clara and San Mateo counties now count over 70 million square feet of office space, as compared to the 40 million square feet in San Francisco. Despite the vigorous growth, the architecture of the valley has been disappointing in its quality. While there have been some highpoints, such as the work of McCue, Boone and Tomsick for IBM and Alza corporations, most high-tech office parks don't reach for high design.[62] Companies are focused on an information- and image-rich product and don't value the communicative powers of architecture. Moreover, their constant mergers and downsizings speaks for the importance of exit strategies–i.e., building plans to incorporate the next tenant. Undifferentiated boxes are thus preferred to articulated shapes. Companies, in their non-stop development mode, prefer to work with local architects. Not a single architect of international renown has designed an office park. Among the few local firms that have tried to spruce up the tilt-up landscape has been Studios Architecture. For Silicon Graphics International, 3Com, and Northern Telecom, they designed colorful buildings in surprising shapes with clip-ons of attached staircases and other sinuous forms.

Overall, the period between 1975 and 2000 was a time of reaction, and not vision.[63] In a broad sense, the Bay Area had rejected the goal of architectural professionalism established in the 1890s and developed through a variety of theoretical approaches in the twentieth century. Development, in the years leading up to the dot-com boom, resembled the bawdy individuality of Gold Rush days. No wonder Victorians became a fetish. Enamored with the past, vocal members of the public and municipal bureaucracies were hostile to any building that would significantly change the look of the region. In Berkeley, the Landmarks Preservation Board approved the preservation of almost any old building. In San Francisco, coercive design guidelines, wielded by the City Planning Department and neighborhood groups, legitimated mediocrity as a design solution. The 1995 San Francisco Main Library, completed by James Ingo Freed, epitomizes the indecisiveness. Two sides of the building look to the past and copy the Beaux-Arts moves of neighboring Civic Center buildings. The other sides are assertively modern, but the whole never comes together. Likewise, for the Giants baseball park, completed in 2000, Hellmuth, Obata & Kassabaum chose to conceal the powerful concrete and steel structure within a historicist veneer of red bricks, cream-colored copings, and a clock tower.

These efforts at recreating a historical cityscape weren't all that different than the marketing strategies for themed parks, resorts, and retail stores popular nationwide. Both municipal design guidelines and corporate theming concentrate on a few visually memorable moments that can be connected to other effects of media exposure–postcards, coffee-table books, Internet browsing. Neither encourages architecture of depth. What results are nostalgic vision-bites. The most notable case of surface design is Santana Row in San Jose. Completed in 2003, a 1500-foot street–containing shops, a hotel, a multiplex, and residences–simulates, if only at the level of fountains and wrought-iron railings, *la dolce vita* of the Mediterranean. Santana Row's fine-grained street set within a mega-complex reveals the Bay Area's schizophrenic design leanings. Many of the same people who drive to shop in suburban malls or power centers celebrate small neighborhood shopping streets created in the era of the trolley. Many of the same people who spend hundreds of thousands of dollars on complete interior remodels fight to keep their neighborhood's facades looking as they did a century ago. Perhaps as distribution centers, hospitals, airports, stores, workplaces, and homes keep ballooning in size, people see "the look" of old styles as their only resort, their only way to maintain a few intimate moments in their lives.

THE NEW MODERNISM

By the mid nineties, the unified aesthetic and purpose of architectural modernism seemed gone for good. But, at the nadir of architectural design both locally and nationally, hints of better things to come could be detected. At the Redevelopment Agency's long-stalled Yerba Buena Center project, important buildings began to rise from the vacant lots. For the first time ever, several international architects were hired to build adjacent to each other: Fumihiko Maki's Center for the Arts, James Polshek's Center for the Arts Theater, and Mario Botta's San Francisco Museum of Modern Art. The new buildings showed citizens that bold architecture could enhance the city and many other projects have followed. There has never been a period when so much energy flowed in from New York, Los Angeles, Mexico, Asia, and Europe as the years from 1993 to 2008. Herzog and de Meuron's Dominus Winery, of

Yerba Buena Center for the Arts Theater (Polshek)

1998, garnered a great deal of acclaim, and led the De Young Museum to hire the firm to design its new building. Between 1998 and 2000, many citizens lamented the passing of the old undistinguished museum, and some groups vociferously fought against the new building. Saner heads prevailed, however, and the magisterial museum opened in 2005. In 2008, new museums will be completed by Renzo Piano, for the California Academy of Sciences, and Daniel Libeskind, for the Contemporary Jewish Museum. From San Jose to Emeryville, Ricardo Legorreta has erected several boldly colored exercises in platonic forms. In the early 2000s, Norman Foster designed two laboratory buildings for Stanford University, and architects from Steven Ehrlich to Will Bruder to Gwathmey-Siegel to Tadao Ando have built (or are building) houses.

Contemporary design shares a great deal in common with mid-century modernism, including a concern for inventing and expressing new materials, and investigating and implementing new organizations of space. Still, it departs from modernism in several significant ways. First, the means of envisioning building, especially on the computer, has led to a preoccupation with customized materials and highly intricate shapes. Second, new buildings occupy a larger slice of the public eye; they play an increasingly important role as generators of visual spectacle (and tourism) within an experience economy. Third, the importance of theory within architectural culture leads architects to fashion a much more nuanced role for themselves as culture providers and mediators; they are increasingly preoccupied with social arenas like community affairs, management, and marketing. And finally, the exploration of site-specificity, influenced by the other visual arts, has erased the epoch of tabula-rasa urban design, at least from most drawing boards and screens.

Landscape architecture has similarly witnessed a major shift in ideology since the happening 1960s. When the Christos set out to erect a 24-mile long fence of white-nylon fabric through the hills of Sonoma County to the Pacific Ocean, they encountered considerable resistance from landowners and bureaucrats. The artwork was nonetheless approved and put into place for two months in 1978. *Running Fence* helped changed the regional attitude toward landscape, which by this point had become mired in cliché. It caused people to see how the insertion of new materials and shapes could deepen the understanding of place. Since then, the best new landscape architecture has embodied a critical engagement with the geology, history, and cultural forces that shape the Bay Area's beloved land.

In particular, George Hargreaves has fought against scenographic garden design that detaches us from the land's fuller meaning in passive, visual perception of beauty. All through the 1980s and 1990s, through the use of found materials, repetition of forms, and the building of strong earthworks, Hargreaves played up urbanized dissonance. He strove to draw attention to a site's natural processes, surrounding context, and historical substrata. His projects for the Guadalupe River in San Jose or Byxbee Park in Palo Alto, as historian Elizabeth K. Meyer describes, "employ land sculpting strategies and spatial sequences as a means to express the temporal characteristics and structure of a particular place such as the geologic time of the region's land formations, or the cyclical time of floods."[64] To Hargreaves, the more wretched a landscape, the more inviting it becomes.

Because the world continues to change, no architect can gain an iron-clad grasp on context. The context for the region's architecture is surely found in older buildings, topography, and the natural environment, but it is also located in the digital economics, explosive social mores, sleek new building technologies, and connoisseur lifestyle of young city dwellers. Among contemporary architects, Stanley Saitowitz's works have crafted a cerebral, industrial, and polished take on context. For his Studio Loft (1992) in San Francisco, Saitowitz married the New York infatuation with industrial lofts to San Francisco's urban condition. In the process he broke apart the fiction of the bay window as the fundamental regional way to heighten illumination for an interior. On Natoma Street in the South of Market, steel beams and strip windows span the entire width of the narrow lot. Interior spaces flow uninterrupted. Light pours in. The hyper-urban architectural language was a killer application, both among artists and a rapidly growing population of high-tech workers enamored with high design.

Since the mid-1990s, loft buildings have been the hottest residential building type in the urban core. Many loft buildings, at least initially, were artist-instigated conversions of old factories and warehouses to live-work spaces. Architect-designed construction followed. The new loft buildings feature open plans and plentiful windows. In the speculative fervor, some of their designs have looked backward as well as forward. Some critics see lofts as alien invaders. In reality, the residential loft building is a home-grown hybrid. It combines not only work and residence, but also modernism and historicism—the long and smooth and glazed walls of the daylight factory, the articulated bays and fine-grain details of the rowhouse.

Saitowitz's innovation with urban building types extends to suburban and rural projects. By boring into earth, spanning a ravine, projecting out over a large drop, aligning (both floors and roofs) to nearby contours, or carefully framing a view, his houses interpret their sites. While his early works often refer to variable landscape shapes, the later bar houses, such as 2002's Lieff House in Rutherford, heighten the landscape through contrasting rectilinear form. As he notes: "Our remaking of the crust of the earth, our efforts to capture space on the horizon, can be viewed as geological. In this process, the chance evolution of nature over eons of time is abbreviated with purposeful acts guided by thought."[65]

Other architects similarly take the trouble to endow houses with exceptional materials and spaces. Jim Jennings has made monolithic artistic statements out of glass block, Korten steel plates, corrugated steel, or poured concrete. For his Visiting Artists House on the Oliver Estate in Geyserville (2003), Jennings sliced two gradually converging concrete walls into a hill, carving out rhythmic spaces for indoor and outdoor living. Each pavilion is a simple structure of glass curtain-walls, steel cross beams, and metal roof decking, set between poured-in-place concrete walls. At angles to each other, the walls distort perspective and turn the building into what might appear as a perceptual telescope.[66] Somewhat differently, Anne Fougeron has explored ways to introduce light into an interior and lightness to an overall mass. Her straight-edged houses soften through contrapuntal rhythms of industrial, earthen and wooden materials, solids and voids, and a variety of semi-enclosed spaces. Fougeron's method of weaving differently clad volumes together to create a complex spatial whole is best illustrated on a weekend house she completed in 2004 in Big Sur.

The new wave of modernism has washed ashore in civic and commer-

Visiting Artists House in Sonoma County (Jennings)

cial architecture. Both Kava Massih and Simon, Martin-Vegue, Winkelstein, Moris (SMWM) have designed numerous buildings that blend industrial materials into a site's context. Craig Hartman, of Skidmore, Owings & Merrill, works in the tradition of the firm's illustrious previous designers in San Francisco—Chuck Bassett and Myron Goldsmith. Hartman's recent office buildings and International Terminal at San Francisco Airport, completed in 2000, return to the vocabulary of glass curtain walls and soaring, truss-supported spaces. Other designers, like Gary Handel and Cesar Pelli, have also brought the San Francisco skyscraper back to its earlier era of curtain-wall elegance. That's not to say the skyscraper's development is over. In 2006, Thom Mayne's Federal Building in San Francisco was completed. Its rippling steel screen, set atop glass walls and a forthright concrete structure, elevates the building's multiple systems into an expressive syntax.

Mayne's high-tech masterpiece is not without local precedent. Beginning in the late 1980s, the firm of Holt, Hinshaw, Pfau, Jones explored ways to express the vast store of form contained in a building's infrastructure. In a few completed structures for houses, bridges, commercial structures and memorials, and a larger number of unrealized projects, the architects animated the machine guts of a building. To Wes Jones, the muscular and articulated forms resulting from these efforts exhibit the integrity and appropriateness common to natural

Federal Building (Morphosis)

forms, such as trees and rocks.[67] After Jones moved to Los Angeles, Holt Hinshaw and Peter Pfau, working independently, have continued to shape, clad and detail buildings in close conjunction with mechanical systems and materials. Another firm that has reveled in industrialized structure and exploited hard-edged surfaces, screens, and joints is Tanner, Leddy, Maytum, Stacy. Their buildings extrude structure into armature, an exoskeleton of nuts and bolts, screens and I-beams, smoothly polished metal, concrete and glass.

Of late, a new architecture school has aided the generation of both machine-age and post-industrial architectural ideas. Founded in 1986 in the industrial lowlands of Potrero Hill, California College of the Arts was first led by Andrew Batey. In subsequent years, David Meckel, John Loomis, Rodolphe El Khoury, and Lisa Findley have directed the school. CCA has garnered a faculty of important young practitioners, among who are Bruce Tomb, Byron Kuth & Elizabeth Ranieri, Neil Schwartz, Sandra Vivanco, Thom Faulders, Cary Bernstein, Craig Scott (of Iwamoto Scott), Christos Marcopoulos and Douglas Burnham. Other up-and-coming local architects include Craig Steely, Addison Strong and Owen Kennerly. The works of these architects have had to balance competing interests. Architects and clients are undeniably fascinated with mid-century design, industrial materials, and post-industrial means

Choy Residence 1 (Bernstein)

of representation ranging from French philosophy to digitization. As could be expected, especially in San Francisco and Berkeley, planning departments and neighborhood groups have resisted experimental design. The best of the new buildings have therefore had to come up with smart, compromise solutions that play off steel and concrete with wood, and explore plate-glass or cantilevered swellings of the bay window. Whenever possible, the new urban buildings have managed to add unusual cladding, prosthetic protuberances, and incisions into walls and roofs that leave memorable shapes.

PUBLIC PRIVATE SPLIT

Both in the city grid and on suburban slopes, sophisticated clients exert a powerful influence on residential architecture of the 21st century. In a region that cultivates fine wine, food, and fashion, houses too must meet gourmet standards. These standards appear in enormous spaces, quality finishes, striking shapes, and, most of all, in the orchestration of visual perception toward bucolic pleasure.

Plaza Apartments (Leddy, Maytum, Stacy / Paulett Taggart)

Wealthy clients and influential magazines (like *Dwell*) encourage architects
to design for the money moment, and
oftentimes that moment springs aloft in
a view. This focus began with the demise
of the front picture window in the 1950s,
and the concurrent opening of the back of
the house to the outdoors. It was exacerbated by the demise of the formal living
room and dining room, starting in the
1980s, and development of the big room
(influenced by loft living), which focused
more attention on the rear of the house.
While luxury houses have long closed
themselves off to the street, their opening to the sides and rear has grown more
complicated as the density of the suburbs
has increased. Designing view corridors
has become something of a science.
Most clients don't want to see the middle
distance of adjacent suburban houses
and prefer to concentrate their gaze on
either close-range nature or long distance
panoramas. Architects have responded,
in cinematic fashion, to highlight certain
view corridors and edit out others. The
house must not only be large, elegant,
and commodious. It must function, like a
machine, to facilitate vision on only what
people want to see.

Houses in the hills are often sold
with captions that state "comes with two
bridge view." Some municipalities, like
El Cerrito and Tiburon, have enacted
hillside design guidelines to protect the
precious view corridors from both new
development and growing trees; in the
panoramic pantheon, an unobstructed
corridor toward a bridge is worth more
than one at a hillside. For instance, a
house by Gwathmey-Siegel in Belvedere,
completed in 2003, took special care
not to block the views from neighboring
houses. Consequently, from the street,
the 12,000 square foot monster home is
hardly visible; the sectional plan steps
down the hillside and culminates in a five-
story glass wall that overlooks a swimming pool and the bay. In San Francisco's
Noe Valley neighborhood, in 2005,
Ogrydziak/Prillinger Architects's 5,600
square-foot "T House" had to be literally

T House (Ogrydziak/Prillinger)

squashed into the hillside in order not to
block neighbors' views.

The protected panoramic view is a
fetish–a seemingly permanent feature
that disavows the disconcerting rate of
societal and technological change. Oddly,
the long, unobstructed view is akin to the
closing of one's eyes during meditation.
Both practices seek to cancel the chaotic
impact of reality. Likewise, it must be
admitted that the plate-glass window
denies its technological materiality just
as much as redwood siding or cedar shingles. One vanishes in utter transparency
while the other grounds itself so closely
to its natural source that it might be seen
as merging with nature–another type of
absence.

This urge toward absence fits the
increasingly private nature of society. In
the left-coast metropolis, paradoxically,
protection of one's private space–consisting not only of view corridors, but
also of on-street parking spaces and less
congested streets–takes priority over the
creation of public space and infrastructure. Thus the encouraging architectural
resurgence has not yielded a concurrent
resurgence of public projects. Despite
the affluence of the dot-com boom, for
instance, very few infrastructural projects were realized. San Jose completed
a couple of light-rail lines and BART was
extended to San Francisco airport and
a few more suburban communities, but
the long-anticipated BART extension to

San Jose seems years off. The replacement span for the Bay Bridge spawned an extremely divisive debate about the value of design that would have been unthinkable in the late 1930s when the Bay Bridge and Golden Gate Bridge were built. The area's freeways are aging, traffic congestion is increasing, but no large-scale transportation plan is in the works. Similarly, despite galloping housing costs and a frightening rate of homelessness, especially in certain parts of San Francisco, the region has not come up with comprehensive housing plans.

TOWARD THE FUTURE

Today, the challenge for the San Francisco Bay Area is to foster visionary design. Without doubt, the moments of positive, collective vision have been few (e.g., the City Beautiful Era, Modernism) and not always oriented toward the future. The more common architectural response has been motivated by backward glances and fear over the complexities of things to come. Such fears have rarely stressed emerging programmatic needs. Instead, they have led architects toward the conventions of a style, or the parameters of a building type, or the textures of a tried and true material. In each case, the search for a comforting design refuge includes too much and thus excludes the possibilities for architecture to shape the turbulent waterfall of contemporary life. Within the historicism of the nineteenth and early twentieth centuries or postmodernism there was too much attention devoted to making a building look like something else, and most often something from the past. Such architecture ended up functioning like a stage set, one thing on the outside and something completely different within. Likewise, over-zealous historic preservationists have over-determined the identity of San Francisco and its region, attempting to fossilize the contemporary city and leaving little room for designers to maneuver in. As Rem Koolhaas warns about cities, "the stronger the identity, the more it imprisons, the more it resists expansion, interpretation, renewal, contradiction."[68]

The long history of architecture teaches us that we know only a small fraction of what buildings may look like and function like. The wonder and relevance of architecture lies in its exploring this vast terrain. Today, digital tools and techniques furnish architectural images as wide-ranging and malleable as the computer-driven exchange of information on the Internet. The new and dynamic architectural image warrants a new and dynamic approach to building. Fixed identity is passé. Architecture must be a creation of change and growth. Especially here in the digital capital of the world, the frontiers of architecture have become more provocative than ever. The region's history of economic booms and busts, social turmoil, technological innovation, and landscape veneration shows no sign of abating. Architects must work harder than ever to construct a beautiful coherence out of these conflicts and opportunities.

The epochal buildings of Bay Area history, those that have had the most local resonance and international influence, have all forged new ground through an interaction with landscape. These include the region's Arts and Crafts Movement; architectural Modernism; the gardens of Church and Eckbo; the flexible school designs of Kump and Reid; the park-like campuses of the Stanford Research Park; Halprin and MLTW's Sea Ranch; Wurster and Esherick's carvings of commerce within old factories; Hargreaves's or Saitowitz's geological investigations. Each of the Bay Area's best buildings deepened their engagement with landscape through exposure to new ideas and materials. A century ago, Maybeck understood architectural design as a cultural endeavor, a means of crafting structure and detail to unify the disparate technologies and symbols of modern society. Almost half a century later, Strauss and Morrow used the Golden Gate Bridge's curves of steel to objectify the sweeping tumble of the coastal ranges and sweeping rush of the automobile.

Chromogenic Dwelling (Faulders)

Recently, Herzog & de Meuron littered the walls of the Dominus Winery and de Young Museum with contextual effects. Wire boxes of stone and copper plates embolden building surfaces with site--specific textures and impressions.

The middle or hybrid condition is the region's contribution to world architectural culture. Think of the incredible, exploding gray zone: the spaces that cannot be classified as wholly interior or exterior; the views that connect home with region and separate home from community; the materials that hover between a natural and fabricated state; the structural innovations that launch building into place and pull place through building; the cultural translations from other places that become saturated with site specificity and radical individuality; the still and moving imagery that informs and deforms place; the sprawl of building against a backdrop of resistance; the fickle glitter of commerce and progress under melancholy banks of fog or searing sunlight.

This engagement with landscape— with its potential to drain across the boundaries of indoors and outdoors, private and public, vision and touch—is the Bay Area's calling card. Most importantly, it demonstrates how architecture always grapples with both concrete entities and atmospheric conditions, with form and material but also with image and emotion, with needs at hand and ideas floating by. Interaction between building, nature, and sensibility must keep growing and flowing. Surely the beauty and dynamism of our natural environment encourages architects to strive for something similarly magnificent in the built environment. Surely architects must experiment with ways to respect context by adding to it and elevating it. Surely the moments when Bay Area architecture has achieved the most are those when it has cast its gaze forward and outward, acting on what lies beyond the horizon of expectation and possibility.

Endnotes

1 William Marlin, "San Francisco," *Architectural Forum* (April 1973), 26.

2 John Hart, *San Francisco Bay: Portrait of an Estuary* (Berkeley: University of California, 2003), 33.

3 Harold Gilliam, *The Natural World of San Francisco* (New York: Doubleday, 1967), 33-34.

4 Malcolm Margolin, (Berkeley: Heyday Books, 1978), 13.

5 See Kurt Baer, *Architecture of the California Missions* (Berkeley: University of California, 1958).

6 On the early history of the city, see James Beach Alexander & James Lee Heig, *San Francisco: Building the Dream City* (San Francisco: Scottwell, 2002), 25-66.

7 John Gregory Dunne, "Eureka! A Celebration of California," *New West* 4 (January 1, 1979), 32.

8 Michael Corbett, *Building California: Technology and the Landscape* (San Francisco: California Historical Society, 1998), 19.

9 Frank Norris, *Blix* (New York: Doubleday, 1900), 27.

10 Anne Vernez Moudon, *Built for Change: Neighborhood Architecture in San Francisco* (Cambridge, Ma.: M.I.T., 1989), 27-35.

11 Randolph Delehanty, *In the Victorian Style* (San Francisco: Chronicle Books, 1991), 103.

12 David Gebhard, *Samuel and Joseph Cather Newsom, Victorian Imaging in California, 1878–1908* (Berkeley: University of California, 1979), 25, 33.

13 Harold Kirker, *California's Architectural Frontier: Style and Tradition in the Nineteenth Century* (Santa Barbara: Peregrine Smith, 1973), 109.

14 Ada Louise Huxtable, "Reinforced-Concrete Construction: The Work of Ernest L. Ransome," *Progressive Architecture* 38 (September 1957), 140-141; Reyner Banham, *A Concrete Atlantis: U.S. Industrial Building and European Modern Architecture* (Cambridge, Ma.: M.I.T., 1986), 32-35.

15 David Gebhard, *Architecture in California* (Santa Barbara: University of California, 1968), 13.

16 See Werner Hegemann, *Report on a City Plan for the Municipalities of Oakland and Berkeley* (Oakland, 1915), 128-134.

17 See Mitchell Schwarzer, "Architectural Magazines in California," *ArcCa* 4.1 (2003), 26-31.

18 Willis Polk, "The Western Addition," in Richard W. Longstreth, ed., *A Matter of Taste: Willis Polk's Writings on Architecture for the Wave* (Berkeley: Book Club of California, 1979), 34.

19 Charles Keeler, *The Simple House* (Santa Barbara: Peregrine Smith, 1979), 5.

20 Richard Longstreth, *At the Edge of the World: Four Architects in San Francisco at the Turn of the Century* (Berkeley: University of California, 1983), 310.

21 John Beach, "The Bay Area Tradition: 1890–1918," in Sally Woodbridge, *Bay Area Houses* (Salt Lake City: Peregrine Smith, 1988), 98.

22 Esther McCoy, *Five California Architects* (New York: Reinhold, 1960), 4.

23 Kenneth Cardwell, *Bernard Maybeck: Artisan, Architect, Artist (*Santa Barbara: Peregrine Smith, 1977), 46, 58.

24 Gwendolyn Wright, *Moralism and the Model Home* (Chicago: University of Chicago, 1980), 3.

25 Robert Winter, *The California Bungalow* (Los Angeles: Hennessey & Ingalls, 1980), 23.

26 Fred Rosenbaum, *Architects of Reform: Congregation and Community Leadership, Emanuel of San Francisco, 1849–1980* (Berkeley: Judah Magnes Museum, 1980), 30.

27 See Michael Corbett, *Splendid Survivors: San Francisco's Downtown Architectural Heritage* (San Francisco: Foundation for San Francisco's Architectural Heritage, 1979), 27-39

28 See William Littmann, "Assault on the Ecole: Student Campaigns Against the Beaux Arts, 1925–1950," *Journal of Architectural Education* 53 (February 2000), 159-166.

29 Elizabeth Mock, ed., *Built in U.S.A., 1932–1944* (New York: the Museum of Modern Art, 1944).

30 Henry Russell Hitchcock & Arthur Drexler, *Built in U.S.A., Post-War Architecture* (New York: Simon & Schuster, 1952).

31 Lewis Mumford, "The Architecture of the Bay Region" in *Domestic Architecture of the San Francisco Bay Area* (San Francisco: San Francisco Museum of Modern Art, 1949), n.p.

32 "Is There a Bay Region Style?" *Architectural Record* 105 (May 1949), 93-96.

33 Paolo Polledri, "The Nearest Thing to a Contemporary Vernacular: the Bay Area's Architectural Tradition in Perspective," *Zodiac* 11 (1994), 19.

34 Garrett Eckbo, "Small Gardens in the City," *Pencil Points* 18 (Sept. 1937), 574.

35 Marc Trieb, ed. *Thomas Church, Landscape Architect: Designing a Modern California Landscape* (San Francisco: William Stout, 2003), 95.

36 Marilynn S. Johnson, *The Second Gold Rush: Oakland and the East Bay in World War II* (Berkeley: University of California, 1993), 31-33.

37 Daniel P. Gregory, "A Vivacious Landscape: Utopian Visions Between the Wars" in *Visionary San Francisco*, ed., Paolo Polledri (Munich: Prestel, 1990), 100.

38 Greg Hise, "Wartime Housing" in *An Everyday Modernism: The Houses of William Wurster* (San Francisco: San Francisco Museum of Modern Art, 1995), 151.

39 John Lyon Reid, "The School Plant Re-examined," *New Pencil Points* 25 (Sept. 1943), 59.

40 John Burchard & Albert Bush-Brown, *The Architecture of America: A Social and Cultural History* (Boston: Little Brown & Co,, 1961), 409.

41 John Jacobus, *Twentieth-Century Architecture: The Middle Years 1940-65* (New York: Frederick A. Praeger, 1966), 47.

42 Alan Hess, *Ranch House* (New York: Harry N. Abrams, 2004), 12.

43 Joseph Esherick, quoted in *Western Architect & Engineer* 222 (Dec. 1961), 26.

44 Pierluigi Serraino, *Norcalmod: Icons of Northern California Modernist Architecture* (San Francisco Chronicle Books, 2006), 258.

45 Miller McClintock, *Report on Citywide Traffic Survey* (San Francisco: Department of Public Works, 1937).

46 Robert O. Self, *American Babylon: Race and the Struggle for Postwar Oakland* (Princeton: Princeton University Press, 2004), 152-153.

47 See Donlyn Lyndon, Jim Alinder, *The Sea Ranch* (New York: Princeton Architectural Press, 2004)

48 Jim Burns, "The How of Creativity: Scores and Scoring" in *Lawrence Halprin: Changing Places* (San Francisco: San Francisco Museum of Modern Art, 1986), 40.

49 See Morley Baer, Elizabeth Pomada, Michael Larsen, *Painted Ladies: San Francisco's Resplendent Victorians* (New York: E.P. Dutton, 1978).

50 See Shelter (Bolinas, Ca.: Shelter Publications, 1973); and Art Boericke, *Handmade Houses: A Guide to the Wood-butcher's Art* (San Francisco: Scrimshaw, 1973).

51 Margaret Crawford, "Alternative Shelter: Countercultural Architecture in Northern California" in *Reading California: Art Image & Identity, 1900-2000*, eds., Stephanie Barron, Sheri Bernstein (Berkeley: University of California, 2000).

52 *A + U* 11 (November 1981), 20-24.

53 Roger Montgomery, "Synanon City," *Architectural Forum* 133 (Nov. 1970), 52.

54 David Gebhard & Susan King, *A View of California Architecture, 1960–1976* (San Francisco: San Francisco Museum of Modern Art, 1976).

55 Allan Temko, "San Francisco's Changing Cityscape," *Architectural Forum* 112 (April 1960), 232.

56 Charles Moore, "The San Francisco Skyline: hard to spoil, but they're working on it," *Architectual Forum* 123 (Nov. 1965), 41.

57 Lawrence Halprin, *Freeways* (New York: Reinhold, 1966), 23.

58 Chester Hartman, *City for Sale: The Transformation of San Francisco* (Berkeley: University of California, 2002), 50-51

59 Allan B. Jacobs, *Making City Planning Work* (Chicago: American Society of Planning Officials, 1978), 189-224.

60 Sim van der Ryn, *Design for Life: The Architecture of Sim van der Ryn* (Salt Lake City: Gibbs Smith, 2005).

61 See Peter Calthorpe, *The Next American Metropolis: Ecology, Community and the American Dream* (New York: Princeton Architectural Press, 1997).

62 Mitchell Schwarzer, "Beyond the Valley of Silicon Architecture," *Harvard Design Magazine* 7 (Winter/Spring 1999), 15-21; and Reyner Banham, "The Architecture of Silicon Valley," *New West* 5 (September 22, 1980), 47-51.

63 Mitchell Schwarzer, "San Francisco in a Age of Reaction" in *Shaping the City: Studies in History, Theory, and Urban Design,* eds. Edward Robbins & Rodolphe El-khoury (London: Routledge, 2004), 177-193.

64 Elizabeth K. Meyer, "Theorizing Hargreaves' work as a post-modern practice," in *Process Architecture* 128 (1996), 139.

65 Stanley Saitowitz, "Geological Architecture," *Harvard Architecture Review* 8 (1992), 93.

66 Catherine Croft, *Concrete Architecture* (Salt Lake City: Gibbs Smith, 2004), 58.

67 Wes Jones, *Instrumental Form: Designs for Words, Buildings, Machines* (New York: Princeton Architectural Press, 1998), 277.

68 Rem Koolhaas, "The Generic City," in *S, M, L, XL* (New York: Monacelli, 1995), 1248.

Map 01

01 Financial District

The history of the area known as the Financial District illustrates the American urban practice whereby the initial mixed-use site of a city gradually becomes limited to offices over time. The Financial District occupies the site of Yerba Buena village and the ramshackle gold-rush boomtown. During the 1870s, a taller (five-story) and more elaborate Victorian city emerged. And by 1890, new technologies of elevators and steel construction resulted in skyscrapers. Over the years the district also expanded geographically— north to the edge of Jackson Square, west to Kearny Street, south to Howard Street, and east (through landfill) into the Bay. The increase in size was accompanied by a crowding out of non-office activities. The city's principal piers and industries first migrated south and north. After 1906, almost all churches and residences were rebuilt outside the district. During the 1960s, the old produce district northeast of the downtown was razed for uses more compatible with the office/service city. Instead of ferries, freeways and BART now funneled commuters from all parts of the Bay Area into the downtown. Since the 1980s, zoning has restricted the height of skyscrapers and historic preservation statutes have resulted in the retention of most older buildings.

20. Transamerica Building (Pereira)

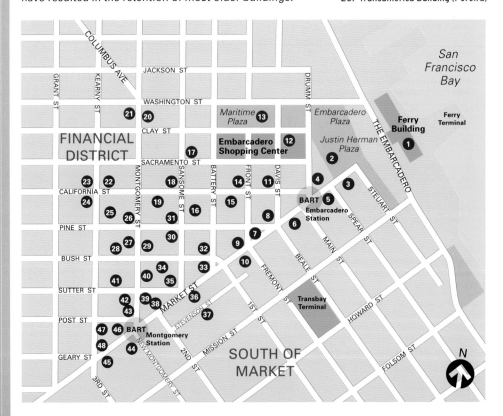

1 Ferry Building (1896)
Arthur Page Brown
For over forty years this terminal was the gateway to San Francisco, one of the busiest transit hubs in the world; up to 170 boats a day used its wharves. Although the building is now a gourmet food hall, it still evokes images of the city's maritime past. The long horizontal lines of its wings, which resemble Roman vaulted halls, continue the smooth sweep of the Bay. The clocktower, consisting of a four-stage belfry culminating in a cupola, introduces sea and city. It is modeled after the Giralda of the Cathedral of Seville, another great port city, whose tower makes a gradual transition from a square shaft to a skyward cylindrical cupola. The tower and Twin Peaks provide fitting bookends for Market Street.

1. Ferry Building (Brown)

2 Justin Hermann Plaza (1971)
Mario Ciampi, Lawrence Halprin
This large asymmetrical plaza unfortunately closes off Market Street, blocking its historic connection to the Embarcadero. The toppling concrete blocks of Armand Vaillancourt's fountain dominate the space. In 2002, the Mid Embarcadero Plaza & Promenades, designed by ROMA Design Group, opened and include an arc of lofty Canary Island Palms and two light towers.

3 Southern Pacific Building (1916)
Bliss & Faville
An appropriately massive building signifies the gargantuan appetite of the railroad, which during the nineteenth century was the greatest economic power in California. The conservative three-part vertical block displays classical ornament and a ground-level arched base. *1 Market St.*

4 Hyatt Regency Hotel (1971)
John Portman
After passing through a tunnel-like entrance, a remarkable explosion of space takes place. The vast skylit atrium reaches a height of 170 feet and discloses tiered floors that resemble an inverted Mayan pyramid. Portman first developed the atrium concept in 1967 for the Hyatt Regency Hotel in Atlanta as a means of bringing excitement to large urban hotels. *5 Embarcadero Center*

5 Federal Reserve Bank Building (1983)
Skidmore, Owings & Merrill
A street-level loggia reinterprets the ground-story arched bases common all over the downtown. Upper stories step back in two-story increments of polished granite and dark strip windows. *100 block Market St.*

6 Matson Building (1921)
Bliss & Faville
& Pacific, Gas & Electric Company (1925)
Bakewell & Brown
This harmonious pair of tall buildings match perfectly in proportion and tripartite composition. Their claddings, however, branch off into cream terra cotta and gray limestone. *215 & 245 Market Sts.*

7 388 Market Street Building (1987)
Skidmore, Owings & Merrill
Sheathed in polished red granite, the building's teardrop shape results from a cylinder dropped into a triangle. The volume is further differentiated through recessed fenestration for the upper-story residential units.

8 101 California Street Building (1982)
Johnson & Burgee
Sawtooth setbacks and cool reflective glass skin on this lofty cylinder combine to create one of the distinctive silhouettes on the skyline. The building mass is sculpted away at the base to reveal forty-foot tall structural piers, dramatically sliced through by a glazed atrium hall.

9 Shaklee Terraces (1982)
Skidmore, Owings & Merrill
The horizontal pattern of extra-smooth dark glass and gray steel is countered by a series of stepped corners that adjust to Market Street and provide a greater number of valued corner offices. *One Front St.*

10 Metropolitan Life Building (1973)
Skidmore, Owings & Merrill
The 525-foot tower rises as a perfectly rectangular slab, and is sheathed in anodized
aluminum. *425 Market St.*

11 Bethlehem Steel Building (1959)
Welton Becket
The facade of this rectangular block is composed of thin concrete strips that orchestrate
gray-tinted glass and panels of black and gray
granite. On two sides, structural columns,
placed outside of wall and faced in white
marble, impart a sense of verticality. *100
California St.*

12 Embarcadero Center (1971–1981)
John Portman
The southern section of the Golden Gateway
Redevelopment Center is a complex of
four towers linked by pedestrian bridges and
walkways; it is the most urbane modernist
environment in the city. The Center's art-
filled network of walkways—enclosed, on
the perimeter, and overhead—updates the
medieval Medina in right angles and surfaces
of rough-faced concrete and sheer glass. The
towers achieve a distinctive profile (especially when lit at night) through their assembly from a series of thin slabs ascending in
size toward the center. *Between Drumm,
Battery, Clay, and Sacramento Sts.*

13 Alcoa Building (1964)
Skidmore, Owings & Merrill
This powerful skyscraper anticipates
Chicago's larger John Hancock Building
and provides a visual guarantee against dis-
ruptive seismic forces. Twelve mammoth
X-braces act as giant trusses. Sheathed
in bronze-colored anodized aluminum,
the raking diagonal exo-skeleton projects
three and one-half feet beyond the window
plane. Chuck Bassett and Myron Goldsmith
intended the diagonals to work solely in tension, thus reducing the weight and mass of
the building. The roof gardens (by landscape
architects Sasaki, Walker Assoc.) open
a series of outdoor rooms, delineated by
fencing, paving, and planters. *Battery St.,
between Clay & Washington Sts.*

14 Home Savings of America Building (1990)
Kohn, Pederson & Fox
A fussy little building aspires to wear a mink
coat within fur-collared dimensions. *200
California St.*

15 Hancock Building (1959)
Skidmore, Owings & Merrill
The current Industrial Indemnity Building
is one of San Francisco's earliest glass-
tinctured skyscrapers, and was designed by
Chuck Bassett. Above the recessed base
is a series of piers resolving into haunched
arches. Polished dark-gray granite panels
with delicate changes of plane sheathe
the reinforced concrete building. *255
California St.*

16 345 California Center (1986)
Skidmore, Owings & Merrill
These Siamese towers are set on angle to
the grid, rising up out of the middle of a block
(between the older Dollar buildings) and
staying connected above via a series of sky
bridges. *345 California St.*

17 Old Federal Reserve Bank Building (1924)
George Kelham
What choice other than classicism could
the Federal government have made in a
city known by this time for its private banking temples? In keeping with a spirit of loose
interpretation, atop the Ionic colonade, government eagles replace the customary
classical antefixes. A large columnar hall
is carved out of the ground floor. *400
Sansome St.*

13. Alcoa Building (Skidmore, Owings & Merrill)

18 Bank of California (1908)
Bliss & Faville
The oldest commercial bank in the state is the grandest of the so-called downtown banking temples, boasting an imposing hall. Outside, a giant-order Corinthian colonnade supports a classical entablature. The pediment, however, is displaced from its customary place atop the temple, and shrunken to serve as the main entrance, an accidental synecdoche for the small banking temple's current subservience to an addition (1967, Anshen & Allen). For the modernist tower, cast-concrete panels with decorative batten strips project between the dark horizontal window rows. *400 California St.*

19 Merchant's Exchange Building (1903)
D.H. Burnham
This facade composition became a prototype for the San Francisco office building through the 1920s—and, as the Wells Fargo Bank across the street (464 California Street) shows, even later. The formula is a three-part vertical composition: with or without a mezzanine level; generous classicist detailing at connecting planes, the cornice line, and especially the entrance; and a rusticated masonry shaft with single- or doubled-punched windows. Interestingly, this attitude marks a retreat from Burnham's earlier work with John Root, where vertical piers and windows emphasized the steel frame. Here, the rough surface and small windows disguise structure and allude to pre-modern building types, an interesting commentary on the visual appearance sought by architects and large businesses for tall buildings during the early twentieth century. Inside, a barrel-vaulted lobby leads to a sumptuous trading hall. *465 California St.*

20 Transamerica Building (1972)
William Pereira
From a distance, this is the building that makes San Francisco look like Oz. The tower's unique pyramidal form is accentuated by flared wings, and tops out–via an aluminum spire—at 853 feet, the city's tallest building; its unique shape allows more light to reach the streets below. From up close, the base resembles old-growth tectonic forest of piers that become a diagonal-truss framework that supports the tapered office tower (faced in pre-cast quartz aggregate). Tom Galli designed the adjacent Redwood Park. *600 Montgomery St.*

20. Transamerica Building (Pereira)

21 655 Montgomery Street Building (1984)
Kaplan, McLaughlin & Diaz
The upper stories of this mixed-use office and residential tower fracture the lower punched-window wall into faceted glass cubes. This intelligent solution to the problem of how to scale back the mass of a skyscraper begins with small balconies, continues through an exposure of the frame in concrete piers and beams, and culminates with distended window surfaces at the penthouse level.

22 580 California Street Building (1984)
Johnson & Burgee
Postmodernism reached San Francisco with a thud in this skyscraper. In front of a glass-roofed mansard stand a row of face-less classical sculptures. The stab at context is further wrinkled by punched windows at the normally solid end bays and curved window bays that don't project much of anything.

23 600 California Street Building (1990)
Kohn, Pederson & Fox
Inside, this office highrise features a mural by Peter Ilyin depicting the dense hilltop city San Francisco might have been; outside, it suffers from over-detailing and a senseless interpretation of the bay window for an office building.

24 International Building (1964)
Anshen & Allen
This early and elegant modernist highrise is enlivened with alternating bands of concrete faced with white quartz and dark gray glass windows. The re-entrant corners allow for the vertical expression of the dark lines of the airshafts. *601 California St.*

25 Bank of America Building (1969)
Skidmore, Owings & Merrill, Wurster,
Bernardi & Emmons, Pietro Belluschi
The 52-story (779 foot) building dominates
the San Francisco skyline with its bulk and
dark color, and was designed by Myron
Goldsmith and Mark Goldstein. On the entire
length of its rise, sawtooth bays on a polished dark-granite skin masterfully pick
up the late afternoon sun, turning the tower
(at least for brief moments) from a menacing
presence above the white city into a purple-
hued march into night. Massive piers support
a glass curtain wall on the separate low-rise
banking hall. Both tower and hall are set
within a raised and austere plaza reached by
a wide cascading stairway. *555 California St.*

30. Pacific Stock Exchange (Dyer, Miller & Pflueger)

**26 California Commercial Union
Building** (1923)
George Kelham & Kenneth MacDonald
Here the compositional motifs of the nearby
Merchant's Exchange are taken a step
further by a grand arched entrance and cul-
minating arcade in the upper attic zone. *315
Montgomery St.*

27 Russ Building (1928)
George Kelham
Kelham's building represented San
Francisco in Francisco Mujica's *History of
the Skyscraper* (1929). Gothic detailing in
travertine accentuates the office tower's
aspirations for the sky (of capital accumulation). Although a sheer profile is maintained
on Montgomery Street, the building steps
back on its sides to create a central tower
that culminates in a castellated profile. Along
with the Pacific Telephone & Telegraph,
Shell, and 450 Sutter buildings, the Russ
Building defined San Francisco's skyline until
the 1960s, and was for many years the city's
tallest building. *235 Montgomery St.*

29. Mills Building (Burnham & Root, Polk, Hobart)

28 San Francisco Mining Exchange (1923)
Miller & Pflueger
A small terra-cotta temple front graces the
second oldest exchange–after New York's—
in the United States. *350 Bush St.*

29 Mills Building (1892)
Burnham & Root (1908), Willis Polk (1931),
Lewis Hobart
The famous architectural partnership's only
visible building in San Francisco is representative of their early work in Chicago, structurally
expressive yet composed of predominant
masonry surfaces. Here, the architects used
deep vertical window rows like those of their
Second Rand McNally Building (1889–1890)
and Woman's Temple (1891–1892) in Chicago.
The severe building lines and horizontal
arches are likewise similar to their Chicago
Masonic Temple (1891–1892). For the Mills
Building, the elevations clearly express the
steel frame upon which they are carried, lend-
ing the building the characteristic Chicago-
school appearance of structural logic and
functional efficiency. *220 Montgomery St.*

30 Pacific Stock Exchange (1915)
J. Milton Dyer (1930), Miller & Pflueger
The Doric colonnade framed by blank end
bays (and attic) resembles the neo-classicism
of Karl Friedrich Schinkel's New Guard House
in Berlin. Two colossal groups of cast stone
sculpture by Ralph Stackpole stand as the
sentinels of *Mother Earth* and *Man and His
Invention.* Adjacent, the twelve-story trading
hall (at 155 Sansome Street) is entered under
moderne bas-reliefs and boasts a lobby of
dark marble and ornate plaster. Diego Rivera's
mural *Allegory of California* graces the stair-
well of the Stock Exchange Club. *301 Pine St.*

31 Royal Globe Insurance Building (1909)
Howell & Stokes
For this multi-part vertical composition, interlaced red brick and green and white terra cotta cladding communicate the lighter side of corporate respectability. *201 Sansome St.*

32 Shell Building (1929)
George Kelham
The vertical thrust of this sleek skyscraper is established by continuous bands of fenestration that culminate in a tapered top. Its capital is accented by generous detailing and a series of projecting plates that, in effect, turn the straight-and-narrow concerns of the lower block into a poetry of the sky. Throughout, the sepia-colored terra-cotta skin throws sobriety aside via a series of elaborate moderne shell designs and vague Egyptian references. *100 Bush St.*

33 Crown Zellerbach Building (1959)
Skidmore, Owings & Merrill,
Hertzka & Knowles
Shimmering surfaces constitute the best glass curtain wall in San Francisco, whose concept was created by Walter Netsch and executed by Chuck Bassett. Two functionally-differentiated slabs make up the highrise, an opaque cube for circulation, and for the offices, a set of stacked lofts.  Thin steel mullions frame the green-tinted–for heat absorption—curtain-wall. The one-story, diamond-shaped glass hall at the southwest corner of the site brilliantly complements the tower. In an urban sense, the buildings do not fully occupy their wedge-shaped site; instead, they are irregularly situated in a garden and plaza. The ground plane is further complicated by opening up the base of the steel column grid and depressing part of the plaza beneath the street level. *1 Bush St.*

34 Standard Oil Co. Building (1922)
George Kelham
This U-shaped highrise employs motifs from Renaissance palace design for the offices of one of the largest oil companies in the nation: a palace of petroleum. *225 Bush St.*

35 Citicorp Center (1910)
Albert Pissis (1984), William Pereira
An alfresco case of taking a one-story building and opening it onto *plein aire* so that it may function as an atrium for a new highrise. *One Sansome St*

36 Chevron Buildings (1964, 1975)
Hertzka & Knowles
A pair of modernist boxes are separated by a small plaza. Above the granite bases, a stark geometry emerges in the rows of rectangular windows set within a terra cotta skin. *555 & 575 Market Sts.*

37 Stevenson Place (1986)
Kaplan, McLaughlin & Diaz
Following guidelines of the city's *Downtown Plan* (1985), this small highrise sculpts away some of the tonnage of earlier office buildings to create a tapered profile that culminates in a hip roof. The variegated skin—patterns of polished brown granite and buff concrete panels—steps away from the severity of the modernist monoliths nearby. *101 Stevenson St.*

38 Hobart Building (1914)
Willis Polk
The architect's flexible massing relates to a polygonal site between Market, Montgomery, and Sutter Streets. The rusticated shaft and Greek ornamental citations on the terra-cotta cladding are standard for a San Francisco office building, but the tower stands out as a series of profiled ornamental courses set within an unusual oval shape. *582 Market St.*

39 Wells Fargo Building (1966)
John Graham
This sleek highrise challenges the straight–forward assumption of glass transparency since its glazing is almost black. The dark curtain wall is framed by smooth granite piers, which are composed into stanzas of projecting aluminum plates. *44 Montgomery St.*

40 Title Insurance Co. Building (1930)
O'Brien Brothers
Clad in cast concrete resembling stone, this small building simplifies classical ornament to its linear essentials, flanking the entrance with columnar fluting, an outsized keystone, and bas-relief figures in the best Moderne manner. *130 Montgomery St.*

41 Hallidie Building (1917)
Willis Polk
Polk's commercial masterpiece was one
of the first buildings in the world to utilize
the steel frame for its potential to support
a transparent glass wall. Indeed, its glass
wall was mentioned by the architectural
historian Siegfried Giedion in *Space, Time,
and Architecture* (1941) as one of the con-
stituent elements of architecture after 1900,
along with the Bauhaus in Dessau! The glass
curtain wall represents one of the great
revolutions in architectural design, turning a
building from an opaque mass into a transparent and reflective presence. Here, cast-
iron tracery and corner fire escapes add to
the impression of a diaphanous curtain pulled
from the sides. *130 Sutter St.*

32. Shell Building (Kelham)

42 Hunter-Dulin Building (1926)
Schultze & Weaver
At 24 stories, this was one of the city's tallest buildings upon its completion, the only
San Francisco building by the New York firm
noted for the Waldorf-Astoria in New York
and the Breakers in Palm Beach. It is set
apart from other San Francisco skyscrapers
by its mansard roof with gabled dormers and
terra cotta roof tiles. *111 Sutter St.*

43 Crocker Center (1983)
Skidmore Owings & Merrill
Two urban gestures emerge alongside this
tower with a graph-paper facade of square
windows. First, the upper-ten stories of
Willis Polk's 1908 building were destroyed
(for the air rights to the new tower), and an
urban garden was inserted on the roof of the
truncated base; the remaining banking hall
contains a banking hall of imperial grandeur.
Second, a retail galleria cuts a pedestrian
walkway between Post and Sutter Streets, a
good idea that is defeated when the sweep
of its interior space is interrupted by escala-
tors and stairways. *One Montgomery St.*

44 Sheraton Palace Hotel (1909)
Trowbridge & Livingston
This namesake is built on the site of the original Palace Hotel (1875), a seven-story mass
of vertical rows of bay windows that once
towered over the Victorian city and acted as
its social nexus. The current building is a large
restrained horizontal block, noted less for
its exterior than for its arched, skylit Garden
Court restaurant, perhaps the city's most
palatial interior space. *633 Market St.*

45 Monadnock Building (1907)
Meyer & O'Brien
This tripartite office block is graced by a
sculpture garden in the interior court. *685
Market St.*

46 Mechanic's Institute (1909)
Albert Pissis
Housing the Mechanic's Institute library, the
reading rooms are set off by their larger windows and enframing pilasters. *57-65 Post St.*

47 San Francisco Federal Savings & Loan
(1986)
Skidmore, Owings & Merrill
A white concrete expression of the steel
frame borrows the technique (seen in the
Flood Building) of inserting a cylindrical tower
at the corner to form an entrance on Market
Street. Minimalist-Japanese detailing graces
the lobby. *88 Kearny St.*

48 Chronicle Building (1889)
Burnham & Root (1962), Hagman & Meyer
The city's first steel-frame skyscraper was
built only a few years after that revolutionary
constructional technique debuted in Chicago.
The building was clad with a sandstone
base and vertically-oriented brick shaft; it
concluded in a bronze-faced clock tower,
destroyed in a 1905 fire. In 1963, the Home
Mutual Savings and Loan Association draped
the historic building in a bland cladding of
vertical window rows and white porcelain
panels. In 2005, work began to restore the
historic exterior and add a setback eight-
story hotel and condo tower. *690 Market St.*

02 Union Square / Civic Center

The city's first retail district was located along Market Street just west of Montgomery Street. By the 1890s, retail uses had divided themselves according to income, migrating in two directions. A working- and middle-class shopping district developed on the stretch of Market Street between Fourth and Sixth Streets, anchored by the Emporium and Hale Brothers Stores. Upper-end stores migrated northwestward to Union Square—the direction of the city's fashionable hotel and residential area, atop Nob Hill. A theater district emerged along Geary Street directly west of the retail zone. Since around 1970,

the fortunes of the retail-theater-hotel uses around Union Square have risen while Market Street has fallen on hard times. Those blocks of Market Street west of Fifth Street, populated by the poor and destitute, have seen their retail uses diminish in quality and their cinemas turn x-rated. Several large legitimate theaters still operate successfully on Mid-Market Street.

One of the largest City Beautiful complexes in the country, Civic Center's development after 1913 continued a series of themes displayed earlier at the 1893 World's

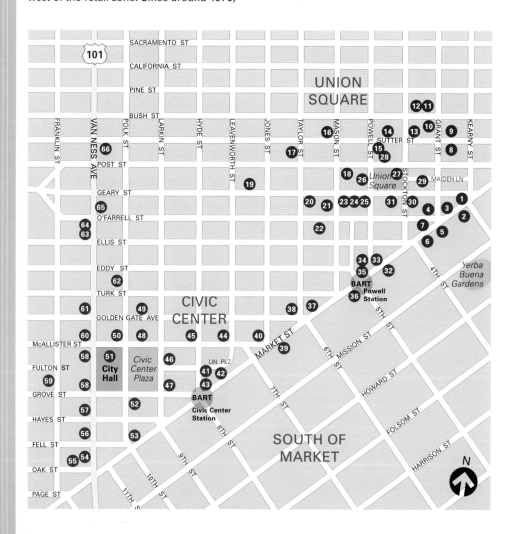

Columbian Exposition in Chicago. In an architectural sense, the buildings of Civic Center follow the example of City Hall to create an ensemble of calculated monumentality. Masses are setback from the street in order to craft the impression of aristocratic remove in a city that never possessed a court society. Likewise, cut-stone masonry facades are composed as imitations of the great works of Beaux-Arts classicism. In an urban sense, Civic Center's designers believed that aesthetic beauty and civic morality could better be designed in a setting removed from commerce. Almost a mile southwest of Union Square, Civic Center forms around a public square, and awkwardly aligns to both the overall city grid and its own internal axes. Unlike Baroque planning through diagonals, these axes are coordinated through frontal disposition. This explains why the corners of Civic Center have received so little attention. But, combined with the large size of Civic Center Plaza and the low elevations of its buildings, these weak corners have meant that the space of the plaza has always been poorly defined. Furthermore, the eastern approach on Fulton Street remains incomplete, marred by insensitive urban design (e.g., square light poles) and the continuing presence of an asphalt street, in the middle of which stands the forlorn Pioneer's Monument.

7. Phelan Building (Curlett)

1 Citizens Savings (1962)
Charles Moore, Clarke & Beuttler
An addition to an older building (1906, William Curlett) fills the corner on Kearny through an epochal postmodern interpretation of older structure's key qualities. In scale, height, belt courses, masonry/glass ratio, and roof mansard, Moore's design matches the feeling of its predecessor while simultaneously creating a totally different impression. *700-704 Market St.*

2 Central Tower (1938)
Albert Roller
The former Reid Brothers' Call Building (1897) once climaxed in a capital section where four corner cupolas surrounded a dome. A desire for additional space led to the replacement of the capital section (and dome) by six additional office floors. The result is a Moderne tower whose plainness is a 180 degree departure from the ostentatious original. *703 Market St.*

3 Wells Fargo Bank Building (1910)
Clinton Day
Once the Union Trust Bank, this Beaux-Arts bank works well with Bliss & Faville's bank across the street to announce an authoritative beginning to Grant Avenue. Its Baroque facade seamlessly turns at just the right moment to join Market Street. *744 Market St.*

4 Emporio Armani (1919)
Bliss & Faville
At one time, this corner banking temple used the classical language of Ionic columns, pediment, and dome to communicate a sanctuary appropriate for the everlasting storage of money. Nowadays, this language has been rewoven to ennoble fashion couture. *1 Grant Ave.*

5 Four Seasons Hotel (2001)
Gary Handel
Rising to 400 feet, this mixed-use hotel,
condominium, retail, and athletic complex
provides a fitting conclusion to the view
corridor south along Grant Avenue, and creates a powerful north wall for Yerba Buena
Gardens. The façade is almost completely
clad in curtain walls of gray-blue tinted glass
and silver-painted aluminum mullions. While
most of the glass surfaces take on a horizontal expression, in selected places a contrasting vertical emphasis differentiates the
massing. *757 Market St.*

6 Humboldt Bank Building (1906)
Meyer & O'Brien
Clad in sandstone and terra cotta, this is the
only domed building designed in the wake of
the Call Building's trend-setting tower. *783-
785 Market St.*

7 Phelan Building (1908)
William Curlett
One of the best flatiron buildings in the city
is more emphatic in its triangulation than the
Flatiron Building at 540 Market Street. The
glazed white terra-cotta surface fashions a
personality for this building that could stand-
in for the white city that San Francisco was
becoming during the City Beautiful Era. *760-
784 Market St. (See pg 71)*

14. Medical-Dental Office Building (Miller &
Pflueger)

8 White House Building (1908)
Albert Pissis
The best department store building in the
city was converted to a parking garage in
1968 and now houses a gigantic Banana
Republic store. On this milky white facade,
the even rhythm of pilaster-ribboned window
units is taken to a higher level by a sweeping
corner bend. *255 Sutter St.*

9 Goldberg Bowen Building (1909)
Meyers & Ward
In a good example of Chicago-school composition, terra-cotta ornament surrounds large
sheets of glass. *250 Sutter St.*

10 Pacific Telephone & Telegraph (1908)
Ernest Coxhead
Paired giant-order Corinthian columns order
the mid-section of this commercial block,
while the arched entrance contains a broken-
scroll pedimental core. *333 Grant Ave.*

11 San Francisco Environmental Center (1916)
W. Garden Mitchell (1982), Storek & Storek
This steam generating plant was converted
into offices and retail space, and utilizes solar
energy panels which are displayed on the
exterior. *530 Bush St.*

12 Notre Dame des Victoires (1913)
Louis Brouchoud
This replica of a church in Lyon, France
is adorned with Romanesque detailing exe–
cuted in gold-colored brick and terra cotta.
An odd composition, the main entrance is
created from two corner towers (with open
belvederes) flanking an extra apsidal exedra,
adding to the apse already located at the far
end of the barrel-vaulted interior. *564 Bush St.*

13 Sutter-Stockton Garage (1960)
John Lord King
Above ground-level shops, this parking
garage rises in a contra-dance of concrete
posts, beams, cantilevers, and checkerboard
screens.

14 Medical-Dental Office Building (1929)
Miller & Pflueger
Here is a tower from which to view the city
while having your teeth or head examined.
Rising as a honed vertical mass, the pale
beige terra-cotta skin and canted window
bays wrap around the steel frame like tight-
fitting jeans. Mayan ornament casts an
exotic spell on panels, around the entrance,
and even on elevator doors in the glistening

lobby. One of the first office buildings in the country to include an indoor garage, its structurally-expressive profile and exotic facade expression make it the most original of San Francisco's pre-war highrises and one of the city's best buildings. *450 Sutter St.*

15 **Sir Francis Drake Hotel** (1928)
Weeks & Day
A setback tower makes gothic allusions that conclude in a series of peaked gables. *432-462 Powell St.*

16 **Sutter Place** (1985)
Moore Lyndon Turnbull, Roger Owen Boyer
A bold classical podium, complete with recessed tympanum, digresses into bay windows and weak pedimental gestures on the upper section. *Sutter & Mason Sts.*

17 **Bohemian Club** (1934)
Lewis Hobart
Anchoring the club district of San Francisco is its *grande homme*, a dark red-brick building whose restrained facade belies the fact that this has long been the cigar-smoking, scotch-drinking retreat for San Francisco businessmen—quite an interesting fate for an association that began its existence as a place for artists and writers. *625 Taylor St.*

18 **First Congregational Church** (1913)
Reid Brothers
Given the location, this classical pavilion looks on the outside more like a theater than a church, but on the inside begins to resemble its ancestors in the New England Meeting Hall. *491 Post St.*

19 **Alcazar Theater** (1918)
T. Patterson Ross
The visual scenography of the Orient (as interpreted through the Alhambra) is a fitting home for the mysterious Shriners. Horseshoe arches, reliefs simulating muqarnas (a honeycomb network of corbels), terra-cotta and brick banding, and a large dome evoke the Arabian nights. *650 Geary St. (See pg 19)*

20 **Clift Hotel** (1913)
MacDonald & Applegarth (1926),
Schultze & Weaver
Within a common brick hotel are the smooth walls of *Sequoia Sempervirens* and gleaming vermilion skies of the Redwood Room (1933), G.A. Lansburgh & Anthony Heinsbergen's design for one of the city's best interior spaces. *491 Geary St.*

21. Downtown Center Garage (Applegarth)

21 **Downtown Center Garage** (1954)
George Applegarth
Great flat plates and thin rows of piers create an exceptional duet between the horizontal and the vertical. The curve introduced by the spiral ramp adds enough movement to take the composition from simplicity to sublimity. *325 Mason St.*

22 **Hilton Hotel Tower** (1971)
John Carl Warnecke
By placing elevator cores at each end, the corners turn solid and the middle becomes a series of strip windows. The matte aluminum skin on the 43-story tower is particularly sensuous. *333 O'Farrell St.*

23 **Curran Theater** (1922)
Alfred Jacobs
A fine companion to the Geary Theater, the projecting pavilion entrance is penetrated by three giant arches, each capped by a keystone and swag. *445 Geary St.*

24 **Geary Theater** (1909)
Bliss & Faville
Home to the American Conservatory Theater, this neo-classical building is conspicuous for its triple-bayed center recess (with metal marquee) framed by engaged Corinthian columns. On a facade where a maximum of wall surface is needed, the architects have wrapped fine decorative brick detailing in a razor-thin framework of terracotta pilasters. *415 Geary St.*

25 Elkan Gunst Building (1908)
G. Albert Lansburgh
At this important site, Baroque ornament and a rounded corner hold in the space of Union Square. *301 Geary St.*

26 St. Francis Hotel (1904)
Bliss & Faville
One of San Francisco's most famous hotels, where people would meet downtown "under the clock," is an E-shaped plan whose wings open toward the square. The steel frame is wrapped by a granite base, sandstone mid-section, and topped with a copper cornice. An arcade and colonnade take up the theme of luxury for visitors arriving at the ground level. *335 Powell St.*

27 Union Square (1849)
Set aside as a public square in William Eddy's 1849 survey, a 1903 Beaux-Arts design created diagonals that formed a circle around a granite shaft supporting a statue celebrating Admiral Dewey's victory over the Spanish at Manila. The rudiments of this plan were preserved when a parking garage (by Timothy Pflueger) was added in 1942, and captured in Francis Ford Coppola's 1972 film *The Conversation*. The square was rede-signed as a much more airy space in 2001 by Philips + Fotheringham.

28 Saks Fifth Avenue Store (1981)
Hellmuth, Obata, & Kassabaum
The precast concrete and granite panels of this department store paraphrase the square windows and white walls of I. Magnin, but soften its exacting edges through long verti-cal piers, recesses, and a curved corner. *384 Post St.*

30. Neiman-Marcus Store (Johnson & Burgee)

33. Flood Building (Pissis)

29 Circle Gallery (1948)
Frank Lloyd Wright
A handsome brick wall is relieved by an arched entrance and an ever-so-slight rise of the central plane. Inside the former V.C. Morris Store a curving ramp ascends toward a luminous ceiling of plastic plates and bub-bles, most likely setting a precedent for the later Guggenheim Museum in New York. *140 Maiden Lane (See also pg 29)*

30 Neiman-Marcus Store (1982)
Johnson & Burgee
Replacing the City of Paris Department Store is a retail building whose cubic/cylin-drical form draws attention to itself (and its architect), but is still responsive to its corner location on the square. Clothed in a tapestry of diagonal wedges, the store is a box into whose corner is inserted a glazed cylindrical entrance. The oval dome from the former building hovers over the entrance. *150 Stockton St.*

31 I. Magnin & Co. Store (1946)
Timothy Pflueger
Classicism is stripped down in this composi-tion of straight rows of sash-less square and rectangular windows flush to a white marble facade. Ironically, this minimalist composi-tion built at the end of the Second World War resembles Marcello Piacentini's fascist University of Rome, and seems to be the inspiration for Skidmore, Owings & Merrill's Qantas Building (1972) across the street. *233 Geary St.*

40. Hibernia Bank (Pissis)

32 **Westfield San Francisco Centre** (2006)
Kohn, Pederson, Fox, RTKL
The colonnaded-façade of the former
Emporium store serves as the frontispiece
for this 1.5 million sq. ft. shopping center,
which includes a Bloomingdales department
store, food emporium, and multiplex cinema.

33 **Flood Building** (1904)
Albert Pissis
The broad hemicycle of this muscular building is interrupted in mid-phrase by the insertion of a cylinder at its corner, stimulating
visual movement toward Hallidie plaza and
leading to a fine interior lobby. The sections
of the five-part block, faced in Colusa sandstone, are vigorously treated by rustication
and giant-order columns. This building would
fit perfectly on a great Neo-Baroque street
like Madrid's Gran Via. *870 Market St.*

34 **One Powell Street Building** (1920)
Bliss & Faville
In this masonry backdrop to the plaza, a
tripartite composition, stone cladding, and
arched windows all too closely resemble
McKim, Mead & White's University Club in
New York.

35 **Hallidie Plaza** (1973)
Mario Ciampi, Lawrence Halprin, John Carl
Warnecke
A depressing plaza's two depressed levels
lose the action at the city's most dynamic
transportation intersection, the place where
BART, trolleys, buses, and cable cars meet.

Michael Willis's 1998 Elevator—enfolded
by two stainless steel and perforated
wings—evokes the kind of tech hardware
Hollywood used for Skynet in the *Terminator*
series.

36 **Former Hale Brothers Department Store**
(1912)
Reid Brothers
Few buildings contribute more to the
grandeur of the mid-section of Market
Street. This building exemplifies the grand
classical palaces erected for the city's
department stores at the turn of the century,
such as Albert Pissis's Emporium Store
(1908), and, more recently, Whisler Patri's
San Francisco Shopping Centre (1989). *901-
919 Market St.*

37 **Fox Warfield Theater** (1921)
G.A. Lansburgh
The facade of this mixed-use office and
theater building gracefully angles with
Market Street. Greek Caryatids overlook the
entrance. *982-998 Market St.*

38 **Golden Gate Theater** (1922)
Albert Lansburgh
At a corner site on Market Street, an
octagonal tower cuts into a rectangular block,
a variation on a common San Francisco
theme. The brick building is enlivened by
a terra cotta base and surmounted by an
ornate dome. On the side, a diagonal
string of windows indicates the auditorium.
1 Taylor St.

39 **Forrest Building** (1908)
MacDonald & Applegarth
The skeletal frame and large windows of the
Chicago School are evident in this small com-
mercial building. *1053-1055 Market St.*

40 **Hibernia Bank** (1892)
Albert Pissis
The first of the city's classical temples for
banking, this Beaux-Arts building buttons
into its corner with a spherical entrance and
staircase capped by a dome. Inside, circular
and oblong domes (1909) cover the vault
area and customer hall. *1 Jones St.*

41 **United Nations Plaza Building** (1980)
Whisler-Patri
A peacefully contextual building's curved
mass, window arches, and cast-concrete
cladding blend into the greater Civic Center
complex. *10 United Nations Plaza*

47. Main Library (Pei Cobb Freed)

42 United Nations Plaza (1978)
Mario Ciampi, Lawrence Halprin
This stage-set for happenings on the edge of Market Street seeks to create an urban space with unconventional elements; instead of formal definition or directionality, Halprin's design of a kinetic landscape features a de-centering granite fountain and sunken pool. *Hyde and Leavenworth Sts.*

43 Orpheum Theater (1926)
B. Marcus Priteca
A Spanish Baroque facade frenzy of Solomonic twisting columns and foliated surfaces (possibly derived from the Cathedral of Leon) unfortunately presents a blank back wall to Civic Center. *1192 Market St.*

44 William Taylor Hotel (1930)
Miller & Pflueger
In this elegant setback tower, the skin is faced in buff terra cotta with green panels. *100 McAllister St.*

45 Hastings College of Law (1980)
Skidmore, Owings & Merrill
The concrete frame of this large horizontal block is the stage for different flavors of minced windows. *200 McAllister St.*

46 Asian Art Museum (1916)
George Kelham (2003), Gae Aulenti
The organizational clarity of the Beaux-Arts method is brought out by this central double-colonnade framed by end bays and attic and elevated upon a rusticated base. The simple, powerful side elevation on Fulton Street takes its inspiration from Henri Labrouste's Bibliothèque Sainte-Geneviève in Paris. The museum renovation ended up decapitating the double-height reading room at the former library and turning the grand catalog room into an orphan. *200 Larkin St.*

47 Main Library (1996)
Pei Cobb Freed + Partners & SMWM
Two interlocking designs, one historicist and the other modernist, fail to cohere into a greater whole. The Civic Center elevation continues the scale and composition of the old library to the point of mimicking its diagonal/checkerboard mullions. At the same time, James Ingo Freed compresses and changes the Beaux-Arts classical language of its neighbors: polished steel plates instead of console brackets, walled-in columns topped by reverse-keystone caps. At the rear, on Hyde Street, the angled compact book storage volume shatters the symmetry and composure established for Civic Center. Inside, irregular geometries continue; an asymmetrical skylight with shifted oculus dominates the open rotunda and staircase. *100 Larkin St.*

46. Asian Art Museum (Kelham, Aulenti)

51. City Hall (Bakewell & Brown)

48 California State Building (1926)
Bliss & Faville
Atop a rusticated base, a continuous window arcade lacks the power of the building it imitates, McKim, Mead, and White's Boston Public Library. Behind the older building, a new "contextual" office tower (1997, Skidmore, Owings & Merrill) replaced a modernist structure dating from the 1950s. *350 McAllister St.*

49 Federal Office Building (1959)
Alfred F. Roller/Stone, Marraccini & Patterson/John Carl Warnecke
The lofty, block-long slab and barren plaza–despite a 1999 update by Della Valle + Bernheimer—symbolize all that is gigantic and forbidding about the government in Washington. *450 Golden Gate Ave.*

50 Civic Center Courthouse (1997)
Hood Miller
Clad in light gray granite from the Sierras (from the same quarry as other Civic Center buildings), this corner building is the latest statement on banal contextualism. *400 McAllister St.*

51 City Hall (1915)
Bakewell & Brown
Centerpiece of Civic Center, the grandest city hall in the United States is worthy of being a state capital. The long rectangular block is articulated by fluted Doric columns, a classical pediment, and capped by a soaring dome. The superb dome, in its dynamic upward movement, pointed lantern, ribs descending

into columnar buttresses, and raised drum, closely resembles Michelangelo's dome for St. Peter's. On the interior, the great rotunda and overflowing staircase are magnificently situated under the visible underside of the dome. *400 Van Ness Ave.*

52 Bill Graham Auditorium (1915)
John Galen Howard, Fred Meyers & John Reid Jr.
On three sides, common brick veneer and fire escapes denote the assembly functions of this hall. On the principal Civic Center side, the auditorium's three-arched windows are framed by projecting end bays; this façade looks like the grand train station San Francisco never had. *99 Grove St.*

53 Fox Plaza (1967)
Victor Gruen
The fenestration of this skyscraper changes from its office levels, windows flush to the frame surface, to its upper residential stories, which feature balconies. It replaced the ultra-ornate Fox Theater, once the second largest auditorium in the country to Radio City Hall in New York City. *1390 Market St.*

54 Masonic Temple (1910)
Bliss & Faville
A fortress-like Venetian Gothic box's unintelligible facade masks a different internal organization, appropriate to the mysterious aims of this businessman's cult. At one of the corners, a niche accommodates a statue of King Solomon. *25 Van Ness Ave.*

55. Façade rendering of the SF Conservatory of Music (SMWM)

57. Davies Symphony Hall (Skidmore, Owings & Merrill)

55 San Francisco Conservatory of Music
(2006)
SMWM
The architects renovated an old building (1916, William Shea) and added an addition of like proportions next door. Along with the adjacent medieval Masonic Temple, the classical and modern facades make this block a case study in the three great moments of Western architectural history. *50 Oak St.* (See pg 77)

56 High School of Commerce (1927)
John Reid Jr.
Built around a courtyard in the Mediterranean fashion, the polychrome terra-cotta ornamental bouquet on the school has an obvious affiliation to the Spanish Baroque. *135 Van Ness Ave.*

57 Davies Symphony Hall (1980)
Skidmore, Owings & Merrill
Another supplement to the western side of Civic Center, Chuck Bassett's concert hall matches its northern neighbors in scale and color. At the same time, its fan-shape form closes off Civic Center by orienting itself on angle toward City Hall. Unfortunately, these urban gestures are not matched by the siting of an immense curved picture window atop a street scene whose vitality is robbed by the building's awkward side entrance—despite the presence of Henry Moore's *Reclining Figures in Four Pieces. 201 Van Ness Ave.*

58 War Memorial Opera House and Veterans Building (1932)
Arthur Brown Jr. &
G. Albert Lansburgh/addition (1979), Skidmore, Owings & Merrill
During the years of the Great Depression, the construction of these substantial Beaux-Arts edifices expanded Civic Center to the west. Not only do they create a commanding setting for City Hall along Van Ness Avenue, but they also shape an exquisite courtyard between them, one that frames a panorama of City Hall's dome. The Opera House is distinguished by the skyward projecting mass of its fourteen-story fly space. Inside, the entrance

foyer is lorded over by an elegant coffered ceiling. Although smaller, Herbst Theater in the Veterans Building is one of the best theater spaces in the city. *301 & 401 Van Ness Ave.*

59 San Francisco Ballet Association Building (1984)
Beverly Willis
The key to this building is a system of structural piers that unfold a gauntlet of cladding ideas. These include opaque planes, recessed windows, and a sculpted entrance loggia lorded over by a window wave. *455 Franklin St.*

60 State Office Building (1986)
Skidmore, Owings & Merrill
The book-end for Davies Symphony Hall features a grand staircase (cut under the curved facade) that leads to a central courtyard. *505 Van Ness Ave.*

61 Opera Plaza (1982)
Jorge de Quesada, John Carl Warnecke
Projecting off a concrete frame, bay windows have never looked so formidable. The multi-use complex features restaurants, matchbox theaters, and a silent inner courtyard. It has inspired numerous imitators further up Van Ness Avenue, such as Daniel Burnham Court. *601 Van Ness Ave.*

62 Das Deutsches Haus (1912)
The intricate gable design developed during the northern Renaissance for narrow townhouses is used here to articulate the entrance of a large meeting hall. *625 Polk St.*

63 British Motors (1927)
Bernard Maybeck, Powers & Ahnden
Not to be outdone by its neighbors, the former Packard showroom eschews industrial associations in favor of giant-order columns. If banks could be temples, why couldn't auto showrooms be palaces? *901 Van Ness Ave.*

64 George Olson Cadillac (1938)
John Dinwiddie
This automobile showroom was one of the first to take advantage of the streamline moderne style's suitability for large glazed showrooms and taut detailing appropriate to the motor car. *999 Van Ness Ave.*

65 Don Lee Building (1923)
Weeks & Day
This former Cadillac showroom confirms that the new industrial economy of the automobile need not forsake an urbane city presence. Upper bays of industrial-sash windows are dramatically contrasted by a whimsical classical base made up of smiling bears atop columns and a dashboard of Cadillac heraldry. *1000 Van Ness Ave.*

66 Galaxy Theater (1984)
Kaplan, McLaughlin & Diaz
The entrance tower, a child's pile of glass cubes, becomes the focus of design, leaving the mass of the theater auditorium to vanish in a gray background. *1285 Sutter St.*

64. George Olson Cadillanc (Dinwiddie)

03 Chinatown / North Beach / Telegraph Hill / Nob Hill / Russian Hill

By the early 1850s, the blocks surrounding Grant Avenue (then called Dupont Street) had become the New World's largest Chinese community. Because of restrictions on Chinese habitation in other areas of San Francisco, Chinatown developed into a homogeneous neighborhood. Later, due to the Chinese Exclusion Acts of the 1880s, the internal economy of Chinatown began to shrink. The destruction of the earthquake presented the opportunity to create a district that would attract tourists and residents from other neighborhoods. Since Chinatown had been viewed negatively by the white community, merchants seized upon the idea of using Asian design motifs to create a positive marketing image. Beginning in 1907, buildings of an "Oriental" character proliferated. Chinese ornament was applied to vernacular commercial and even residential buildings. Paradoxically, at the same time that Chinese cities like Shanghai were being built in a European image, San Francisco's Chinatown was constructed in an Asian image.

2. Sing Sing Building (Ross & Burgren)

This practice followed upon centuries of secularization of classical architecture. In other words, Chinese architectural elements were integrated into buildings in a manner that recalled the practices of the European architectural styles, and, most significantly for California, the example of the contemporaneous Mediterranean and Mission Revivals. Throughout Chinatown, buildings began to receive corner pagoda towers formed by successive rings of projecting eaves. Other ornamental features were iron balconies, colored electric lights along belt courses and cornices, Tuo-kung brackets, and carved columns decorated with dragons. Through these and other efforts, Chinatown became a merchandizing stage set, one of the nation's first examples of an entire neighborhood recast through the imagery of tourism and exoticism.

In North Beach, the beat north of the downtown leaves the rush-rush tempo of the marketplace behind for solos of prodigious eccentricity. The Barbary Coast along Pacific Avenue was a collection of bawdy dancehalls and day-less bars in the days when the waterfront teemed with sailors and prostitutes. Later, in 1964, the Condor Club at the corner of Broadway and Columbus Avenue made topless and then bottomless dancing infamous. North of Broadway, and centered on Columbus and Grant Avenues, North Beach was historically an Italian neighborhood, home to workers on the fishing fleets and Embarcadero piers as well as groceries, restaurants, and cafes. In the 1950s, the area spawned the Beat Movement, expressed at Lawrence Ferlinghetti's City Lights Bookstore, Cafe Trieste, and the Co-Existence Bagel Shop. East of North Beach, Telegraph Hill's blocks are subdivided by alleys with flat-faced clapboard row houses. Further north, the 1950s decline of maritime industries led to the piecemeal emergence of a tourism district, as former factories, canneries, and piers were converted to restaurant and shopping arcades.

The hills west of downtown early on became home to some of the city's wealthi-

Map 03

81

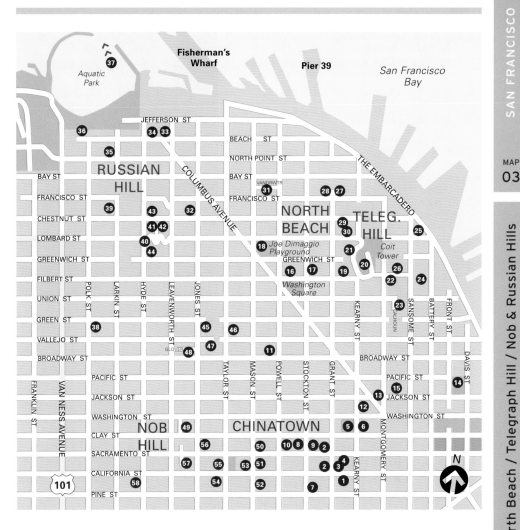

est citizens, and have remained so to this day. Beginning in 1873, the introduction of cable car service permitted development of the steep slopes. The top of Nob Hill became San Francisco's Valhalla to the titans of commerce, the site of Victorian mansions whose scale was never replicated anywhere else. Here were the homes of the Big Four who built California's railroad: Leland Stanford, Mark Huntington, Charles Crocker, and Mark Hopkins. After 1906, the sites of these mansions were redeveloped for hotels and large apartment buildings, the brick and terra-cotta mountains of elegant San Francisco. Russian Hill was also an important spot for exclusive residential development. Altogether, these hills boast

an architecture ranging from two-story rowhouses to great apartment towers. More cohesive architecturally are the streets of lower Nob Hill, south of Pine Street reaching down into the Tenderloin. Here is found the densest residential fabric in San Francisco, and the most powerful evocation of midrise urbanity west of New York City.

1 St. Mary's Square (1906–1955)
The original ground-level park was replaced by a parking garage whose pleasant yet deserted rooftop greenspace was designed by Eckbo, Royston, & Williams (1960).

2 Sing Chong Building & Sing Fat Building (1907 & 1908)
T. Patterson Ross & A.W. Burgren
These buildings were most responsible for popularizing the "Oriental look" of Chinatown. Selling Chinese arts and antiques, the bazaars quickly became among the great tourist sights of the district. They are embellished with pagoda towers that establish the Chinese look of Grant Avenue. *601 & 717 Grant Ave.*

3 Old St. Mary's Church (1854, 1906)
This was the original Catholic Cathedral of San Francisco, and a rare surviving example of the Gothic tendencies that characterized early San Francisco. The combination of a simple (in this case red-brick and stone) block penetrated and crowned by a rectangular spire is characteristic of English-inspired design since Christopher Wren's London city churches of the seventeenth century. *660 California St.*

4 Nam Kue School (1925)
Charles Rogers
The Mission Revival "eaved" at the last moment toward the pagoda uplift of China. *765 Sacramento St.*

5 Portsmouth Square (1844)
The original square in Vioget's plan for San Francisco became for a short while the center of the early American city. Later, as a part of Chinatown, it was turned into a city park. In 1963, an unfortunate park-atop-parking garage scheme was approved, leading to the current plan of small parks on two levels–designed by Royston, Hanamoto, Mayes & Beck. A further indignity was foisted on the park in 1971 when a concrete bridge was rammed into it from the new Holiday Inn across Kearny Street.

6 Holiday Inn (1971)
Clemmet Chen, John Carl Warnecke
On the site of the former Hall of Records facing Portsmouth Square rises a concrete behemoth—in the best of the brutalism style—of vertical trusses and giant steel girders. *750 Kearny St.*

2 & 3. Sing Chong Building & Old St. Mary's Church

7 Ritz Carlton Hotel (1909)
LeBrun & Son (1930), Miller & Pflueger
Built originally for the Metropolitan Life Insurance Company, this Beaux-Arts composition stands out for its pedimented entrance flanked by symmetrical colonnades and end bays. The formal design in gleaming terra cotta seems more appropriate for a public function than either an insurance company or hotel. *600 Stockton St.*

8 Chinese Consolidated Benevolent Association (1908)
Built for use by the Six Companies, a Chinese school and other organizations, the small brick building is accentuated by green tiles, and entered beneath a gate framed on either side by sculptures of lions. *843 Stockton St.*

9 Presbyterian Mission House (1908)
Julia Morgan
This building sheltered Chinese women rescued from the nineteenth-century slave trade. On the façade clinker bricks and austere links underscore the seriousness of this enterprise. *920 Sacramento St.*

10 Clay Street Center and Residence Club (1932)
Julia Morgan
This brick complex, replete with an Oriental tower, expresses the Occidental image of the Orient. *940 Powell St.*

11 Jean Parker Elementary School (1999)
Kwan Henmi
Pieces from the earthquake-damaged building are used as punctuation marks along the otherwise quiet walls of this new structure. Classical columns stand as sentinels around the courtyard. An arched terra-cotta portal, bolted to new masonry, frames the entrance. *840 Broadway*

12 International Hotel (2005)
Gordon Chong, Herman & Coliver
In 1977, in one of the most publicized cases of tenant abuse, approximately 50 largely Filipino and elderly residents of the old International Hotel were evicted; two years later the hotel was torn down. The new building, cream colored and 14 stories in height, contains 114 apartments for low-income seniors as well as the Manilatown Center, a focal point for the Bay Area's large Filipino population. *838-848 Kearny St.*

13 Old Transamerica Building (1911)
Salfield & Kohlberg
Dwarfed by its corporate incarnation across the street, this small flatiron building encased in elegant terracotta detailing was originally the Fugazi Bank of Italy. *Four Columbus Ave.*

14 Golden Gateway Commons (1961–1968)
Wurster, Bernardi & Emmons (1980–1983), Fisher, Friedman
In a project by the San Francisco Redevelopment Authority, the old produce district was razed to create a small city within a city, arranged around a pleasant greenspace of lawns on stylized hills and valleys—Sidney Walton Park (Sasaki Walker). In the first phase, square and slab towers

18. North Beach Pool and Clubhouse (Taggart)

are connected by overhead walkways to create an above-ground pedestrian network that opens onto landscaping and small townhouses. The second phase features low-rise townhouses arranged around courtyards and mid-block alleys. *Between Front & Davis Sts., Jackson & Pacific Sts.*

15 Jackson Square District
The city's first historic district preserves the largest collection of older commercial buildings to survive the Earthquake and Fire. Many of them date back to the 1850s and 1860s. Architecturally, the district is made up of small, brick-bearing wall buildings with wooden frames, and faced with classicizing ornament in either wood or stone.

16 SS. Peter & Paul Church (1924)
Charles Fantoni (1939), John Poporato
The soaring towers and crisp lines of this split personality speak Gothic, but the rich details, especially around the main portal, reveal Romanesque accents. *666 Filbert St.*

17 Telegraph Hill Neighborhood Association (1908–1909)
Bernard Maybeck, (additions 1913, 1928)
The gabled-roof, projecting beams, and balustraded balconies holding flower boxes almost start to resemble Heidi's farmhouse in the Alps. *1736 Stockton St.*

18 North Beach Pool and Clubhouse (2005)
Paulett Taggart
A new butterfly roof covers the addition (to the 1927 structure), and lends the complex a sharper profile along the street. *Lombard & Mason Sts.*

13. Old Transamerica Building (Salfield & Kohlberg)

20. Coit Tower (Brown, Jr.)

23. Kahn House (Neutra)

19 **Garfield School** (1981)
Esherick, Homsey, Dodge & Davis
This stucco-clad building ambles up the hillside, opening up windows to catch great views. *420 Filbert St.*

20 **Coit Tower** (1934)
Arthur Brown Jr.
Rising from the top of Telegraph Hill (on the site of earlier telegraphic structures) is one of San Francisco's signature monuments. The design of the tower is an abstraction of a column in which a massive fluted-Doric shaft gives way not to a capital, but to an set of open arcades used as viewing platforms. Instead of supporting a beam and roof enclosure, the column grows into a tourist viewing platform: San Francisco's architecture acting as a foundation for its number one industry. Inside, the tower contains a series of W.P.A. murals depicting life in California. *Telegraph Hill Blvd.*

21 **House** (1942)
Gardner Dailey
Anchoring a complex of residences by the architect, canted window bays and balconies exploit views of Telegraph Hill for the architect's own home. *275 Telegraph Hill Blvd.*

22 **Apartment House** (1937)
J.S. Malloch
One of the best moderne apartment buildings expresses the period's adoration of curving white surfaces and motifs of movement: in this case, nautical and bridge scenes within silver plaster murals and smoked-glass etchings. The lit glass-block elevator transported a bandaged Humphrey Bogart to Lauren Bacall's apartment in *Dark Passage*. *1360 Montgomery St.*

23 **Kahn House** (1939)
Richard Neutra
The Austrian-born architect was partially responsible for bringing the European "New Objectivity" to San Francisco, the creation of architecture within abstract three-dimensional space. From the simplicity of its white walls to its horizontal windows looking out onto the Bay, and to its balconies that storm the sky as great slabs of volume, this house epitomizes that contribution. *66 Calhoun Terrace*

24 **Levi's Plaza** (1982)
Hellmuth, Obata & Kassabaum
Landscaped plazas and fountains by Lawrence Halprin surround this early office campus. A meandering stream of water-washed rocks recalls the streams of the Gold Rush Days. Three separate buildings step down from the bottom of Telegraph Hill to the Bay, mimicking the terraced character of houses on the hill's shattered eastern side. The recollection of historic warehouses by the red-brick facades is defeated, however, by dark strip glazing and rounded corners. *1155 Battery St.*

25 **Belt Line Railroad Roundhouse** (1914)
A series of acutely-angled concrete buildings curve in places to meet functional demands. The ample planes of industrial-sash glazing further define these demands. *1500 Sansome St.*

26 **Townhouse** (1986)
Ace Architects
In this archaeology of traditional styles, individual elements stand apart. A three-story wooden bay mass crashes down upon the ochre and flat facade plane, itself eroded by a recessed entrance under a curving, incomplete arch. *34 Darrell Pl.*

27 Telegraph Terrace (1984)
Backen, Arrigoni & Ross
Earthbound textures of red-tiles and plaster walls renew the flame of Bay Area Mediterraneanism. *Francisco St. at Grant Ave.*

28 Glickman House (1988)
Backen, Arrigoni & Ross
Steel piers and beams allow for a free facade, almost all of which is glazed in plate-glass windows and glass block. *Francisco St. at Grant Ave.*

29 Martin House (1999)
Leddy, Maytum, Stacy
Set atop a concrete base that frames a steel garage door, the architects have crafted a modern-looking house of gray stucco walls, glazed asymmetries, and industrial accents. Paradoxically, when nods to the residential context are made—such as an open steel framework at the roof that mimics older cornices—they transport the house further into the industrial age. *281 Chestnut St.*

29. Martin House (Leddy, Maytum, Stacy)

30 House (1996)
Jim Jennings
The modernist preoccupation with differentiating living and circulation spaces receives a twist here. Instead of locating the server spaces on the periphery, elevator and stairs are enclosed in a white, concrete cylinder at dead center of this composition. Steel bridges join the cylinder to two rectilinear volumes containing the served spaces, which in turn freely sling out slab masses and windows as expressions of the vivid moments of lived behavior. *340 Lombard St.*

31 Apartments (1981)
Dan Solomon
Bay windows are grouped around a frail center which can't decide whether it is an arch, a recess, or a window. *55 Vandewater St.*

32. San Francisco Art Institute (Bakewell & Brown, Clay)

32 San Francisco Art Institute (1926)
Bakewell & Brown (1970), Paffard Clay
Reinforced concrete is used alternatively for very different ends in this two-building complex. In the older part, Bakewell and Brown crafted the modern material as an affectation of historical surfaces, a textured evocation of a Mediterraneanism otherwise brought out by the bell tower, red tiles roofs, classical entrance, and courtyard. Inside, there is a mural by Diego Rivera. The later building, in addition to its marauding staircase and roof deck, owes its presence to the strong, even rhythms of the studio wall. Forming balconies within angled concrete plates, this wall and window design is indebted to Le Corbusier's Carpenter Center for the Visual Arts in Cambridge, Massachusetts. *800 Chestnut St.*

33 The Cannery (1968)
Joseph Esherick
Here is a different way to transform an old working building (1909) into a complex for shops and restaurants. Stairs, elevators, and passageways create a sense of perpetual movement from one place of accumulation to another—an oriental shopping bazaar within the skeleton of the old Del Monte Fruit plant. *2801 Leavenworth St.*

34 Haslett Warehouse (1909)
A rhythmic series of parapets and well-executed brickwork make this large brick warehouse one of the more evocative remnants of San Francisco's maritime history on the northern waterfront. *680 Beach St.*

35 Ghirardelli Company and Square (1967)
Wurster, Bernardi & Emmons
Sharing the block with the Pioneer Woolen Mill (1859), the Ghirardelli Chocolate Factory and French chateau-inspired Clocktower (1916, William Mooser) was one of the grandest industrial complexes on the waterfront. It was later remodeled into a complex of shops and restaurants that surround a multi-leveled plaza, designed by Lawrence Halprin, and featured a circular fountain and statue by Ruth Asawa. The renovation of factory into specialty shopping center stirred imitators around the country. *900 North Point*

35. Ghirardelli Square (Wurster, Bernardi & Emmons)

36 National Maritime Museum (1939)
William Mooser
Inspired by Eric Mendelsohn's De la Warr Pavilion in England, the white museum looks like an oceanliner. *900 Beach St.*

37 Alcatraz Island.
Soon after Americans raised the flag over California, artillery batteries went up on this small island in the Bay. In 1861, it became the nation's first military prison and served as a Federal Penitentiary between 1934 and 1963. Now a part of the National Park Service, the sheer cliffs of the Rock rise out of the Bay, and are dominated by a light-house, water tower, two-story, reinforced concrete cellhouse (1909) and the Model Industries Building (1929).

38. Alhambra Theater (Miller & Pflueger)

38 Alhambra Theater (1930)
Miller & Pflueger
A pair of minarets announces the call to the silver screen from a building that is no less fantastical. This Moorish movie palace is festooned with horseshoe arches and arabesques, but brought out of the medieval shadows by Alexander Cantin's neon sign. Now used for a gym. *2330 Polk St.*

39 Walters House (1951)
Wurster, Bernardi & Emmons
A vivid contrast between the house's solid and dark redwood siding and its large bayward windows clarifies the architects' attention to site and view. *2745 Larkin St.*

40 Lombard Street (1920s)
In the 1920s, a fusilli-noodle jiggle replaced a straight precipice and became one of the city's most popular tourist attractions. If they twist it, they will come.

41 House (1938)
Gardner Dailey
Instead of small-scale detailing, this early modernist house achieves distinction thorough the interpenetration of volumes, and a bold curving balcony. A balance is achieved between the cubic nature of the house's form and the peculiarities of its individual parts. *65 Montclair Terrace*

42 House (1956)
Henry Hill
Although a second story has been added which detracts from the original horizontal sweep, the hovering window strip and semicircular overhang, reminiscent of Eric Mendelsohn's San Francisco work, are still quite dramatic. *66 Montclair Terrace*

43 House (1948)
John Funk
A reservoir of modernist spatial conceptions reaches back to the Dutch De Stijl movement, where volumes of space and masses of form become one and the same thing. Counterpoint to the distinct cubic volumes of pre-modernist composition are a series of intersecting planes that act as solid walls, horizontal balconies, or transparent windows, all expressed in different materials and shades of white and gray. *998 Chestnut St.*

44 Southard Place (1981)
Daniel Solomon
The glass-block surfaces, recessed planes, balcony, and various window shapes were most likely inspired by turn-of-the-century compositions like the apartments at 1425-1429 Clay Street. *Southard Pl. & Greenwich Street*

45 Summit Apartments (1965)
Neil Smith
This muscular concrete highrise, 32 stories in height and supported by massive buttresses, was built by Joseph Eichler. *999 Green St.*

46 Royal Towers (1961)
Chin & Hensel
One of the first modernist residential skyscrapers, the steel-frame construction is heightened through generous glass curtain walls. *1750 Taylor St.*

47. Polk-Williams House (Polk)

47 Russian Hill Place.
A gathering of buildings and small off-grid streets responds beautifully to its hilltop setting. From Jones Street, an automobile ramp opens a passage within a long, irregular wall of plaster surfaces, balconies, and red-tile roofs. This earth-colored wall is composed of buildings by Willis Polk *(1, 3, 5, 7 Russian Hill Place)* and Charles Whittlesey *(30, 35, 37, 39 Florence Place)* that together create a facsimile of a small Mediterranean village. On the other side, from Taylor Street, the shingled surfaces and gables of Joseph Esherick's Livermore Condominiums present an atmosphere (of unpainted shingles, gabled roofs, extended flue pipes, bays, and balconies) appropriate to the North Coast of California. Within the precinct, the most important design is Willis Polk's Polk-Williams House (1892, *1013-1019 Russian Hill Pl)* whose elevation is treated as a single residence, and whose facade has been compared to a condensed Norman streetscape. Polk's intentional-ramshackle design is reminiscent of the Shingle-style houses on the East Coast designed by McKim, Mead & White and H.H. Richardson. Also noteworthy for the longevity of this tradition is the Berggruen House, earlier designed by Willis Polk, and given a reconfigured entrance on *40 Florence Place* by Robert A.M. Stern in 1985.

48 Duplex (1982)
Dan Solomon
On a narrow lot, a bay-window divides into two parts, an ascending square and a descending industrial-sash face for the living room. *15 & 17 Glover St.*

JE 88

47. Russian Hill Place

49 Iann-Stolz House (2000)
Kuth-Ranieri

Relating to its context of small buildings and intimate gardens, the surface is clad with mahogany wood panels that surround a central plate glass window accented in steel. A grid of horizontal wooden strips, spaced two-feet apart at the base, gradually compress as they ascend to the roofline. This compositional device introduces a rhythmic movement that is well contrasted by the absolute stasis of the central window. Across the street, at 17 Reed Street, the clients' commissioned an art gallery and guest cottage (2005) topped by a corrugated-metal gable. *44 Reed St.*

53. Pacific Union Club (Laver, Polk)

50 Brocklebank Apartments (1926)
Weeks & Day

This apartment tower is by the same architects who designed the Mark Hopkins Hotel. The building's angle and automobile court provide an admirable counterpoint in elegance and detailing, appropriate to the residence of Carlotta Valdez in Alfred Hitchcock's *Vertigo*. *1000 Mason St.*

51 Fairmount Hotel (1906)
Reid Bros.

The grand dame of San Francisco hotels is a huge horizontal block that feathers its granite surfaces by a projecting porte cochere entrance. A rusticated base and slightly projecting central and end-bay colonnades delineate the composition. *950 Mason St.*

52 Mark Hopkins Hotel (1925)
Weeks & Day

The quintessence of a large urban hotel where a remote tower and stately brick and terra-cotta walls elevate the experience of travel into a noble act. The hotel's angular siting provides an automobile entrance court and establishes a center for Nob Hill in the direction of the Pacific Union Club and Huntington Park. Also noteworthy is the view afforded from the Top of the Mark lounge, designed by Timothy Pflueger. *850 Mason St.*

53 Pacific Union Club (1886)
Augustus Laver (1908), Willis Polk

The former Flood Mansion occupies the choicest spot atop Nob Hill and does so with aplomb. Faced in brownstone from a Connecticut quarry, this urban villa is a survivor from the Earthquake and a rare San Francisco example of the stone-faced urban townhouse popular on the East Coast. The composure of the mansion derives from its bilateral symmetry, projecting front porch, and framed stairway and street wall. Willis Polk's addition of projecting one-story wings only adds to the splendor of the composition. *1000 California St.*

54 Masonic Temple Auditorium (1958)
Alfred Roller

A marble composition of solid wall masses played off against minimalist columns evokes both the classical and geometrical aspects of modernism. Tall, unrelenting entrance piers create striking rhythms of shadows and sun-draped form. *1111 California St.*

49. Iann-Stolz House (Kuth-Ranieri)

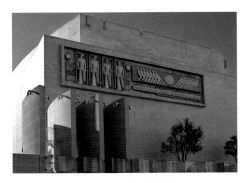

54. Masonic Temple Auditorium (Roller)

58. Cala Store (Wynkoop & Imada)

55 Grace Episcopal Cathedral (1910)
George Bodley & Lewis Hobart (1964),
Weihe, Frick & Cruse
Third largest Episcopal Cathedral (after
the Cathedrals of St. John the Divine in
New York and the National Cathedral in
Washington) in the United States, San
Francisco's is an cast-concrete interpretation of the early French Gothic style, taking
its tower design from Notre Dame in Paris,
but refraining from an imitation of flying
buttresses. The east-front doors are casts
from Lorenzo Ghiberti's Doors of Paradise
on Florence's Baptistery. Inside, the Chapel
of Grace recalls the sparkling glass walls of
Sainte-Chapelle in Paris. *1051 Taylor St.*

56 Chambord Apartments (1921)
James Francis Dunn
An apartment building of bright white surfaces and bulging balconies speaks of the
good life along the Mediterranean and could
look comfortable in Nice or Cannes. *1298
Sacramento St.*

57 House (1990)
Hood Miller
The acrylic-paneled garage of this bow-
fronted facade mimics the facing of upper-
bay windows, one solution toward masking
the truth of the automobile-inflected house-
hold. *14-16 Leroy Pl.*

58 Cala Store (1960)
Wynkoop & Imada
A concrete butterfly roof encloses giant win-
dow walls in this supermarket for the space
age that appears in the movie *Petulia*. *1095
Hyde St.*

55. Grace Episcopal Cathedral (Bodley & Hobart,
Weihe, Frick & Cruse)

04 South of Market

South of Market was long home to working-class housing, light industry, wholesaling, and the port. Because of the demands of the Gold Rush and California's distance from other American cities, industrial activities proliferated in San Francisco, and included: ironworks, tool and machine shops, shipbuilding, wholesaling and warehousing. Because of the large size of South-of-Market blocks, numerous mid-block streets and alleys were introduced to provide interior access and additional frontage for parcelization. This development of inner-block space resulted in a pattern of residential areas surrounded by industry on the main streets, the opposite of Central European arrangements that feature residential buildings on exterior avenues and light industry within inner courtyards. The decline of the port during the 1960s eventually paved the way for the district's redevelopment as a center of art, entertainment, conventions, and loft living. The southern waterfront, now called South Beach, has become a swanky residential area and includes the Giants' baseball stadium.

5. Hills Brothers Coffee Building (Kelham, Whisler-Patri)

1 Rincon Center (1939)
Gilbert Stanley Underwood
Once a post office, this streamline moderne building is made up of smooth surfaces divided by colossal piers and ornamented with flying dolphins and eagles. The interior features a fresco by Anton Refriger that depicts his vision of the course of civilization. *90 Mission St.*

2 Rincon Towers (1989)
William Pereira
Upper surfaces are treated as curtain walls while lower ones feature punched windows. A distinctive form is further created by free-form interpretations of machine parts as ornament. *88 Howard St. & 101 Spear St.*

3 135 Main Street Building (1989)
Robinson, Mills & Williams
A segmental arch carries two superimposed columns in this curious postmodern base.

4 The Gap Building (2000)
Robert A.M Stern
Here the historical and contextual references fly in many directions—to the great Chicago high-rises of the 1890s, to classical office downtowns of the 1920s, to warehouses of the late nineteenth century, and to the monumental state architecture of Mussolini's Rome. Stern begins with a two-story stone

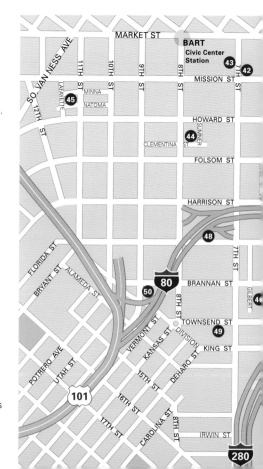

base, and continues with large Chicago-style windows surrounded by Expressionist brick patterns and classical stone accents. At two of the base entrances and the thin tower, blank surfaces and stripped piers evoke an abstracted classicism. *Two Folsom St.*

5 **Hills Brothers Coffee Building** (1924)
George Kelham (1992), Whisler-Patri
From the bay, the tower and arcade evoke the illusion that one has just embarked at a Mediterranean port, or, given the company's old advertisement of itself through a coffee-sipping Arab, the island of Zanzibar. The addition is one of the more tasteful contextual designs in recent memory. *Two Harrison St.*

6 **San Francisco-Oakland Bay Bridge** (1936)
Charles Purcell
Once the world's longest bridge at over seven miles in length, the crowded lanes of the Bay Bridge are in a sense the center of the ever-mobile Bay Area. The western end of Interstate 80, the bridge is comprised of two sections connected by a tunnel through

6. San Francisco-Oakland Bay Bridge (Purcell)

Yerba Buena Island. On the San Francisco side, a huge concrete pier was erected midway to the island to reduce the two-mile distance for the suspension bridge of four towers, each 518'. Painted battleship gray, the x-braced towers create a profound march over water into the city. A new bridge is currently under construction to replace the eastern span.

11. Oriental Warehouse

7 Treasure Island.
In 1939, these marshy shoals were claimed from the Bay to serve as the site for the Golden Gate International Exposition. Centered on the Court of the Pacific and Ralph Stackpole's 80' goddess "Pacifica," architects (including George Kelham, Timothy Pflueger, Lewis Hobart) looked to the lands of the Pacific Basin for design motifs. After the fair, the island was to have served as San Francisco's new airport. But, the Second World War intervened, and Treasure Island became a naval base, which finally ceased operations in 1997. Almost nothing of the fair remains. One structure, Kelham's streamline, crescent-shaped administration building, is now the Treasure Island Museum.

8 Portside II (1997)
HKS, Fisher Friedman
A colony of Miami Beach is growing up under the Bay Bridge. This new condominium complex replicates almost exactly the luscious curves, maritime deco motifs, and immaculate white surfaces of the earlier Portside I building (1994, John Towers). *401 Main St.*

9 The Watermark (2005)
Moore, Ruble, Yudell
This condominium tower sports glass and metal curtain walls and very direct Bay Bridge views. *501 Beale Sts.*

10 Delancey Street Center (1992)
Backen Arrigoni & Ross
A jumble of midrise and highrise buildings establishes an urbane edge for the South Beach neighborhood. Towers, setbacks, a red-tile roof supported by wooden eave brackets, and abrupt changes in veneer (from red to pink) scale down the real dimensions of this large center for individuals in recovery. *600 Embarcadero*

11 Oriental Warehouse (1868)
Built by the Pacific Mail Steamship Company, the brick building was long used for the storage and distribution of coffee, tea, silk and rice from Asia. In 1997, Fisher Friedman inserted housing units into the empty shell. *650 Delancey Street*

12 South End Warehouses.
Here, in the vicinity of the great Pacific Mail Steamship Company's dock, a concentration of buildings (most constructed between the 1870s and 1920s) reflects San Francisco's former maritime identity. Among building types, the forms of these warehouses are particularly dictated by function, needs for structural strength, safe storage of goods, expansive floorplates, and protection against fire. Structural systems range from initial brick-bearing walls to reinforced-concrete frames. Inside, heavy-mill timber-frames gradually gave way to iron (and later steel) posts and beams. In terms of artistic expression, their facades are articulated by parapets, pediments, patterned surfaces, arched openings, corbelled cornices, and painted signs. Among the oldest of the warehouses are Morton's South End (1874) and the California (1882). *First to Third, Bryant to Townsend Streets*

13 Giants Baseball Park (2000)
Hellmuth Obata & Kassabaum
Designed by Joe Spear, whose earlier works include the ballparks in Baltimore, Cleveland, and Denver, one time Pacific Bell Park continued the trend in nostalgia—red brick walls, dark green seats, and an asymmetrical outfield whose right field wall is just 306 feet from home plate. This enthusiasm for the past results in a design that obscures the

13. Giants Baseball Park (Hellmuth Obata & Kassabaum)

building's powerful concrete and steel structure—which is fortunately visible from south of the channel. Along King Street, however, the brick walls, corner tower, and faux-stone moldings are ornaments that refer less to the context of San Francisco than a corporate idea of what a baseball stadium should look like. Inside, almost every one of the 40,800 seats is good, and the view from the upper decks includes not just the ballgame, but ships passing along the Bay. *King Street between Second and Third Sts.*

14 Mission Place (2003-2004)
Skidmore, Owings & Merrill, HKS Architects
Eight concrete towers rise between seven and sixteen stories, and bring urban amenities to the new South Beach neighborhood. *201-250 King St.*

15 Third Street Bridge (1933)
Joseph Strauss
On this heel-trunnion bascule Bridge with exposed steel girders, one end is weighted to counterbalance the other end.

16 China Basin Building (1922)
Bliss and Faville
The city's longest building fronts the partially abandoned Mission Creek. *185 Berry St.*

17 South Park (1856)
George Gordon
A notable alteration to the South-of-Market grid, South Park was modeled after the private squares of London. Located entirely within the confines of a single block, this venture introduced new streets upon which residential townhouses faced an oval park. *Second to Third Sts., Bryant to Brannan Sts.*

18 Office/Condominium (1996)
Toby Levy
This small metal, stucco, and slate building introduces spatial tension into its orthogonal lot by rotating a set of interior spaces 45 degrees. The architect's ecological concern emerges through the use of recycled sawdust panels and compressed rubber for floors and cotton batting for walls. *90 South Park*

19 Corson-Heinser Live/Work Building (1992)
Tanner, Leddy, Maytum, Stacy
A wood-frame structure is paradoxically accented by steel beams and glistening glass and steel surfaces. On a narrow lot, the circulation zone is expressed as

an opaque, steel-faced slab while the living zone becomes a transparent window wall. Throughout, the architects' delight in exposing and unfurling constructional joints, screws, metal-gratings, studs, and beams. *25 Zoe St.*

20 Sailors' Union of the Pacific Building (1950)
William Merchant
Broken up by office wings sporting horizontal window rows, the central pavilion is a soliloquy on the elongated lines and planes of stripped classicism. It gives us the basics of column and wall and no more, and provides an impressive entrance for this center of union activity in maritime San Francisco. *450 Harrison St.*

21 Foundry Square (2003)
Studios Architecture/Jennings
A superblock development, only partially completed, creates a plaza within the city grid. An undulating roof tops this complex of varying facades–masonry clad panels and double glass walls. *405 Howard St.*

22 Transbay Terminal (1939)
Timothy Pflueger, Arthur Brown Jr.
Built to accommodate electric trains using the recently completed Bay Bridge, the terminal was soon converted into a bus station. The inner warren of ramps and stairs is encased within an austere concrete cladding of gray granite and tall window bays. *Mission St. at First St.*

19. Corson-Heinser Live/Work Building (Tanner, Leddy, Maytum, Stacy)

26. 101 Second Street (Skidmore, Owings & Merrill)

25. J.P. Morgan/Chase Building (Pelli)

23 Residential Lofts (2001)
Jim Jennings
Instead of a roof set atop walls at a ninety-degree angle, the steel frame curves into a roof and arched penthouse. Beneath this bend, large glass bay windows project from painted metal walls. *85 Natoma St.*

24 100 First Street Building (1989)
Skidmore, Owings & Merrill/Heller & Leake
Above this pile of setbacks and off-beat rhythms in glass and masonry, a pointless top-with-spire becomes a case study for not requiring crowns on buildings with immense floorplates.

25 J.P. Morgan/Chase Building (2002)
Cesar Pelli
The 31-story highrise is clad in glass and aluminum. The aluminum frame is painted dark green, and its lines, along with other projecting aluminum lines within the window bays, weave a rich orthogonal tapestry atop the glass. *560 Mission St.*

26 101 Second Street Building (2000)
Skidmore Owings & Merrill
Large surfaces of glass emphasize the 26-story building's verticality and reflect the changeable luminosities of the sun. Unlike the mid-century office towers, each of the four sides of the tower, designed by Craig Hartman, is composed differently, and some

surfaces are clad in limestone panels. At lower levels, belt courses and punched window walls relate to the nearby small, older buildings. A glazed four-story pavilion is attached to the tower.

27 Call Building (1914)
Reid Brothers
Paradoxically, a glazed base gives way to a rusticated mezzanine. Fluted Corinthian pilasters delimit the shaft. *74 New Montgomery St.*

28 Pacific Telephone & Telegraph Building (1925)
Miller & Pflueger, A.A. Cantin
One of the city's most delicate skyscrapers is clad in light gray terra cotta. In plan an F-shape, the tapered mass was influenced by Eliel Saarinen's Chicago Tribune Tower competition entry (1922), and is ornamented at each setback level with art-deco bands and bracelets, stylized flowers, bells, and eagles. The entrance lobby features black marble walls and bronze elevator doors. *134-140 New Montgomery St.*

29 St. Regis Tower (2002)
Skidmore, Owings & Merrill
The 42-story mixed-use hotel and condominium building peels open at its corner, turning its two major facades into flat sheets. *125 Third St.*

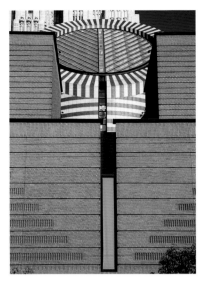

30. San Francisco Museum of Modern Art (Botta)

30 San Francisco Museum of Modern Art
(1995)
Mario Botta

The Swiss architect has given us a blow-up of the encounter between simple geometry and classical order that is present in his Ticino houses. The tension between the wholeness of primary volumes and the demand for symmetry lends the museum seismic monumentality, made evident by the pared window strip that slices down from the truncated cylindrical tower into the lowest of the stepped walls of rusticated red brick. At the base and then leading inside, zebra stripes of black and gray granite provide a setting for another object-creation, the central, top-lit staircase, whose solidity here is broken apart by stacked trays of balconies. After passing through the unfilled lobby and confining staircase, the best interior experience is at the top, a footbridge showered in light. *151 Third St.*

31 Yerba Buena Gardens.

Demolition of a workingman's neighborhood of single-room-occupancy hotels and taverns began shortly after the site was designated a redevelopment area in 1966. Redevelopment of the central ten-acre block, however, did not take place until the early 1990s, as proposal after proposal was scaled down from the initial vision of megastructures. The centerpiece of the new vision is a finely-landscaped esplanade park (designed by Romaldo Giurgola) that gently rises from Mission Street toward a twenty-foot high waterfall hiding the Moscone Center extension. *Fourth and Mission Sts.*

32 Yerba Buena Center for the Arts (1994)
Fumihiko Maki

A welcome addition of quality international modernism to San Francisco houses exhibition spaces and a screening room. A double-height glass lobby links the disparate parts of this L-shaped building. The aluminum-clad exterior walls, a trademark of Maki's design, might refer to the former industrial character of the district or equally to a Japanese suit of armor. *701 Mission St.*

33 Yerba Buena Center for the Arts Theater
(1994)
James Stewart Polshek

The best of the Yerba Buena Gardens buildings is a collage of cubist volumes, solid and glass, and colors occupying the white-gray-black spectrum. Creatively extending a tradition in theater design, Polshek arranges and garnishes the volumes as expressions of internal uses. The fly loft is faced with aluminum panels, the auditorium becomes a solid gray box, and the lobby is treated as a glass cube. Above the lobby is a perforated metal screen intended for video displays. *700 Howard St.*

33. Center for the Arts Theater (Polshek)

34 Metreon (1999)
SMWM, Gary Handel + Associates
The Metreon's main entrance is highlighted by a trapezoidal slice of mosaic-scored concrete and a giant neon sign hovering over the corner of Fourth and Mission Streets. Entered through a sixty-foot glass atrium, interior spaces flow off of the 270-foot long lobby flooded with special-effects signs, poles, and overhangs. With numerous stores, restaurants, attractions, 15 movie screens, and an IMAX theater, the Metreon is a shopper-tainment paradise for bundled, high-voltage experiences. Fortunately, these experiences continue beyond the commercial interior through a great window curtain wall on the eastern side, opening onto viewing terraces of the downtown skyline. The architects have done an impressive job of enlivening the four different facades of what would ordinarily be an enormous box with blank walls. *101 Fourth St.*

35 The Contemporary Jewish Museum (2008)
Daniel Libeskind
This angular outgrowth from the old Pacific Gas and Electric Substation (1907, Willis Polk) exposes the act of construction as consisting of material, shape, light, history, and the word of God. The museum's massing is based on the two Hebrew letters of the word L'Chaim (to life). *Chet* provides an overall continuity for the core exhibition, while the *Yud,* located on the pedestrian connector, gives a new identity to the power station. A couple of blue metal cubes tumble and crash against the side of the old brick substation. *Mission St., between Third and Fourth Sts.*

39. House (Jennings)

36 Marriott Hotel (1989)
Anthony Lumsden
To the chagrin of architects, the buildings most popular with the general public are often those looking like other things. In this case, San Francisco has added a blown-up Wurlitzer jukebox to its skyline, the Dr. Jekyll and Mr. Hyde of architecture. The sober side of the hotel is neo-1930s highrise whose windows recall the McGraw Hill Building in New York. The mad invention is a staccato phrasing of glass-arched windows, dramatically reflecting the evening sunlight and "glazenly" paraphrasing the art deco era. *55 Fourth St.*

37 Moscone Convention Center (1981)
Hellmuth, Obata & Kassabaum (1988),
North Gensler/DMJM
West Gensler/Michael Willis/Kwan Henmi
Upon opening, the underground hall, engineered by T. Y. Lin, was the largest column-free space in the world. Sixteen post-tensioned concrete arches span the 260,000 square foot hall. Over time, Moscone South has become a mound for other buildings. Rising on its western flank are the whimsical shapes of the Children's Center (1998, Adele Santos). Gensler was involved in two extensions: the underground Moscone North in 1992, and Moscone West in 2003. The latter's black-box interior is wrapped with three levels of glass curtain walls that curve at the corner and form canted bays along Howard Street. *Howard & Fourth Sts.*

38 Old U.S. Mint (1869–1876)
A.B. Mullett
The oldest stone building in the city is one of the only remaining examples of Greek Revival architecture for an institutional building. Side wings with unfluted pilasters surround the central entrance, reached via a set of stairs and distinguished by a Doric colonnade topped by a pediment. *88 Fifth St.*

39 House (2001)
Jim Jennings
On a rectangular façade clad in Korten steel panels, holes drilled into the surface create a grid of nocturnal light patterns. Inside, there's no need for a media entertainment. The holes function as a grid of camera obscuras, projecting the passing outdoor scene onto domestic walls. One section of the wall is recessed and fitted with translucent glass windows. *967 Howard St.*

43. Federal Building (Morphosis)

40 Yerba Buena Lofts (2002)
Stanley Saitowitz
The interiors of these live-work buildings are crafted as large single spaces that can be flexibly adapted (or sub-divided) for a wide range of uses—antithesis to the cramped quarters of Victorians. On the concrete-framed exterior, artistic expression is given to constructional and seismic systems, dominated by the forthright exhibition of the concrete frame. The frame, which the architect likens to a giant egg crate, is divided into 16 x 16 foot bays, each of which contains a two-story loft that is further divided into an open terrace and floor-ceiling channel glass. Two large recessed areas segment the long façade into three parts. *855 Folsom St.*

41 Columbia Square Housing (1999)
David Baker
Organized around a central courtyard, the 50-unit apartment complex serves up a multicourse decorative perimeter. Colors range from gray to mustard to burnt Siena. The mass is broken down into vertical sections (reminiscent of San Francisco row houses) of different shapes and heights. The cladding shifts back and forth from horizontal wood-composite siding to vertical galvanized steel to painted cement plaster. Wooden staircases and trellises further turn up the decorative heat. *1035 Folsom St.*

42 Post Office and U.S. Court of Appeals Building (1905)
James Knox Taylor (1931), George Kelham (1997), Skidmore, Owings & Merrill
A granite facade is framed by projecting end bays whose banding and rustication stresses the sought-after weightiness of Beaux-Arts classicism. The interiors, especially the lobby and courtrooms, are opulent and decorated with motifs from Californian culture. *Seventh St. at Mission St.*

43 Federal Building (2006)
Morphosis
An 18-story slab and four-story annex shape a large plaza along a desolate stretch of the South of Market. Designed by Thom Mayne, the tower—120 feet long and 65 feet wide—is constructed out of reinforced concrete and is punctured by a three-story sky garden. The radical treatment of the skyscraper skin includes a vertical row of projecting windows along with a wrinkled fabric of steel mesh draped over the glass. This metal screen will draw heat up and away from the building. Natural ventilation will be enhanced by operable windows, fluted undersides on the concrete floor slabs, and a concrete core that should keep the interior cool during the day. The elimination of corner offices and use of skip-stop elevators will presumably enforce workplace solidarity and community. *Seventh & Mission Sts.*

44 Rowhouses (1993)
Donald McDonald
An architect famous for creating a formula of Liliputian living in San Francisco dresses it up in a sci-fi treatment. Similar ideas can be seen in more pedestrian attire at the architect's other housing complexes, such as the Hermann Garden Cottages (1983–1985) at Duboce and Hermann Streets. Here, the exceedingly narrow (twelve foot wide) buildings are stamped in sheet metal and allowed to explode wide-angled bay windows on the upper floors. *Summer St., between Howard & Clementina Sts.*

45 Studio/Apartments (1992)
Stanley Saitowitz
A modernist challenge is issued against the design constraints that have long existed for the city's railroad flats. Steel braces at the front and rear ends allow for the creation of a open central space, breaking open the

40. Yerba Buena Lofts (Saitowitz)

45. Studio/Apartments (Saitowitz)

prototypical sequence of sarcophagus-like rooms. On the sides, thick party walls contain the infrastructure, the stairs, bathrooms, and kitchens. The exposed steel frame supports a set of windows that straddle the territory between the bay and the horizontal strip. Next door at 1028 Natoma Street is a new neighbor (2005) whose mute concrete and window screen politely mocks the earlier act of structural expressiveness. *1022 Natoma St.*

46 Live-Work Loft Projects (1995–1997)
Sternberg Benjamin
An early representative of the loft-living phenomenon in San Francisco housing, these residences provide double-height living areas with mezzanines. Their external appearance is a curious fusion of features drawn from nearby residences and industrial buildings. Domesticity and productivity come together to create a hybrid aesthetic for the cyber-artist age: bay windows faced in sheet metal; small balconies framed in wiremesh; and wooden French doors that lead to raw steel staircases. *5-45 & 50 Lucerne St., 111, 125, & 161 Gilbert St.*

47 Hart Production Studios (2000)
Michael Graves
Entered through a cylindrical pavilion, the small building is faced with a checkerboard concrete façade. It was constructed many years after the architect's original design. *772 Bryant St.*

48 New Sheriff's Facility (1992)
Del Campo & Maru
Visible from the 101 Freeway, a recent city jail represents its functions not through thick walls and watchtowers, but with a frosted, undulating curtain wall. Visible behind this curtain wall is a service corridor with bathrooms and mechanical functions. Behind the corridor is a concrete wall whose small windows open onto the prisoner's cells. The undulating curve is created by the organization of the cellblock into three connected circles, allowing all cells to be clearly visible from a central supervisory booth—an up-to-date interpretation of Jeremy Bentham's Enlightenment Panopticon prison. *Harrison & Seventh Sts.*

49 Office Building (2002)
Leddy, Maytum, Stacy
An exoskeleton of steel beams, aluminum sunscreens and clay cladding hangs in front of the (partially exposed) concrete structure in order to relate the new structure to older brick buildings nearby. *625 Townsend St.*

50 Diamond and Jewelry Mart (1985)
Tanner & Van Dine
On a triangular site, walls are almost completely faced in glass block, creating an arctic tundra of translucent stone and ice. *999 Brannan St.*

51 Plaza Apartments (2006)
Leddy, Maytem, Stacy/ Paulett Taggart
A concrete frame infilled with glazing and wood/resin panels provides 106 units of supportive housing. *6th & Howard Sts.*
(See pg 56)

05 Western Addition / Haight-Ashbury

The Western Addition was a Victorian neighborhood destabilized by rapid development (and conversions of houses to multi-unit buildings) after 1906, when for a short time Fillmore Street became the commercial artery of the city. During the 1940s, the area became home to a large African-American community and the city's jazz scene. Later, during the 1960s, the designation of "blight" by the San Francisco Redevelopment Authority led to demolition of almost 1,000 buildings—many of them Victorians—and redevelopment with slab structures on superblocks. During the early 1960s, the Haight-Ashbury neighborhood was a quiet working-class district whose inexpensive housing became an attraction for young people. Stores like the Thelin Brother's Psychedelic Shop, which Timothy Leary termed "a holy place," turned the district into the laboratory for America's hippie culture that still leaves a pungent scent aloft in the neighborhood.

Row Houses

1 First Unitarian Church & School (1888)
George Percy (1970), Callister Payne & Rosse
A heavy Gothic Revival church that could be encountered on an English country road is instead located on an island between two of the city's most trafficked arteries. More interesting is the modern school addition, crafting a pleasant courtyard of glass porticoes, timber-grained concrete surfaces, and Japanese-inflected redwood posts. *1187 Franklin St.*

2 St. Mark's Lutheran Church (1895)
Henry Geilfuss
A survivor of both the Earthquake and Western Addition urban renewal, this German Romanesque church exudes great power through its solid walled geometries of congregation hall and (conical and square) corner towers. *1135 O'Farrell St.*

3 St. Mary's Cathedral (1971)
Pier Luigi Nervi, Pietro Belluschi
An apparently simple form discloses complex intentions for this 2,500 seat sanctuary. In common language, what one sees here is a white ship turned upside down to become the rotating device seen inside of washing machines. Or, through the language of futurist geometry, four 190-foot up-ended paraboloids rise from a square plan to create

a spatiality of elliptical and hyperbolic curves, which is then intersected by a skylit cross of stained-glass windows. The four muscular piers at ground level make palpable the plasticity of this roof, while the thin poured-concrete shell is covered in travertine. The expansive forecourts lie barren in even the most glorious of weather. *1111 Gough St.*

4 Cathedral Professional Building (1915)
Frederick Meyer
The former Green's Eye Hospital unfolds as an L-shaped Mediterranean-revival building that is highlighted by a bell tower. *1801 Bush St.*

3. St. Mary's Cathedral (Nervi, Beluschi)

Map 05

101

5 Trinity Episcopal Church (1892)
A. Page Brown
Here is a West Coast example of the nation-wide return to the Gothic Style led by Ralph Adams Cram after years of Richardsonian Romanesque. The exterior is a fortress of gray sandstone whose deeply-incised and simple details express the workmanlike construction typical of this design outlook. *1668 Bush St.*

6 Congregation Ohabai Shalome (1895)
Moses Lyon
Now the Kokoro senior housing building, this wooden *shul* features pointed arches and an elevation borrowed from a Venetian palace. *1881 Bush St.*

7 Stanyan House (1852)
A prefabricated wooden house exhibits a puritanical severity. *2006 Bush St.*

8 House (1885)
Samuel & Joseph Cather Newsom
Investing its form with a redwood over-growth of detailing, this Stick Style house culminates in a projecting sunburst gable and steeple. *1735 Webster St.*

9 Nihonmachi Mall (1976)
Okamoto & Murata/Van Bourg Nakamura
Across the street from the mall, out alone in the fog-enshrouded streets, is a recre-ated Japanese village street. *Buchanan St., between Post & Sutter Sts.*

10 Japan Center (1968)
Minoru Yamasaki
Here the traditional Japanese vernacular architecture of large plaster surfaces neatly framed by wooden beams is enacted on a massive scale. This collection of spare yet elegant buildings frames T.Y. Lin's five-roofed, cylindrical peace pagoda. *Post St., between Buchanan & Webster Sts.*

11 St. Francis Apartments (1961)
Marquis & Stoller
A superblock development for 299 garden apartments is arranged in orthogonal geometries that update the city's rowhouse traditions. The project is sited around communal gardens and landscaping by Lawrence Halprin. Across Laguna street to the east are other notable modern apartments: to the north, the Laguna/O'Farrell Apartments (1964, Jones & Emmons); and south, Laguna Heights (1963, Claude Oakland). *Laguna St. between Geary Blvd. and Ellis St.*

12 Fillmore Auditorium (1912)
Reid Brothers
The most famous dance hall of the 1960s was home to light shows and the San Francisco sound of the Jefferson Airplane and Big Brother and the Holding Company, the scene "of psychotropic substances," at least according to Wavy Gravy. *1805 Geary Blvd.*

13 Fillmore Center (1991)
Daniel, Mann, Johnson, & Mendenhall
A multi-block mixed-use development attempts to restore an urban atmosphere to what had been the heart of the Fillmore

16. Westerfield House (Geilfuss)

District. The large, bulky towers are an example of design-by-committee, repeating the mantras of traditional urbanism: bays, setback profiles, ground-level retail, and distinctive tops. *Fillmore St., between Turk St. & Geary Blvd.*

14 UCSF/Mt. Zion Hospital (1950)
Eric Mendelsohn (1953), Hertzka & Knowles
Formerly the Maimonides Health Center, the expression of paper-like concrete slabs turned into decorative curving balconies has regrettably been lost to an insensitive infill. *1600 Divisadero St.*

15 Holy Cross Parish Hall (1854)
The oldest wood-frame church in the city is simply decorated by plain pilasters. *1820 Eddy St.*

16 Westerfield House (1889)
Henry Geilfuss
This Stick Eastlake house is inflated beyond the style's normal liveliness and widely regarded as one of San Francisco's definitive Victorians. This walk down the high ornamental wire rises or falls through its right-angled bays, decorative wooden ribbons, and dominating tower. *1198 Fulton St.*

11. St. Francis Apartments (Marquis & Stoller)

17 700 Block of Steiner Street
Matthew Kavanaugh
Why not see the movie set of San Francisco that happens to be real? Viewed from Alamo Square, these Queen Anne row houses in evening gowns have become one of the city's trademark photo opportunities, damsels of color and decoration atop the working city.

18 Zen Center (1922)
Julia Morgan
This stately block communicates a curious contrast of colonial impressions from England and Spain—red-brick walls beneath a red-tiled roof—linked together by the liberal use of classical elements. *300 Page St.*

19 Houses (1984)
Donald McDonald
An attempt is made to craft super-small buildings (800 square feet) on super-small lots. *496-498 Germania Sts.*

20 Haight Street Lofts (1996)
Tanner, Leddy, Maytum, Stacy
Large, industrial sash windows continue above the cornice to become dormers for this loft complex. *625 Haight St.*

21 Phelps House (1850)
Constructed of local redwood, this one-time farmhouse is notable for its long balustrades, capped dormers, and central decorative gable. *1111 Oak St.*

22 Haus Martin (2004)
Cass Calder Smith
This minimal house steps back from its ostentatious older neighbors. The façade consists largely of slats of cedar that encase a long, horizontal window. *611 Buena Vista Avenue West.*

23 House (1910)
Bernard Maybeck
A sloping roof sets off an interesting dialogue with the front elevation. *1526 Masonic Ave.*

24 Bransten Residence (2006)
Addison Strong
The steel frame that carves out the large interior volume is visible on the busy façade, which consists of a steel openwork garage, horizontal cedar panels, vertical ceramic tiles, and black steel panels. *510 Belvedere St.*

27. Darling House (Neutra)

25 House (2005)
Anne Fougeron
On a narrow and deep lot, the architect carved out a number of diverse outdoor spaces. The house was cut into two, allowing a courtyard to be inserted in the middle. Other outdoor spaces include a roof deck, rear courtyard, and garden. The façade is clad in wooden boards that open as slats on the second floor to accompany a projecting plate-glass window. *1532 Cole St. (See pg 104)*

26 Kurlander House (1980)
Ira Kurlander
Dramatically backing off from its corner to reveal a thin columnar support, this modernist house is a remodelling of an older building. The original windows are visible on the first floor, but dominated by a series of cubist windows and balconies at the entrance and upper level. *1401-1403 Shrader St.*

27 Darling House (1936)
Richard Neutra
Industrial details like a steel door and silver-gray trim enliven the redwood facing, a cladding solution Neutra used for his early works in the Bay Area. On the north and east sides, great horizontal windows are the dominant planar element. *90 Woodland Ave.*

28 Grims House (1911)
Louis Mullgardt
Great plaster walls give way to an open wooden porch and create echoes of Frank Lloyd Wright's Prairie period. *226 Edgewood Ave.*

31. St. Ignatius (Devlin)

29 Shay House (1985)
James Shay
Aside from siding references to Esherick's reductive Goldman House, this house is distinguished by the nuanced push and pull of the asymmetrical front facade plane, where a bay window is covered in sheetmetal. The use of metal finishes and flush detailing point to the early houses of Shin Takematsu. *276 Edgewood Ave.*

30 Parkview Commons (1990)
David Baker
Replacing the monumental bulk of Polytechnic High School is a dull complex of three-story neo-Edwardian residences grouped around a courtyard. The flashy Art-Deco gymnasiums of the former high school (1929, G. Alfred Lansburgh/ 1937, Charles Sawyer) frame the project. *Frederick & Willard Sts.*

31 St. Ignatius (1914)
Charles Devlin
One of the landmarks of the western half of the city crowns the southern slope of Lone Mountain. The Jesuit Church of the University of San Francisco boasts all the compositional features of a great church: two front towers, a pedimented colonnade, a dome, and a campanile. The principal facade is fashioned by Ionic and Corinthian colonnades that rise up to a pediment, and are framed by corner towers which progress in stature from large to small octagons, a cupola, and finally a lantern. The buff-colored brick and cream/yellow terra cotta cladding atop a steel frame resembles the neo-classical compositional formula created by Servandoni's St. Sulpice in Paris. Inside, the sanctuary culminates in a coffered ceiling and large apse where the dome might have been visible. *650 Parker Ave.*

32 San Francisco Columbarium (1898)
Bernard Cahill
At the end of a provincial street of stucco houses is a non-denominational cemetery for cremated remains, splendidly housed in a Beaux-Arts chapel capped by a green-copper dome. A remnant of a 167-acre cemetery and crematorium, the building is the last functioning columbarium in the country. *1 Loraine Ct., between Stanyan St. & Arguello Blvd.*

32. San Francisco Columbarium (Cahill)

06 Pacific Heights / Marina / Presidio Heights

Even more than Nob Hill, the crest of Pacific Heights reaching west to Presidio Terrace dominates the social register of San Francisco, containing the homes of the haute bourgeoisie that appear in the conspicuously-large social columns of the *San Francisco Chronicle*. The range of architecture here is perhaps wider than anywhere else in the city. Represented are all the Victorian periods, the Shingle

Style, the Beaux Arts, and many impressive modern and contemporary houses. Pacific Heights boasts two superb mid-sized parks. Lafayette Park (1867) is conspicuous for a large white building situated on its eastern end, the remains of a greater complex of private property (among them, the Holladay Mansion) that uneasily co-existed with the park. Alta Plaza, constructed by John McLaren on the site of an old quarry, is

notable for its four great staircases that zig and zag the steep slopes in order to connect U-shaped terraces. Below Pacific Heights is the Marina District, constructed on landfill that initially was the site for the Panama-Pacific International Exposition (P.P.I.E.) of 1915. The Marina District, built on the fair's site, contains scores of Art-Deco buildings and businesses as well as Mediterranean-style residences.

1. McElroy Octagon House

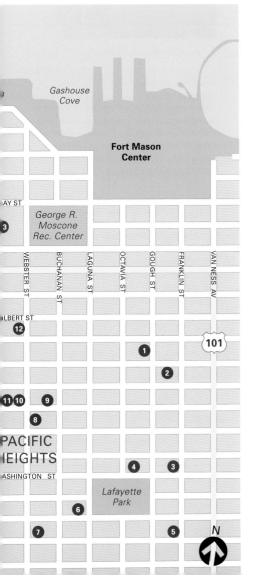

1 McElroy Octagon House (1857–1861)
This is one of two remaining eight-sided houses in San Francisco; the other is the Kenny House at 1067 Green Street. In these homes, geometrical rationality (or, alternatively, mysticism) overcomes the functions of domesticity, except perhaps for the fact that the unusual plan allows sunlight to enter all rooms. *2645 Gough St.*

2 House (1940)
William Wurster
The architect's challenge to formal monumentality could not be better illustrated than in this redwood-hued retreat into the pastoral vernacular. *1641 Green St.*

3 Haas-Lilienthal House (1886)
Peter Schmidt
Painted in gray tones reminiscent of the nineteenth-century chromatic palette, this Victorian more than makes up for these grave hues in its transition from horizontal lap siding to fish-scale shingles, or in its mastery over projecting gables, angled and rounded bays, and a four-story corner tower. In a city where ornamental excess was the name of the game, this house dealt the cards. Open to the public. *2007 Franklin St.*

4 Spreckels Mansion (1913)
George Applegarth
On one of the largest Beaux-Arts residences in the city, stylized Ionic columns order a series of arched window bays below garlands that drip from balconies, fitting tribute to the sugar baron who resided here. *2080 Washington St.*

5 Coleman House (1895)
W.H. Lillie
Great outbursts of gables, turrets, porches, and rounded bays emphasize the volumetric eccentricities of the Queen Anne style. *1701 Franklin St.*

6 Pacific Heights Conference Center & Culinary Arts Institute (1895)
Arthur Page Brown
The feeling of a palazzo is established by a hemispherical portico supported by Ionic columns and an outline punctuated by fluted pilasters. *2212 Sacramento St.*

7 Temple Sherith Israel (1905)
San Francisco's oldest Jewish congregation is the embodiment of frenzied historicism. Where the whole is less than the sum of its parts, particulars anxiously scurry along a number of medieval and classical ornamental tracks and culminate in a blazing sun on the dome's intrados. Inside, the great half-circle window shows Moses bringing the Ten Commandments down from Yosemite's Half Dome. *2266 California St.*

8 Bourne House (1896)
Willis Polk
Faced with ample walls of clinker brick, this composition is apprehensively balanced around a single, diminutive piano-nobile window, and enclosed by an elaborate set of pilasters, segmented arch, and balustrade. *2550 Webster St.*

9 James Flood Mansion (1901)
Julius Krafft
Broadway's classical banks are anchored by one of the early trendsetters in copious detailing. *2120 Broadway*

10 Joseph Grant Mansion (1910)
Hiss & Weekes
Resounding from the weighty red-brick surfaces, classical quoins and columns, and weathered mansard roof, is the self-conscious stab for immortality of the business elite. *2200 Broadway*

11 Convent of the Sacred Heart (1912)
Bliss & Faville
Formerly the Second James Flood Mansion, this stone-faced paean to Italian classicism is a tranquil reflection of an earlier time. *2222 Broadway*

3. Haas-Lilienthal House (Schmidt)

12 Vedanta Society (1905)
Joseph Leonard
Expressing the Vedanta belief that all religions are paths to God, this architectural smorgasbord features a medieval crenelated tower, Russian Orthodox multiple onion domes, and bulbous domes of Bengali origin, among other peculiarities. *2963 Webster St.*

13 Marina Middle School (1936)
George Kelham, William Day
Crisp planes and cool colors announce the Streamline Moderne style. *3500 Fillmore St.*

14 Schiff House (1937)
Richard Neutra & Otto Winkler
The principal two floors of this rowhouse—on a standard San Francisco lot—are a gleaming glass curtain wall framed in steel sash. The recessed third floor allows for a front roof terrace. *2056-2058 Jefferson St.*

15 Palace of Fine Arts (1915)
Bernard Maybeck
The only built remains of the grandiose P.P.I.E. is a concrete structure rebuilt during the early 1960s after the original wood-lathe and plaster design. Maybeck's most Piranesian fantasy, the architect designed this stage set as an intentional ruin, a gesture to the Fair's evocation of California as a land of romantic longing and ancient mystery. The open octagon and dome are reminiscent of Rome's Temple of Minerva Medici, a decagonal structure that similarly merged

acute angles to form a circular conclusion. The rotunda stands at the midpoint of a free-standing peristyle, which together form a backdrop for the lagoon. From the Lyon stairs above, the view of redwood trees, the Palace, and the Bay looks almost like a painting by Thomas Cole of the westward course of American Empire. *3601 Lyon St.*

16 **St. Vincent de Paul** (1916)
Shea & Lofquist
An avalanche of snow-balling detail and over-crafted woodwork is most outrageous for its projecting, bracketed gambrel roof. *2350 Green St.*

17 **Casebolt House** (1866)
An Italianate mansion framed by Canary Island palms looks like a plantation house set amid the great fields of the Central Valley. The projecting central porch is supported by paired Doric columns on the ground floor, Corinthian columns on the second floor, and is terminated by a gable. *2727 Pierce St.*

18 **Houses** (1893, 1895)
Ernest Coxhead
These transplanted English cottages feature large expanses of shingled wall and roof. *2421 & 2423 Green St.*

19 **House** (1938)
John Dinwiddie
On this early modernist composition, the opposed bearings of horizontal and vertical wood siding animate all surfaces—garage, lower levels, upper section. These linear games redefine the artistic representation of a facade from a traditional reliance on applied ornament to a new emphasis on geometry. *2660 Divisadero St.*

20 **House** (1939)
William Wurster
This house bases its architecture on the movements of regular lines that break apart the idea of a house as a cubic box, and reveal domestic space as a dynamic interpenetration of planes and volumes developed from these lines. A wood lattice network forms balconies and frames the entrance. *2633 Green St.*

21 **House** (1938)
Wurster, Bernardi & Emmons
A wood-frame house painted yellow exhibits a flat roof and windows that turn corners. *2795 Vallejo St.*

27. Church of the New Jerusalem (Brown)

22 **Raycliff Terrace.**
On a cul-de-sac off Pacific Avenue, houses by Gardner Dailey (#1, 1951), Wurster, Bernardi & Emmons (#25, 1959), and Joseph Esherick (#75, 1951) express the modernist drive toward abstract, volumetric form using local materials such as redwood siding and shingles. The block of Pacific Avenue contains other noteworthy houses: #2800 (1899, Ernest Coxhead); #2820 (1912, Willis Polk); #2870 (1951, Wurster, Bernardi & Emmons); #2889 (1890, Arthur Brown, Jr.).

23 **Howard House** (1939)
Henry Howard
And for the reflective and plastic qualities of glass and concrete, modernist vengeance is wrought upon the box. Beginning above the flat plane of the ground story, each successive balcony and window row makes a systematic and curvilinear retreat from the street wall. *2944 Jackson St.*

24 **Cottage Row** (1989)
Kotas & Pantaleoni
Instead of expressing the house as a unified bulk, the architects have opted for small irresolute masses, cottages that fold back from the street, exposing peaked roofs, a variety of angular (and bay window) forms, clapboard and shingle sidings, and muted and dramatic colors. *2910 California St.*

25 **House** (1959)
Wurster, Bernardi & Emmons
A simple cubic volume is composed of corner windows and capped by a projecting flat roof. *3095 Pacific Ave.*

29. Roos House (Maybeck)

26 House (1912)
Ernest Coxhead
On a large site, the gable becomes an experiment in compositional order, reaching down from the roof to form the second-story bay and then dissolving within the complex outline of the entrance porch. *3151 Pacific Ave.*

27 Church of the New Jerusalem (1894)
Arthur Page Brown
The Swedenborgian Church of Joseph Worcester, a prime mover in California's Arts and Crafts Movement, was a testing ground for the idea that the craft of building should be joined to the qualities inherent in natural materials. Entered through a low arch, the small brick and stucco structure is situated in a walled garden reminiscent of old mission compounds. While modeled on an Italian church near Verona, the interior hall makes an original statement of California, using bark-covered Madrone logs to support a gabled roof clad in tiles. *2107 Lyon St.*

28 3200 Block of Pacific Avenue.
Houses by Bernard Maybeck, Willis Polk, Ernest Coxhead, and William Knowles (all built between 1901 and 1913) employ dark shingles and generate picturesque outlines of bays, gables, and chimneys. The most harmonious visual effect is seen from the adjacent Presidio, where an enlightened flat wall of shingles and windows looks out at the sprightly dance of branches and boughs in the Monterey Cypress Forest.

29 Roos House (1909)
Bernard Maybeck
Irregular outlines and projecting eaves mesh somehow an ornamental half-timber framework and stucco skin. Structural beams beneath the roofline support quatrefoil tracery. Quite idiosyncratically, the house manages to be ornamental and structural all at the same time. *3500 Jackson St.*

30 House (1940)
Michael Goodman
The flat roof, white walls, and volumetric plasticity of the modern movement are all present on this small townhouse. *3550 Jackson St.*

31 Goldman House (1951)
Joseph Esherick
Breaking apart the idea of the house as a closed cube fronting the street, this residence is entered via a long recessed path alongside a garden. For the L-shaped plan, concrete piers support wood beams that in turn prop up a dominating flat roof. The recessed house well illustrates Esherick's design philosophy: "A house isn't the same as trying to do a storefront on Market Street, where you're competing for identification. In a way I like being able to be indifferent to things, to push some things into the background. I always thought it was kind of nice to have things sort of disappear, not see them, but make life better for their being there." *3700 Washington St.*

28. 3200 Block of Pacific Avenue

32 Fisher Residence (1996)
Butler, Armsden
This house acts like a blue-jean and tee-shirt visitor arriving at a high-class party and promptly putting on a tie and dinner jacket. In this sense, an industrial-looking penthouse and raw concrete cladding are juxtaposed by residential massing and window composition as well as mahogany sash. *3757 Washington St.*

33 Russell House (1952)
Erich Mendelsohn
This Redwood mansion generates a forceful dialogue between the enclosed and disclosed. Entered through a depressed ground plane, Mendelsohn composes floor slabs and walls as free-form dividers between interior and exterior, above and below. Each of the four floors reads as a different plan, ceilings on one level becoming balconies on the next, floors covering open-air verandas below. The northwest corner of the house, remarkable for its great rounded room and balcony, recalls the architect's love of the curve, as seen elsewhere in his 1920s work. *3778 Washington St.*

33. Russell House (Mendelsohn)

34 Koshland House (1902)
Frank S. Van Trees
Well-mannered classical detailing (including a projecting Corinthian portico) and a flowing staircase evoke the Petit Trianon at Versailles. *3800 Washington St.*

35 Batten House (1892)
Willis Polk
Polk's idiosyncratic classicism goes further in this unusually wide, seven-part bay window.

116 Cherry St.
36 Lem House (1986)
Dan Solomon
In the midst of an ordinary block, a night-clubbing facade is created through an odd assortment of window shapes, surfaces, and transparencies. *Cherry St., between Sacramento & Clay Sts.*

37 Presidio Terrace (1905–1910)
Fernando Nelson, developer
This exclusive enclave is a textbook case of the historicism that was rampant in San Francisco at the time. Represented (by architects including Julia Morgan, George Applegarth, Lewis Hobart, and Bakewell and Brown) are the styles of the Beaux-Arts, Spanish-Colonial Revival, Craftsman, French Colonial, and even Pueblo. There is no charge for walking around this exclusive backlot of

38. Congregation Emanu-el (Brown)

heartsick dreams.
38 Congregation Emanu-el (1926)
Arthur Page Brown
For this reform Jewish congregation, the architecture of Byzantium was used to identify Judaism's eastern origins and differences from the architectural languages that define Roman Catholicism and Protestantism. Entered via a cloistered courtyard, whose arches are supported by columns with lion-headed capitals, the domed-central plan and drum windows set between buttresses resemble the great churches of Justinian in Constantinople. Not surprisingly, the massive red-tiled dome strikes an imperious chord within San Francisco's western reaches. *Two Lake St.*

39 Drew College Preparatory School (2001)
SMWM
Attempting to relate to older cityscape, the great curving curtain-glass windows of the library are set within a framework of solid walls

07 Eureka Valley / Noe Valley / Mission / Bernal Heights / Potrero Hill

Here are found many of the city's best blocks of Victorians, thankfully spared the ravages of the 1906 Fire. In Eureka Valley (or, the Castro District), the largest Gay neighborhood in the United States has flourished over the past thirty years. Below in the Mission, a bohemian culture has spread far beyond its origins around the Roxie Theater on 16th and Valencia Streets. The Mission is also the nexus for San Francisco's Latino families, fittingly since this was the area of original Spanish-Mexican settlement. Further east, on Potrero Hill and the flatlands along the Bay, artists have layered overtones onto a former industrial canvas. Overall, these neighborhoods are described by the main character of Arturo Isla's novel *The Rain God* (1984), who moves from Texas to California, completes his education, gives up all forms of organized religion, and decides to live in the Mission District.

5. Mission San Francisco de Asis

1 Capp Street Project House (1981)
David Ireland
Looking like a banzai meditation on an industrial building, this artists' space is covered in corrugated metal walls that fold into cubist shapes and openings. *65 Capp St.*

2 Mission Plaza Housing (1981)
Jorge de Quesada
On a busy street, a flush facade steps back in places to generate balconies and store entrances. *2017 Mission St.*

3 Tanforan Cottages (1853)

Among the oldest residential buildings in the city, these two small cottages are also among the first buildings in San Francisco to adopt an eastern—meaning England and New England—outlook, even though they are located only a block away from the Spanish Mission. *214 & 220 Dolores St.*

4 Mission Dolores Basilica (1918)
Willis Polk

The density of detailing around key points on this Churrigueresque composition—a Spanish Baroque phenomenon—draws its power from the surrounding spotless stucco surfaces. *3321 16th St.*

5 Mission San Francisco de Asis (1776)

One of the smallest of California's 21 missions, all that remains of a larger complex of fields and outbuildings is the church and graveyard. Aside from several engaged Tuscan columns on the front, the building is an exercise in the depth and clarity of its walls, whose four-foot thick adobe bricks are covered by plaster. Redwood timbers, held together by rawhide and manzanita pegs, support the sloping red-tile roof. Inside, the modest exterior gives way to a lavish Baroque altarpiece. *320 Dolores St.*

6. Mission High School (Reid Jr.)

6 Mission High School (1926)
John Reid Jr.
One of the city's best Churrigueresque compositions has spiraling columns and blooms of flower and vine that mark the upward movement around the entrance, upper windows, and polychrome tower. The vertical thrust of the well-detailed tower effectively counters the long horizontal blocks of the school. *3750 18th St.*

7 Triplex (2004)
Kennerly Strong
This corner building choreographs the transition from a residential street to a busy automotive artery. The 14th Street façade consists mainly of a pair of glazed bays, while the other wall, faced in corrugated copper, is a sweeping curve that boomerangs attention back from the sharp corner onto busy Guerrero Street. In an intriguing interpretation of the corner building, the entry court occupies the small rear yard space, and the true backyard emerges as a roof deck. *201 Guerrero St.*

8 Lesbian-Gay-Bisexual-Transgender Community Center (2001)
Peter Pfau, Jane Cee
The spaces of the LGBT Community Center revolve around a courtyard covered in translucent paneled walls. Several architectural maneuvers play off the complex histories—closets, stereotypes, epidemics—that underlie the meaning of this building. For the Market Street glass curtain wall,

sliding sunscreens can be moved to expose or screen the activities of the interior. At night, illuminated to high intensity, the center looks like a giant glowing candle, a fitting metaphor for the innumerable candles flamed during the struggles and memorials of the past decades. *1800 Market St.*

9 United States Mint (1937)
Gilbert Stanley Underwood
Standing atop a 100 foot cliff is an architectural crag of weighty reinforced concrete walls faced in granite. *155 Hermann St.*

10 Davies Hospital (1970)
Stone, Marraccini & Patterson
The close-knit lines of the bare concrete frame impress clear overall form and one of the city's unusual examples of "New Brutalism." *45 Castro St.*

11 Everett Middle School (1925)
John Reid Jr.
Walls of glazed tiles are broached through an entrance loggia supported by giant, medieval columns. *450 Church St.*

12 Castro Theater (1922)
Pflueger & Miller
On the facade of the grandest of San Francisco's neighborhood movie theaters, Spanish Baroque ornament never travels in straight lines. The vertical neon sign (1935) by Alexander Cantin has become the symbol of a neighborhood. *429 Castro St.*

13 Castro Condominiums (1982)
Dan Solomon with Paulett Taggart
Stepped boxes and industrial-square windows fit snugly into an irregular site. *2425 Market St.*

8. Lesbian-Gay-Bisexual-Transgender Community Center (Pfau, Cee)

14 Clarke Mansion (1891)
Smooth choreography takes a back seat in this Queen Anne house, whose ornament is pumped up on steroids. The roof profile is an intoxicated roar of turrets, cupolas, gables, dormers, more turrets, and more gables. *250 Douglass St.*

15 Lewis-Letton Residence (1995)
James Shay
Changing domestic temperaments and the shortage of empty lots in the city are both illustrated by this rebuilding of a vernacular house into an immense curtain wall that transforms living space into a perch for the long view of downtown. *51 Eagle St.*

16 Brown Residence (1997)
Frank Israel
Knife-edge corners and insidious geometries interrupt the stucco and metal façade, and unfold a cast of irregularly shaped windows. *69 Grandview St.*

17 House (1952)
Wurster, Bernardi & Emmons
Composed in an exterior asymmetry which reflects freer planning on the interior, the projecting eaves are a leitmotif for the sprawling ranch houses then proliferating all through the United States. *4015 21st St.*

18 James Lick Middle School (1929)
William Crim
The school building's white cubic forms reflect the different volumes of classroom wings, auditorium, and gymnasium. Stylized forms etched in low relief and moderne detailing accent major entrances. *1220 Noe St.*

19 Diamond Heights.
The second-largest of San Francisco's Redevelopment Zones did not actually need "redevelopment" since it was largely undeveloped in the 1950s. Planned for much higher densities, the 330-acre site is nonetheless a departure for San Francisco in more ways than one. Breaking off the grid, Diamond Heights's serpentine streets contain a range of residential types from attached Eichler homes to multiple-unit townhouse complexes. The best design emerged earliest, in the Red Rock Hill townhouses (1962, Cohen & Leverson), where overhanging balconies and floor-to-ceiling windows offer a logical regional alternative to the bay window. The twelve pier buttresses

7. Triplex (Kennerly Strong)

supporting a copper-clad dome at the Holy Trinity Greek Orthodox Church (1964, Reid, Rockwell, Banwell, & Taries) are also noteworthy.

20 Houses (1981–1991)
Jeremy Kotas, Kotas Pantaleoni, Kotas & Shaffer
These brightly-painted houses are either a second-coming of the Poole-Bell House (1872) down the block or a fitting act for an architectural drag show. Over-dressed in found materials, an eyebrow cornice, decorative I-beams, and running commentaries on different cladding materials, they are so completely out of bounds that they fit perfectly in San Francisco. *102, 123, 134, 135, & 140 Laidley St.*

21 St. Paul's Catholic Church (1911)
Frank Shea
Similar to the architect's design for St. Brigid's on Van Ness Avenue, this large Gothic Revival Church is faced with massive granite stone blocks that abruptly unfold into soaring wooden towers. These thick walls hid Whoopi Goldberg in *Sister Act*. *221 Valley St.*

22 Holy Innocents Episcopal Church (1890)
Ernest Coxhead
A soliloquy on the dark-brown shingle comes to a swirling-tongued conclusion around the arched entrance. The interior features the Arts and Crafts Movement's infatuation with dark woodwork. *455 Fair Oaks St.*

23 Collegio de la Mission (1939)
Masten & Hurd
On the rear wall, what amounts to an industrial facade is relieved in three locations by cylindrical stair towers faced in glass block. *22nd & Bartlett Sts.*

24 Del Carlo Court (1994)
Dan Solomon
An apartment complex grouped around a courtyard and reached through a right-angled arc reveals the architect's interest in creating mid-block urban environments. Other such projects are his Amancio Ergina Village (1985) in the Western Addition and Fulton-Grove Townhouses (1992) near Civic Center. This type of site planning represents a major departure from San Francisco's customary streetscapes where cubic boxes create a solid street perimeter that encloses private gardens. By contrast, courtyard buildings of the Mediterranean or Latin American variety create public inner-block open spaces by sculpting out their insides. Here, the dark-brown and white exterior is dominated by roof-brackets supporting an oversized cornice. *3330 Cesar Chavez St.*

25 Barnes-Tenazas House (1999)
Stanley Saitowitz
Three great curves ripple into the upper floor of the house: first, a sixteen foot skylight shaped like the lid of a grand piano; then, a gently bowed bay window that cuts inside of the frame to isolate vividly a steel pier at the northwest corner; and finally, a curled interior staircase lined by factory-style steel mesh. From the street above the house, the skylight resembles the prow of a ship floating high above the city. *1401 Shotwell St.*

31. La Cocina & Housing (Taggart)

26 Houses (1986)
William Stout, Peter Van Dine
Inside, the three residences are orchestrated by courtyards at each level. On the exterior, pristine white surfaces, open-air windows, and hard volumes flawlessly match the arid clarity of the San Francisco sky. *170-180 Manchester St.*

27 Market Heights Residences (1997)
Herman Stoller Coliver
This large housing development bridges the spatial differences between the residential neighborhood of Bernal Heights and the open spaces of the Allemany Farmer's Market. Looking like a California version of a Yemini walled town, the architects have used projecting and receding wall planes, and contrasting colors and materials, to create the ambiance of a caravansary. The overall impression would have been stronger had the concern for neighborhood context (especially in the form of pitched roofs) not dominated to such a great extent. *Ellsworth & Crescent Sts.*

28 House F/R (2003)
Craig Steely
A deep blue row house on a narrow lot opens up at the third floor via a large balcony and overhanging eave punctured dramatically by a circular cutout. *187 Peralta Ave.*

29 House B (2004)
Craig Steely
A dense wooden lattice fence wraps around the base of this corner house. The third story projects a prow, sheathed in wood and plate glass windows. *104 Franconia St.*

30 Good Samaritan Housing and Community Center (1997)
Mark Horton & SMWM
Changes in geometry, height, siding, color, and fenestration strive to disguise the institutional nature of this institution, and lend it instead a time-worn village appearance. *1290 Potrero Ave.*

31 La Cocina & Housing (2003)
Paulett Taggart
A street-front kitchen is faced in bands of glass and aluminum, atop of which is a horizontal curtain wall and slatted screen of ipe, a South American hardwood. Three townhouses occupy the rear of the lot. *2940 Folsom St.*

34. California College of the Arts (Skidmore, Owings & Merrill)

33. Office Building (Pfau)

32 San Francisco General Hospital (1909–1915)
Newton Tharp, John Galen Howard,
Frederick Meyer, John Reid Jr. (1976),
Stone, Marraccini & Patterson
Few buildings in the city signify the immensity and impersonality of institution more than this half-mile long procession of hospital buildings. The emphasis on rich details—patterned red brick, tile roofs, and terra-cotta bays—is awkwardly contrasted by concrete staircases that wrap around their host buildings like a replicating virus. *1001 Potrero Ave.*

33 Office Building (2001)
Peter Pfau
Two skin treatments are used for each of the intersecting L-shaped buildings; the first, glass curtain walls with translucent louvers and panels; the second, punched windows opening on a textured, concrete surface. *350 Rhode Island St.*

34 California College of the Arts (1951)
Skidmore, Owings, & Merrill
Designed by Walter Netsch during the early years of the glass-curtain wall, the former Greyhound Bus Company Building is now the center of the college's San Francisco campus. Bountiful glass walls wrap around reinforced-concrete frames and reduce the building to the artistic terms of exposed construction. The long-span roof of the northerly building is supported by bent concrete beams, which are pinned together at the building's apex. The enclosed space is one of the largest and most dramatic in the city. In 1999, renovations and additions to the great shed were completed by Tanner, Leddy, Maytum, Stacy. In 2004, Jensen & Macy completed the Graduate Center

across Hooper Street, an old frame structure wrapped in corrugated cement-board panels on the bottom and corrugated polycarbonate on top, creating a translucent clerestory. *1111 Eighth St.*

35 Mission Bay.
For decades, visions for this desolate area of former rail yards and freight terminals failed to get off the drawing board. At least three major plans for a city-within-a-city were drafted and eventually dropped. Finally, starting in 2000, the fourth plan, developed in 1998 by Silvetti & Machado, began to bear fruit. It consists of a 43-acre biotechnology research campus for the University of California at San Francisco, approximately 6,000 housing units, 6.8 million square feet of commercial space, a 500-room hotel, and 43 acres of parks. One of the first buildings was located at the eastern edge of the vast site; designed by Studios Architecture in 2002, its glass walls tautly cover a concrete frame. In the center, the Community Center Building (2003, Riccardo Legorreta) and its bold red-orange color and attached campanile provide a contrast to sober, academic buildings by Robert Frasca and Cesar Pelli. Finally, a parking garage, completed in 2006 by Stanley Saitowitz, livens things up with a DNA-patterned skin of glass and voids.

36 Gleeson-Jeanrenaud House (1991)
Dan Solomon
In this tonal composition of expressionistic miniatures in black asphalt shingles, symmetrical windows are divided by an exposed metal flue and right-angled bays. In the movie *The Joy Luck Club,* Lena's mother

complains that while the house cost a million dollars, the walls are still crooked. *610 Rhode Island Ave.*

37 Musilek Residence (2006)
Leddy, Maytum, Stacy
Set back on its lot to form a sunny forecourt, the three-story house is clad in glass, metal and cement-board panels, and features high-finish concrete-block sidewalls. *1218 Mariposa St.*

38 Potrero Hill Neighborhood House (1922)
Julia Morgan
A dark shingled building wraps around a small entrance courtyard. *953 De Haro St.*

39 House (1991)
Kotas, Pantaleoni
For this postmodern house, diverse siding materials (white and light orange plaster and dark brown shingles) are fitted onto an angular profile. *782 Wisconsin St.*

40 Victoria Mews (1979)
A nostalgic Victorian village was built on the hillside where a factory once stood. The complex avoids large-scale massing and industrial materials in favor of wood siding, balconies, and fine detailing—tops and tails prevail over nuts and bolts. *20th & Wisconsin Sts.*

41 Townhouses & Lofts (1995)
David Baker
Stepping down a steep hillside, this large complex strives to create unity out of different architectures. Gable roofs and clapboard siding give way to stucco walls and finally galvanized sheet metal, reassembling the upper residential neighborhood and factory district below into a single entity. *559-609 18th St.*

36. Gleeson-Jeanrenaud House (Solomon)

42 Adams House (1868)
Grace and restraint are the hallmarks of this Italianate residence, set behind a wall on a large lot and boasting luxuriant plantings. *300 Pennsylvania St.*

43 San Francisco Drydock.
The largest industrial complex in San Francisco, and for many years one of the largest in the entire American West, was noted for its construction of steamships, cruisers, battleships, as well as locomotives and steel machinery. Operations of Union Iron Works began at this site in 1883, and continued after the company was purchased by Bethlehem Steel in 1905. The buildings along 20th Street convey the atmosphere of an old industrial town, and notably include the machine shop (1886), a clear-span brick building covered by a steel truss roof. The highlights are the two drydocks, u-shaped steel beds on the waters of the Bay. Either occupied by ships or not, the hardboiled rust surfaces of the drydocks set off by the vertical girders of their associated cranes make for one of the most spectacular industrial landscapes anywhere. *420, 449, 462, & 548 20th St.*

35. Community Center Building (Legorreta)

08 Outside Lands / Golden Gate Park / Richmond / Sunset

The lands west of the coastal divide and south of Interstate 280 were the last parts of the city built for residences, in part because real estate developers were reluctant to construct in these fogbound sectors. Yet the spectacular construction of Golden Gate Park on coastal sage-scrub, despite Frederick Law Olmsted's recommendations to the contrary, changed the image of the Outside lands. By the 1920s, streetcars and automobiles provided access to these lands, leading to the rowhouse development of the Richmond and Sunset Districts. In general, the density and verticality of the inner districts of San Francisco gives way here to a looser, lower, and more automobile-oriented urbanism. Stucco is more common than clapboard siding, parking garages are ubiquitous, and front lawns quite frequent. Grids typically give way to serpentine streets when there are hills.

Doggie Diner Head, (National Historic Landmark) on Sloat Blvd.

1 Golden Gate Bridge (1937)
Joseph Strauss, Irving Morrow
Within the landscape of the Bay Area there is no spot more commanding than the Golden Gate and no human creation so inspiring as this bridge, symbolizing the aspirations and emotions of an entire region. An enlightened instance of human technology and willpower improving one of the world's most beautiful natural sites, the bridge stands in the face of dramatic winds and churning waters. Its 4,200-foot length is supported by two towers (746 feet high) that suspend great cables whose slopes rise and fall in tune with the surrounding Coast Ranges. The structure of the stepped-back towers is concealed by faceted steel panels that diminish in size as the towers climb toward the sky, and embellished by spandrels containing prism-like streamline detailing. The striking color has been alternatively called International Orange or red-lead primer.

2 Fort Point (1853)
U.S. Army Engineers
Forty-foot thick brick walls encase an interior courtyard, whose galleries of tiered arches create dramatic shadows as evocative as the paintings of Giorgio De Chirico. Everything, from the bold granite staircases to the bonding of bricks, is laid out in rigorous and ravishing simplicity. This former artillery fortress was used for the final confrontation in *Point Blank* starring Lee Marvin. *Long Ave. & Marine Dr.*

3 Crissy Field (2001)
George Hargreaves
The 100 acres of this former military airstrip faces the bay just east of the Golden Gate Bridge. The park project restored dunes and wetlands as well as created a huge grassy field as a memory of aviation days.

4 Presidio.
Now a national park, the Presidio contains hundreds of buildings reaching back to the Spanish Commandant's Quarters (1792), now incorporated into a 1930s Officer's Club. The former military base is a singular example of how architectural tastes have changed from the time of San Francisco's origin in the 1840s to the modern era. Wood-frame buildings from the 1860s (the Cavalry Barracks, Old Post Hospital, Officer's Row) are succeeded by brick structures with red-slate roofs during the 1890s, most notably the long line of ascending colonnaded barracks along Montgomery Street. The stucco facades and red-tile roofs of the Post Chapel (1932) succeeded these Anglo-references. Most recently, George Lucas's Letterman Digital Arts Center (2005, Gensler), with landscaping by Lawrence Halprin, gets stuck a long time ago in a galaxy one wishes were far, far away.

1. Golden Gate Bridge

5 House (1958)
Wurster, Bernardi & Emmons
Faced in stucco, great overhanging eaves become balconies as the view toward the Golden Gate grows in immensity. *850 El Camino del Mar*

6 House (1963)
Esherick Homsey Dodge & Davis
At the edge of Lincoln Park and its cliffs cascading down to the sea, the recessed entrance under a great beam announces a harmonious monologue in redwood surfaces. *890 El Camino del Mar*

7 House (1963)
Joseph Esherick
An irregular massing of cubes and window patterns are covered in unpainted shingles. *100 32nd Ave.*

8 Palace of the Legion of Honor (1916)
George Applegarth
At Land's End is a museum that houses the city's European art collections in a time-honored Neo-Classical outfit. The U-shaped building is entered under a triumphal arch flanked by colonnades, a modified version of a palace of the same name in Paris. Oddly enough, this architecture of Cartesian reason works well atop a landscape mesmerized by the wild radiance of nature. The building was rebuilt in 1995, adding an underground level. George Segal's Holocaust Memorial is located slightly northeast of the museum. *Lincoln Park*

9 Sutro Heights Park.
Site of the former mansion of Adolph Sutro, this landscaped garden's plants, gazebo, fragments of statuary, and stone lookout evoke romantic allusions. The park towers above the ocean and the ruins of the old Sutro Baths (1896), whose glass and iron structure enclosed a complex of swimming pools until it burned down in 1966. The old atmosphere is captured in Don Siegel's film *The Lineup.*

10 Holy Virgin Cathedral of the Russian Church in Exile (1977)
Oleg Ivanitsky
Five onion domes on drums and ornamental *kokoshniki* (Russian corbels) set a traditional tone for this Orthodox church. The cavernous interior is quite unlike the cramped, mysterious confines of old Russian Churches, but walls covered with icons might persuade the old believers. *6210 Geary Blvd.*

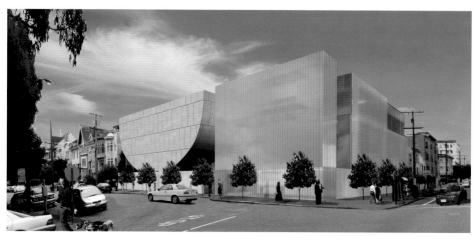

11. Congregation Beth Sholom (Saitowitz)

13. Roosevelt Middle School (Miller & Pflueger)

11 Congregation Beth Sholom (2008)
Stanley Saitowitz
Two striking shapes sit side by side: the utterly opaque concrete sanctuary, whose semi-circle flattening at the ends recalls a watermelon; and the administrative block, a sliced box of translucent glass. The sanctuary reverts to Jewish tradition by placing the Bimah–the table where the Torah is read—in the center of the room between rows of raked seating. It also evokes the internalized, spiritual quality of Jewish synagogues; the only openings for light are in the upper skylights. *1301 Clement St.*

12 Former French Hospital (1971)
Paffard Clay
Bold concrete lines and infill windows sound the call for strict structural expression. *Geary Blvd. & 6th Ave.*

13 Roosevelt Middle School (1934)
Miller & Pflueger
This meditation on the structural and expressive power of brick masonry, replete with faceted brickwork and redoubled distortions of the tower, recalls German or Dutch Expressionist design. The south-facing glass walls and copper spandrels underneath a pediment allude to Peter Behrens's AEG factory complex in Berlin. *460 Arguello Blvd.*

14 Golden Gate Park.
Beginning in 1871, the city's largest park (1,023 acres) was created on the site of the Great Sand Waste, a place many people thought utterly inhospitable for a great urban park. Through the arduous efforts of William Hammond Hall, the park's first superintendent, and John McLaren plantings of lupine and other groundcovers began the task of claiming the parkland from the sand. Monterey pine and cypress trees, Torrey pines, and different species of Eucalyptus were subsequently cultivated to provide a

barrier from the wind. In the English manner, the nature of Golden Gate Park is encouraged to grow toward the appearance of manicured wildness. Aside from the formal Music Concourse, the park's roads and paths meander, following the bends of glades or the shores of ponds and lakes. As one proceeds westward, the park gets wilder, and the trees less towering as scraggly forests replace meadows and the high canopy. The park ends abruptly under the gaze of two windmills, where thickets open up to the Great Highway and the Pacific Ocean.

15 Alvord Lake Bridge (1889)
Ernest Ransome
The first reinforced concrete bridge built in the United States derives its strength from twisted steel bars bonded into the concrete. Since these bars are not visible the design question becomes: how should the surfaces of the bridge be expressed? The solution here veered in two directions, each of which expresses concrete's inherent plasticity: the two exterior sides were treated like arches, and the concrete furrowed to create the impression of stone blocks, archivolts, and keystones; on the intrados, however, Ransome crafted concrete to resemble the dripping limestone stalagmites of a cave. *Golden Gate Park*

16 McLaren Lodge (1896)
E.R. Swain
The first Bay Area attempt to evoke the design vocabulary of the Mediterranean region was inspired by A. Page Brown's Spanish-Colonial pavilion for the State of California at the World's Columbian Exposition in Chicago (1893). Mediterraneanism is suggested for this low-slung building by arcades and a second-story loggia, a rugged sandstone exterior, and, most of all, the prominent red-tile roof. *Golden Gate Park*

14. Golden Gate Park

21. Japanese Tea Garden (Marsh, Hagiwara)

17 Conservatory of Flowers (1878)
Hammersmith Works/2004, Architectural
Resources Group
Fronted by the most sumptuous formal
garden in the park, this glass house is an
architectural anachronism, evoking the age
of great iron glasshouses, but supporting
its small sheets of glass within wooden
frames. Nonetheless, this house for tropical
flowers strikes an elegant profile. It was the
first large structure erected in Golden Gate
Park and the first municipal greenhouse in
California. *Golden Gate Park*

18 Spreckels Music Pavilion (1900)
Reid Brothers
A triumphal apse, flanked by double colon-
nades, conducts the spaces of the Music
Concourse. *Golden Gate Park*

19 De Young Museum (2005)
Herzog & de Meuron
One of the most important buildings ever
constructed in San Francisco raises the
stakes for architecture in the region. The
Swiss architects began by laying down three
parallel pavilions and then carefully twisting
them to create courtyards as wells as points
of crossing and separation. This subtle commentary on the cultural harmony and friction
among the collections displayed extends
to the shaping of the galleries: more classi-
cally proportioned spaces for Western Art;
a looser, flowing arrangement for the art of
Latin America, Africa, and Oceania. A unity
among all the collections emerges through
the use of a uniform roof, which boldly cantilevers over part of the landscaped garden.
A torqued education tower establishes a
citywide presence; its upper viewing plat-

form, whose geometry is aligned to the grid
of the neighboring Richmond and Sunset
districts, provides some of the best views
of the western part of the city. Most of all,
the museum is memorable for its cladding,
approximately 7,200 copper plates perforated, embossed, or debossed to provide a
textural counterpart to the surrounding park
forest at the golden hour before sunset. As
the copper turns green through oxidation
the impressions will stand out even more
and bring the sensual qualities of nature and
architecture as close together as they have
ever been. Finally, Walter Hood has created
varied landscapes on each side of the building—ranging from rhythmic bands of grass
and concrete in front of the principal façade
to a sculpture garden on the west side that
includes, behind black bamboo, a folly by
James Turrell. *50 Hagiwara Tea Garden Drive
Golden Gate Park*

20 California Academy of Sciences (2008)
Renzo Piano
A different approach to integrating a building
with nature is underway at this complete
restructuring of the varied parts of the natural
science museum. Only the African Hall and
Aquarium Vault will be retained from the old
museum. The 2 1/2 -acre roof of the unified
structure is rectangular in plan and undulating
in section. This profile echoes the contours
of the park's landscape, and also reflects the
common disciplinary standards and remarkable paradigm shifts that characterize scientific discovery and investigation. The organic
roof will be covered in vegetation, well over a
million plants, sloping gently over the interior
galleries, and opened at selective places to
allow for ventilation. Sides of the building will
be draped with glass curtain walls. *Golden
Gate Park*

21 Japanese Tea Garden (1894)
George Turner Marsh, Makoto Hagiwara
Part of the garden remains from the 1894
Midwinter Fair while the other half was
constructed in 1916. The garden is entered
through a two-story *ro-mon* (gate) and contains a tea house as well as a large statue of
the Buddha. *Golden Gate Park*

22 Beach Chalet (1921)
Willis Polk
For this small building, paired rustic Doric
columns lead into a hall adorned with fres-
coes by Lucien Labault (1936–1937). *Golden
Gate Park*

23 St. Anne of the Sunset (1904–1970)
Denis Shanagher
Massed sculptural colonnades of worshipers
and soft pink, rose, and white tones create
in this French Romanesque Church a visual
pageant for the Inner Sunset District. *850
Judah St.*

**24 University of California, San Francisco
Medical Center.**
The 107-acre campus contains a wide variety
of buildings dating from the 1920s to the
contemporary era. Its overpowering scale
hovers over Golden Gate Park and the surrounding neighborhoods like a laboratory
experiment gone awry. Most notable for
their architecture are the Health Sciences
Instruction & Research Buildings (1967,
Reid, Rockwell, Banwell & Tarics), which
exemplify the distinct artistic possibilities
of a square concrete box: rough-faced concrete set atop great piers with cantilevered
arches, concrete and black glass in continuous rows, where overhanging eaves reveal
the structural pattern of the beams. *500
Parnassus Ave.*

25. Sutro Tower

25 Sutro Tower (1968)
San Francisco's tallest structure is an
ungainly concatenation of steel girders.
Perhaps we would all rather know this omni-
present television and radio tower as Vikram
Seth saw it one evening or morning: "And
hand in hand they stroll below the fog-trans-
figured Sutro Tower, a masted galleon at this
hour." *1 La Avanzada Street*

26 House (1948)
John Funk
A modernist design clarified by its thin
slab roof and horizontal window rows.
2 Glenbrook Ave.

27 House (1958)
George Rockrise
This shingled structure relies heavily on
horizontal lines, redwood construction, and
wood lattices and framing details that recall
traditional Japanese construction. In Blake
Edward's *Experiment in Terror,* the entire
block was staked out by the FBI to protect
Lee Remick. *150 St. Germain Ave.*

28 House (1959)
Campbell & Wong
Visible from Glenbrook Ave, the backside of
this long horizontal box turns into patterns of
applied redwood strips. *175 Palo Alto Ave.*

29 House (1959)
Charles Warren Callister
A curved roof hangs over the head of this
house otherwise orchestrated by rectilinear
projecting beams. *176 Palo Alto Ave.*

30 Clarendon School (1959)
Wurster, Bernardi & Emmons
In this excellent articulation of a reinforced-
concrete frame, flanges artfully support the
flat floor slabs. Epitomizing school architecture of the modernist era, the separate
masses of classrooms, auditoria, and administration are connected by glass corridors.
500 Clarendon Ave.

31 Hibbs Gray House (2006)
Bruce Tomb
This addition to a mid-century modern house
adds a second story that turns a horizontal
band of windows to a vertical cadence.
The money moment is a dramatic projecting
bathroom, shaped like a teacup and clad in
a greenish fiber monocoque composite.
29 Mendoza Ave.

32 House (1933)
Irving Morrow
Window frames and moldings, painted
International Orange, accent the serene walls
of redwood. The house's sectional design
and large windows were trendsetters locally.
171 San Marcos Ave.

33 Forest Hill Association Clubhouse (1919)
Bernard Maybeck
Ever searching for the beauty of architecture in personalized memories, Maybeck here contrasts an English half-timber facade with large industrial-sash windows. *381 Magellan Ave.*

34 Erlanger House (1916)
Bernard Maybeck
Paired gables, leaded glass windows, shingle siding, and projecting beams all work to make this one of the best of his houses in the city. *270 Castenada Ave.*

35 E.C. Young House (1913)
Bernard Maybeck
An orange sensation (in the painted woodwork) expresses the architect's usual exuberance. *51 Sotelo Ave.*

36 House (1951)
Ernest Born
On a wide lot, two windows break the concentration of vertical redwood siding. *2020 Great Highway*

37 Oceanside Water Pollution Control Plant (1994)
SMWM
Almost all the sewage regalia is buried in a 1,000 foot-long man-made canyon. Inside this industry gorge, polished stack cylinders, a maze of steel walkways, and half-egg shaped anaerobic digesters reverberate the precision and complexity apropos a communal city bathroom. *Great Highway & Sloat Blvd.*

38 San Francisco Zoo (1925)
Lewis Hobart (1976), Esherick Homsey Dodge & Davis
For the Thelma Dolger Primate Center, the architects (1985, SMWM) crafted a series of multi-tiered walkways to engage the climbing habits of primates. *Sloat Blvd. at Great Highway.*

39 Lakeside Medical Center (1941)
Harold Stoner
On one of the city's earliest automobile shopping strips, this streamline moderne tower's spasmodic lines and folds evoke a space-age architecture later seen in venues like the Jetsons' television show. *2501 Ocean Ave.*

40 Commodore Sloat School (1977)
Marquis Assoc.
Behind an older Spanish Colonial building, this modern addition guides students through a concrete threshold of knowledge. *50 Darien Way*

41 San Francisco State University.
This 95-acre campus opened in 1954, and was designed by the Office of State Architecture. Originally organized around a series of low-slung slab buildings whose white plaster walls revealed horizontal window rows, many buildings have been added subsequently. The most notable is the Cesar Chavez Student Center (1980, Paffard Clay), perhaps the most sculptural building in all of San Francisco. In a reinforced concrete structure articulated by V-shaped cross braces and overhanging beams, disembodied staircases are flung out from the main volume, great projecting prows that look like the underside of a ship's bow (one supporting an outdoor amphitheater) are launched from the roof line. *1600 Holloway Ave.*

42 Montessori Children's Center (2005)
Mark Horton
Located on the site of the Park Merced Apartments, this steel-frame box is covered by corrugated metal walls and topped by a prominent overhanging roof that slants toward the back of the property. *80 Juan Bautista Circle*

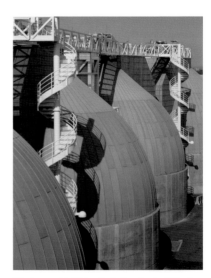

37. Oceanside Water Pollution Control Plant (SMWM)

43. Lick Wilmerding High School (Pfau)

47. Hunter's Point Crane

43 **Lick Wilmerding High School** (2003)
Peter Pfau
The core of the addition to the campus is a
quartet of industrial shops that face out onto
an open courtyard. Set below grade, their
terraced roofs are covered with grass that
provides students with precious open space.
Wooden louvers modulate solar penetration for the cafeteria, the most prominent
feature above ground level. Solar panels and
proposed windmills set along Interstate 280
complete the eco-friendly design. *755 Ocean
Ave.*

44 **City College of San Francisco.**
Opened in 1940, this 49-acre campus is
organized around Timothy Pflueger's
monumental multi-winged block, classicized
by three giant-order stripped colonnades.
The nearby theater building contains Diego
Rivera's "Pan American Unity" mural. *50
Phelan Ave.*

45 **Corpus Christi Church** (1953)
Mario Ciampi
A curtain wall of dark and clear windows
enlivens the plain white exterior. Inside the
sanctuary, concrete columns, clad in bronze
tiles, separate the nave from side aisles,
themselves covered by louvered skylights.
62 Santa Rosa Ave.

46 **South San Francisco Opera House** (1888)
Built for the Masons, this Victorian theater
contains an excellent array of the standardized wooden ornamental vocabulary popular
in nineteenth century San Francisco. *4705
Third St.*

47 **San Francisco Naval Shipyard at
Hunter's Point.**
The southernmost of San Francisco's prom-
ontories was inaugurated as a shipyard during the Civil War. In 1941, the U.S. Navy took
over the private Bethlehem Steel yards and
created a 520 acre complex for the overhaul
of ships taking part in the war against Japan.
The most prominent structure on the site
is Dry-Dock Four whose 450-ton battleship
gun crane (1945), visible from throughout
San Francisco, was the largest such crane in
the world. On each of its four piers, diagonal
bracings assist in supporting two horizontal
beams that in turn support the red-and-
white crane. The green-glass Ordinance and
Optical Building (1956, Ernest Kump) is also
striking; the six-story edifice was equipped
with cranes that could hoist a submarine
periscope to the upper floors. The Navy
closed the shipyard in 1973.

48 **Candlestick Point Park** (1985-93)
George Hargreaves
The 30-acre landfill features a series of sites
meant to orient the visitor to the sites cultural
and natural history, including: shallow chan-
nels that fill with water at high tides; furniture
constructed out of architecture rubble found
at the site.

South Bay

The South Bay has come a long way since the founding of the pueblo of San Jose in 1777. The peninsula south of San Francisco and the broad Santa Clara valley were largely agricultural well into the twentieth century, first dotted with cattle ranchos and then with cherry and apricot orchards. Urban development followed the railroad, whose route between San Francisco and San Jose was completed by 1864. Towns like Burlingame, San Mateo and Palo Alto are the region's prototypical commuter rail suburbs. El Camino Real, the route of the Missions, also bisects the South Bay and has been its commercial heart since the nineteenth century. In 1926, the parallel Highway 101 was commissioned as one of the original US highways, and converted to freeway in the 1950s. During the 1960s and 1970s, a freeway net was laid over the Santa Clara Valley.

20. San Jose Repertory Theater (Holt Hinshaw)

The founding of Stanford Research Park in the early 1950s brought about a singular style of urbanization fueled by high-technology research and production. Owing to the lightning success of the personal computer, beginning in the 1970s, and the Internet, in the 1990s, a new geographical designation was born: Silicon Valley. Instead of urbanism centered in vertical downtowns, the Valley has featured an all-around urbanism in low-rise scale. Office campuses are ubiquitous, as common as gas stations and shopping centers. The one counterpart to the prevailing sprawl is downtown San Jose. Since 1985, San Jose has added a host of office buildings, hotels, civic projects, museums, sports facilities, and light-rail lines. Now one of the nation's ten largest cities, San Jose is acquiring an urbane, cosmopolitan core. But emblematic of the South Bay's ongoing decentralized urbanism, the recent and wildly successful "city street" mall at Santana Row is located several miles from the downtown.

1 IBM Santa Teresa Programming Center (1976)
MBT
On a 50-acre site in the Santa Teresa foot-hills is an office campus that could be the setting for a sci-fi flick. The complex of eight cruciform buildings rests on a Spartan plinth—underneath of which is a gigantic bank of computers–to form a futuristic open plaza. In this minimalist creation, forms, colors, and spaces all emanate from an axiomatic pattern that oscillates between whole and the smallest part. For instance, polished aluminum and glass surfaces are contrasted by eight vivid colors at the corners where different towers meet. *555 Bailey Ave., San Jose*

2 IBM Almaden Research Center (1985)
MBT
A rectangular block joined by four angled office wings, is clad in dark-green ribbon aluminum. Like the Santa Teresa facility, the Almaden Research Center stands out as as an ideal object in rugged terrain. The hard edges, regular forms, and industrial materials contrast the rational operations of the human mind (and technological machine) with the random forces of nature. *650 Harry Rd., San Jose*

3 DiNapoli House (1990)
Stanley Saitowitz
On a promontory of the Santa Cruz Mountains, a large house's straight lines arrest the landscape's rough and tumble contours. Even planar surfaces–a platform,

Map 09 Santa Clara County

131

SOUTH BAY

MAP
09

Santa Clara County

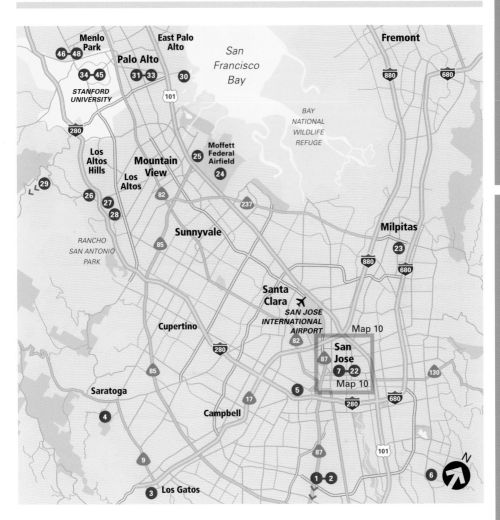

walls, and roof–give way to open-air terraces overlooking bracing views. Inside, hovering glass sheets envelop living volumes in light and the outstanding outdoors. *17986 Foster Rd., Los Gatos*

4 Villa Montalvo (1912)
William Curlett

In 2004, an orchard of live-work studios for visiting artists, designed by an "A list" of architects, was planted on the former Phelan estate. The most delicious are a pair of contrasting cottage by Hodgetts & Fung—the rectilinear introvert and the angular extrovert–done up in bright contrasting colors. Among the other architects whose work is represented are Jim Jennings, Mark Mack, Adele Santos, and Dan Solomon. *15400 Montalvo Rd., Saratoga*

3. DiNapoli House (Saitowitz)

5 Winchester Mystery House (1884–1922)
When Sarah Winchester purchased the house it had six rooms. Over the years the heiress to the repeating-rifle fortune rebuilt the house into a maze of 160 rooms, 40 staircases, 467 doorways, and approximately 10,000 windows. Staircases lead nowhere, doors open onto two-story drops, and cupboards and closets open onto walls. Multiple skylights and clerestory windows admit diffuse light. Snaking corridors define the troubled spirit of the house. Like the occult world that captivated Sarah for the last four decades of her life, the architecture stretches the mind's urge for pattern to the breaking point. Next door are the space age Century theaters, a set of domical pods that landed during the early 1960s. *525. S. Winchester Blvd., San Jose*

6 Student Center, Evergreen Valley College (2001)
Fernau & Hartman
A hyperactive intersection of form, material, and color brings life to this staid campus. *3095 Yerba Buena Rd., San Jose*

7 Biblioteca Latinamerica (2000)
Steven Ehrlich
On the exterior, a projecting glass and steel reading bay interrupts the façade's concrete block and brick wall. On the interior, curving, laminated wood beams span the high space. A metal-grilled tower prods upward and marks the entrance to the adjacent youth center. *921 South First St., San Jose*

8 Guadalupe River Park (1988)
George Hargreaves
The banks of the largely-channeled river are overlaid with berms whose curves recall the sandbars of the river's wild past. *San Jose*

9 Children's Discovery Museum (1990)
Ricardo Legorreta
The architect's magical handling of color splashes over this Jacaranda-purple museum. From afar, the tumbling combination of angular and boxy forms suggests a set of children's building blocks balanced between construction and destruction. *180 Woz Way, San Jose*

10 McEnery Convention Center (1990)
Mitchell/Giurgola
The muscular concrete piers and walls of this black-box building are fronted by a giant mural. *180 W. San Carlos St., San Jose*

11 California Theater (1927)
Weeks & Day
The narrow structure sports Churriguerresque detailing and a neon sign. *345 S. First St., San Jose*

12 Plaza Park (1986–1989)
George Hargreaves
The new park layers its forms atop the history of the site and region. A central promenade traces the former square of the Spanish pueblo. A grid of Jacaranda trees reminds one of the Santa Clara Valley's once-bountiful orchares. And, lastly, a glass-block grid of fog jets recalls both the Pacific fog and, when illuminated at night, the screens of the computer industry. *San Jose*

13 Tech Museum of Innovation (1998)
Ricardo Legorreta
The Tech consists of a simple rectangular block broken open by some of the museum's manifold activities. At street level the façade opens to reveal the IMAX theater, whose metal dome crowns the building. On the façade, Legorreta juxtaposes complementary colors, including mango stucco walls and a blue cylinder and dome composed of glazed tiles. *201 S. Market St., San Jose*

14 San Jose Museum of Art (1892)
**Wiloughby Edbrooke (1991),
Skidmore, Owings & Merrill**
A Romanesque sandstone mansion is married to a modern addition clad in sandstone and concrete. Skylights illuminate the principal barrel-vaulted gallery. *110 S. Market St., San Jose*

15 Hotel de Anza (1931)
William Weeks
A frosting of zigzag, moderne ornament covers this mid-rise hotel. *233 West Santa Clara St., San Jose*

9. **Children's Discovery Museum (Legorreta)**

Map 10 Downtown San Jose

133

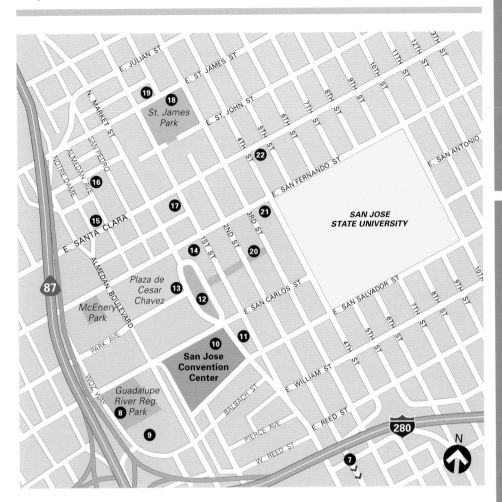

16 Peralta Adobe (1805)
A remnant from the original pueblo, the tiny adobe may be the oldest house in the Bay Area. *184 W. St. John St., San Jose*

17 Bank of America Building (1926)
H.A. Minton
At 227 feet, the narrow spire of this bank tower was the tallest building in San Jose until the late 1980s. *12 S. First St., San Jose*

18 St. James Park (1848)
Arrayed around this historic square are a mixed bag of civic buildings, by architects including Willis Polk, A. Page Brown, and Daniel Solomon. *N. Second St. & E. St. James St., San Jose*

19 First Church Christ Scientist (1905)
Willis Polk
An Ionic portico and pediment lead to a crossing surmounted by a dome atop a drum. *43 E. St. James St., San Jose*

20 San Jose Repertory Theater (1998)
Holt Hinshaw
The skin covering this 529-seat theater isn't smooth or simple. Rather, the architects have carefully wrapped a series of intersecting and overlaying planes around the auditorium and stage. Consisting of blue-steel, the panels are pierced occasionally by small rectangular windows as well as an indented balcony. The result is a theater building that looks like a blow-up of stage-set machinery. *101 Paseo de San Antonio, San Jose*

21 Dr. Martin Luther King Jr. Library (2003)
Gunnar Birkerts
A clash of angular and rectilinear geometries defines this ungainly structure. Inside, a six-story skylit atrium space is wasted on circulation space, and not a reading room. *125 E. San Fernando St., San Jose*

22 City Hall (2005)
Richard Meier
This large civic space, which includes an 18-story tower, rotunda, low-rise offices, and parking garage, combined several city blocks. The architecture emerges from an encounter of basic geometries–the tower slab and the cylindrical, domed rotunda–clad in glass, steel and concrete. A rich variety of cloaks are applied to the refined surfaces. For instance, the pristine steel and glass rotunda, which has no identifiable purpose, is partially covered by steel plates. Likewise, on the east side of the tower, stairways and balconies lend a vertical counterpart to the horizontal strip windows. And on the tower's west side, in the most dramatic move of all, curving lattices and plates are attached to the façade. A curving sandstone wall provides a backdrop to the plaza. *200 E. Santa Clara St., San Jose*

23 Milpitas City Hall (2002)
Studios Architecture
Two huge glass walls surround the lobby and frame the view of the nearby hills, ending a momentary sense of place to the surrounding suburban sprawl. *455 E. Calaveras Blvd., Milpitas*

25. Silicon Graphics Internationa (Studios Architecture)

MAP
09

24 Dirigible Hanger (1933)
Built to house the U.S.S. Macon, a giant dirigible, the hanger is gargantuan—1,138 feet long and 308 feet wide, covering over eight acres. Visible throughout the South Bay, it rises to a height of 211 feet. Nearby, a slightly smaller pair of hangers, built in 1942, stored anti-submarine dirigibles. *Moffett Field, Sunnyvale (See pg 32)*

25 Silicon Graphics International
(1991, 1996, 1999)
Studios Architecture
The three buildings that once formed SGI's campus raise formal distortion and aggravated imagery to feverish temperatures. (While the Crittenden Lane Building is still occupied by SGI, the Shoreline Building is now the Computer History Museum and the Charleston Road Building contains the headquarters for Google.) The complexes share certain features. Circulation towers are set apart from office blocks by bright turquoise, lime, or fuscia colors. Over-scaled overhangs, rotated geometries, and collages of stone, brick, metal, and glass create dizzying refractions and reflections. Angular walls and emancipated corridors and bridges invade the serenity of the courtyards between buildings. The architecture calls to mind the logic of computer graphics—non-linear, branching, and intersecting. *1401 N. Shoreline Blvd., 1545 Charleston Rd., 1500 Crittenden Ln., Mountain View*

23. Milpitas City Hall (Studios Architecture)

26 Foothill College (1962)
Ernest Kump

The 122-acre site preserves the hill as a
pedestrian sanctuary, as roads and parking
lots are distributed around the perimeter
bottom. The college is notable for Kump's
mastery of his space-module system. All the
original 40 buildings were designed according to a 60-foot x 68-foot module, with the
larger structures multiplying it as much as
twelve times, as in the case of the library. In
each, powerful, V-shaped concrete piers support hipped roofs that culminate in parapets.
The redwood-faced (and occasionally brick-
faced) buildings send out large eaves. These
partially covered spaces work well with the
planted patios and sunken courts designed
by the landscape team of Sasaki Walker.
12345 El Monte Rd., Los Altos

27 Eurich House (1939)
Richard Neutra

One of the more forceful International Style
buildings in the Bay Area is this L-shaped
house, clad in white stucco and topped with
a flat roof. Two variations on clerestory windows face the street, and surround a bright
red entrance door. Out back, walls emerge
from the house to become screens and dividers in the garden. *13081 W. Sunset Dr., Los
Altos Hills*

31. 440 House (Fougeron)

28 House (2000)
Douglas Burnham

Importing the loft idea to the suburbs, the
architect designed a large multi-use space
that opens out, through three movable doors,
to the rear yard. Like many contemporary
houses, walls, roof, and other elements (such
as hedges) screen out the suburban middle
ground in favor of long-distance views. *1640
Crestview Dr., Los Altos*

30. Byxbee Park (Hargreaves)

29 Gregory Farmhouse (1927)
William Wurster

Inspired by Gold Rush towns as well as early
Monterey adobes, Wurster pared away the
excesses of 1920s architecture to come up
with a simple house fitting for its clients
and site. The architect's breakthrough building has since become a landmark of a vernacular sensibility in architecture–informal
and unpretentious ranch living in harmony
with the landscape. The walled compound,
entered via a gate, contains an L-shaped
house and tall wooden water tower. A
continuous veranda outlines the courtyard.
Whitewashed and irregular vertical boards
give the house a look of the ages. *Canman
Rd., (off Glenwood Dr.), Scotts Valley*

30 Byxbee Park (1988–1992)
George Hargreaves

Numerous earthworks, interpreting the
history and geography of the site, occupy
this bleak bayside site, built atop a garbage
dump. Small tear-drop moguls recall Ohlone
shellmounds. A grid of truncated telephone
poles traces the sun's journey through shadows on the land. Pairs of pre-cast highway
median dividers are arrayed in the form of
chevrons, and mark the flight path of the
nearby airport. *2775 Embarcadero Way,
Palo Alto*

31 440 House (2000)
Anne Fougeron

A chief aim of the architect and clients was
to draw the outdoors indoors through multiple portals. Accordingly, light penetrates
this house both vertically and horizontally—
though plate-glass windows, glass floors,
skylights, and a stair tower enclosed in
Reglit, a channel-glass cladding system.
440 Marlow St., Palo Alto

32 Waldfogel House (2004)
Steven Ehrlich
A pinwheel plan sends out two separate wings and encloses four courtyards. Two stucco boxes on the second floor float above the mahogany-clad ground floor. Their glass corners and sliding doors open the interior to the outdoors. *300 Santa Rita Ave., Palo Alto*

33 Gideon Hausner Jewish Day School (2003)
SMWM
A curved roof turns into a twenty-foot overhang that wraps around much of the building. Supported by a double colonnade, this loggia shelters walkways and exterior staircases. At the back, the roof resolves into a series of projecting bays covered in bright yellow aluminum panels. *450 San Antonio Rd., Palo Alto*

34 Stanford University Campus.
In 1886, railroad magnate Leland Stanford engaged Frederick Law Olmsted to plan a site for a future university. Against the landscape architects' wishes, the university was located on the flatlands instead of the nearby hills. Olmsted's boldest stroke, however, was the platting of the mile-long Palm Drive as a monumental entrance to the campus from downtown Palo Alto. Although curving paths criss-cross the adjacent arboretum, Palm Drive culminates in a transverse plan involving seven interrelated and geometrically-rigid quadrangles. During the late 1950s and 1960s, Thomas Church attempted to bring some order and good design to a campus plan that had been disregarded for decades. Church developed landscaped malls to tie together dispersed islands of building. He also designed a number of intimate courtyards, sunken fountains, curvilinear seating, and paths that weave between lawns and trees. Alas, much of Olmsted and Churchs' work has been disrupted by the ceaseless and chaotic addition of more buildings and parking structures.

35 Inner and Outer Quadrangles (1887–1891, 1898–1906)
Shepley, Rutan & Coolidge
The centerpiece for the campus is an inner and outer quadrangle whose buildings are linked by a system of arcades. The buildings are designed in a manner owing to the Richardsonian Romanesque, where the impression of solidity and strength of rough unadorned sandstone is contrasted to rich moments of ornamentation. Memorial Church forms the focal point of the inner quad and resembles H.H. Richardson's Trinity Church in Boston. The Mission Revival was stimulated in part by this design, which features deep-window reveals and red-tile roofs. *Stanford University (See pg 136)*

36 Green Library (1919)
Bakewell & Brown
This building continued the campus's founding design motif of buff-colored sandstone, arcades, and red-tile roofs. It went on to influence many later buildings and provided the campus with a sense of visual unity. *Stanford University*

37. Hanna House (Wright)

37 Hanna House (1937)
Frank Lloyd Wright
This Usonian—an adjective developed for the United States—house was intended by Wright as a prototype for moderate-income, mass-produced suburban development. Often called the honeycomb house, the remarkable experiment represents the architect's earliest use of a non-rectangular geometry, the hexagon. Clusters of hexa-gons form the basis for the plan, and both internal partitions and external brick walls conform to their 120 degree angles. Wright believed that the hexagon had a more human rhythm than the rectangle. Thus, whereas diagonal movement leads to overlapping activities and energizing interaction, the obtuse corners are intended to lend a sense of repose. *737 Frenchman's Rd., Palo Alto*

38 Hoover Tower (1938–1941)
Arthur Brown Jr.
The 285-foot tower is topped by a domed carillon and modeled on the towers of Spanish and Mexican cathedrals. *Stanford University*

39 Maples Pavilion (1969)
John Carl Warnecke
Four huge reinforced-concrete columns hold
up a steel-truss roof. The underside of the
concrete stepped seating is visible on the
exterior. *Stanford University*

40 Cantor Center for the Visual Arts
(1894, 1899)
Percy & Hamilton (1998), James Polshek
The original Stanford Junior Museum pioneered classical design for the American
museum and also featured engineer Ernest
Ransome's revolutionary use of reinforced
concrete. Stanford allowed Ransome
to experiment with the new technology
because of the building's tight construction
schedule and a concern for better structural resistance to earthquakes. Although
the walls were meant to look like stone,
Ransome left the concrete aggregate
exposed. *Stanford University*

41 Science Engineering Quad (2002)
Pei Freed Cobb
The Hewlett and Packard twins form the
most recent quadrangle on the campus. The
Packard building is sliced diagonally by a
glass wall to reveal an interior stairway; by
contrast, the Hewlett classroom building is
punched out to reveal the metal-clad shape
of the auditoriums. *Stanford University*

42 Paul Allen Center for Integrated Systems
(1995)
Antoine Predock
Clad in smooth sandstone veneer, the most
interesting feature is a copper-shingled roof
that appears to float atop the clerestory glazing line. *Stanford University*

43 Clark Center (2003)
Norman Foster/MBT
The curvilinear courtyards are hollowed out
by three wave-like curtain-wall laboratories.
Stanford University

44 Center for Clinical Sciences Research
(2001)
Norman Foster
In an homage to Louis Kahn's Salk Institute
in La Jolla, Foster places two slabs of laboratories far enough apart to create a central
plaza. This time the central community
space, articulated by rows of half cylinders
of glass projecting from each side, turns
into a dark oasis of bamboo groves and the
soothing sounds of birds. On the exterior,

44. Center for Clinical Sciences Research
(Foster)

a steel lattice encircles virtually the entire
complex of elegant glass curtain walls and
pre-cast concrete panels. The south wall
is shaded by an attached structure of lightweight perforated steel sails, while a latticed
steel colonnade juts out from the north wall
and turns to fill the courtyard filled with filtered light. *Stanford University*

45 University Hospital (1959)
Edward Durrell Stone
Stone's penchant for texturing a building
with squares containing abstract patterns
reaches an apogee in this low-rise hospital.
Only a few of the surfaces are treated with
openwork concrete grills, however.
For the vast majority of walls and piers,
Stone incises the symbol, vaguely resem-
bling a Sanskrit symbol gone awry during
the Third Reich, directly into the concrete.
Stanford University

46 Varian Associates (1953)
Erich Mendelsohn
The first building of the Research Park is a
single-story, loping glass building that looks
like a ranch house blown out of proportion.
3100 Hansen Way, Palo Alto

47 Alza Corporation (1969)
McCue, Boone & Tomsick
Exposed steel I-beams orchestrate the
rhythms of this brick-infill office complex.
For much of the façade, volumes are
recessed to allow a more forthright expression of the steel structure as well as permit
space for the angular counterpoint of angled
brick brise soleils in the bays. *950 Page Mill
Rd., Palo Alto*

47. Alza Corporation (McCue, Boone & Tomsick)

48 Hewlett-Packard (1970)
Clark, Stromquist, Sandstrom
In 1942, shortly after outgrowing the now-legendary one-car garage behind 367 Addison Ave, Palo Alto, Dave Packard and Bill Hewlett built an office/laboratory/factory at 395 Page Mill Road that they reasoned could be converted to a grocery store if the business failed. Decades later, the multinational corporation built this glass-curtain wall structure, with butterfly skylights, up the road as the corporate headquarters. *1501 Page Mill Rd., Palo Alto*

49 Sunset Magazine Headquarters (1952)
Cliff May
These office buildings were designed to bridge indoor and outdoor spaces, and epitomize the work of the father of ranch-house design. The botanical gardens were designed by Thomas Church and echo the contours of San Francisquito Creek. *80 Willow Rd., Menlo Park*

50 Hilmer House (1954)
Don Knorr
Built on the site intended for Case Study House #19 is a different house by the same architect. The fascinating encounter of old and new technologies presents an infill of adobe bricks fitted inside the visible I-beams of a steel frame. *One Mercedes Ln., Atherton*

51 Mathews House (1954)
Frank Lloyd Wright
A redwood shake roof with wide eaves covers this all-brick house. Floor-ceiling windows open onto the garden, while on the driveway side the windows are reduced to a row of small rectangular portals. *83 Wisteria Way, Atherton*

52 Scoren House (1971)
Don Knorr
A pair of linked pavilions are brightened by a tiled wall executed by Alexander Girard. *568 Mountain Home Rd., Woodside*

53 Filoli (1916)
Willis Polk
Country estates of the fabulously wealthy have long come in extra-large sizes; witness this 43-room, 35,000 square foot retreat house for William Bourn. Known less for the massive Georgian-Revival mansion, the country estate–Filoli stands for fight, love, live—is made memorable by its 16-acre formal garden. 8*6 Canada Rd., Woodside*

54 Oracle (1989–1998)
Gensler
Visible from Highway 101, the six office buildings are known locally as the Emerald City. Most of the reflecting-glass buildings feature a 45-degree encounter of a cylinder with a rectangular block. Behind the high-rises are four trapezoidal parking garages, clad in precast concrete grids that continue the design motif. *500 Oracle Pkwy., Redwood City*

55 Schwind House (1952)
Richard Neutra
Recently renovated, this small redwood house features a horizontal glass wall facing a swimming pool. *1430 Carlton Rd., Hillsborough*

50. Hilmer House (Knorr)

56 Hofmann House (1937)
Richard Neutra
A stack of cubes step back from the hillside, clad in alternating bands of white stucco and silver-painted casement windows. *1048 La Cuesta, Hillsborough*

Map 11 San Mateo County

141

54. Oracle (Gensler)

57 Bazett House (1939)
Frank Lloyd Wright

A covered entrance separates the studio wing from the main house. The triangular composition has a brick base with faceted corners, redwood siding and clerestory windows with sculptural designs, and a flat roof with generous overhangs. Joseph Eichler lived in the house for a few years. It is alleged that he was so inspired by the experience that he came up with his eventual enterprise of developing modern houses for the middle classes. *101 Reservoir Rd., Hillsborough*

58 House (1956)
Mario Ciampi & Germano Milano

For this California ranch house the high moment comes in a tall gable that projects outward to cover an ample terrace. *760 Chiltern Rd., Hillsborough*

59 Daphne House (1964)
Craig Ellwood

In this West Coast version of Mies van der Rohe's Farnsworth House, the entire white structure hovers, supported on a grid of 32 steel columns, over a field of black pebbles. Walls are recessed behind the col-

umns to create shadows from the structural frame. The U-shaped plan, enclosing a pool, is faced in gray glass, white marble, plastic laminate, and stucco. *20 Madrone Pl., Hillsborough*

60 Coxhead House (1891)

Ernest Coxhead
Built as a summer home for the architect, the house is now a bed & breakfast. The Tudor Revival design includes a double bowed roof, scaly shingles, and large projecting bay windows divided by leaded glass. *37 E. Santa Inez St., San Mateo*

61 College of San Mateo (1965)
John Carl Warnecke
On a 153-acre site in the foothills, two pedestrian malls intersect to create a center for the campus. The roofing system unifies the predominantly two-story buildings, and consists of folded concrete terminating in hyperbolic-paraboloid shapes. This motif was also used for the top of the covered colonnades. *1700 W. Hillsdale Blvd., San Mateo*

62 X-100 House (1956)
Quincy Jones
This one-of-a-kind house was intended to promote Joseph Eichler's hope to market steel-frame houses—a dream never realized. The cinnamon-colored, heavy-gauge steel piers and beams that hold up a corrugated metal roof are all visible. Electronic sliding doors eliminated the need for windows. The house also contained a number of built-ins: rooftop spotlights that did away with the need for lamps; reversible kitchen cabinet doors for color changes between white and yellow; and a Formica kitchen table that parted in the middle to reveal two burners. *1586 Lexington Ave., San Mateo*

63 San Mateo County Courthouse (1904)

66. San Francisco Airport (Skidmore, Owings & Merrill)

64 Hillsdale High School (1952)
John Lyon Reid
For this exceptional experiment in school design, Reid eliminated all fixed features. His goal was a building whose spaces could meet changing pedagogical mandates. Accordingly, movable partitions and exterior walls shape the spaces of both rooms and corridors. A series of ramps and courtyards marks a formal axis down the middle of the massive complex. *3115 Del Monte St., San Mateo*

62. X-100 House (Jones)

64. Hillsdale High School (Reid)

Dodge & Dolliver
This tripartite block with projecting center is entered under a colonnaded portico, and crowned by a stained-glass dome and lantern. A 1939 addition mars the proportions. *Broadway & Hamilton St., Redwood City*

65 Burlington Station (1894)
George H. Howard & J.B. Matthews
One of the first Mission Revival buildings in California, the station used red tiles, open arcades, and stucco walls as a primary design idiom. *Burlingame Ave. & California Dr., Burlingame*

66 **San Francisco International Airport.**
Originally called Mills Field, the airport was inaugurated in 1927 with the purchase by the City of over 1300 acres of bay front property. The most impressive older building is the United Airlines Hanger (1956, Skidmore, Owings & Merrill), which once provided berth for four DC-8 jets. Seven pairs of muscular reinforced-concrete piers support cantilevered girders. Unfortunately, the airline, choosing to cut costs and aesthetics, chose to sheathe the structure in metal and not glass. In 2000, the International Terminal opened, also designed by Skidmore Owings & Merrill, with Craig Hartman as lead architect. The new terminal's centrality, size and unusual form gives the airport a pivot around which its turbulence can revolve. The western side of the building features a pixel-fretted glass wall that announces the airport's entrance as the front door to the city. The five-story terminal contains a 1,200-foot long rectilinear hall containing ticketing and check-in areas. A double-cantilevered truss roof linked by bowstring trusses, spans 380 feet at the center. Some might think the roof inspired by the arched sheds of European rail stations. Others may reflect on the resemblance to the famous Firth of Forth Bridge in Scotland. Still others might see the interlocking silhouettes as a flock of birds in flight.

67 **Cypress Lawn Memorial Park** (1892)
In addition to a wealth of monuments, mausoleums, statues and stained glass, the protestant cemetery is the final resting place for magnates like William Randolph Hearst and over 35,000 old-time San Franciscans "relocated" from the city's Laurel Hill, Masonic, Odd Fellows and Calvary Cemeteries between 1939 and 1942, one of the most poignant illustrations of the transient mentality of San Francisco. *1370 El Camino Real, Colma*

70. Vista Mar Elementary School (Ciampi)

68 **Hope Lutheran Church** (1955)
Mario Corbett
Eight A-frames support the tall sanctuary and are pierced in a couple of places by diamond-shaped skylights. The altar wall is a grid of glass panels marked by the shape of a leaning cross, a reference perhaps to the cross laid upon Christ on the Via Dolorosa. *55 San Fernando Way, Daly City*

69 **Westmoor High School** (1958)
Mario Ciampi
In response to Daly City's persistent fog (as well as fifties' fears of youthful vandalism), Ciampi developed compact school plans organized around interior courts; altogether he built 10 schools in Daly City. The high school contains several small interior courts as well as a great central court. It is notable for its barrel-vaulted gymnasiums, constructed out of pre-cast concrete shells. *131 Westmoor Ave., Daly City*

70 **Vista Mar Elementary School** (1959)
Mario Ciampi
Renamed the Marjorie Tobias School, two round buildings announce the space age on a hill in Daly City. The smaller, multi-purpose hall is supported by a ring of concrete piers that slant inward at the roof level to form an intricate ribbed structure. For the larger school building, a thin circle of classrooms, offices, and a library surrounds an open core, replete with a raised bed of pine trees. A folded-shell roof tops the reinforced concrete structure. *725 Southgate Ave., Daly City*

68. Hope Lutheran Church (Corbett)

East Bay

Until the twentieth century, the bulk of the Bay Area's population resided in four cities, three of which were located across from San Francisco in the East Bay–Oakland, Berkeley, and Alameda. The East Bay's early development owes to its bayside location, but also to the routes taken by the transcontinental railroad. In 1869, from the Central Valley, the former Southern Pacific railroad plowed through Jameson Canyon, west of Fairfield to the Carquinez Straits, from which point ferries took passengers and goods to San Francisco. The Western Pacific direct land route to Oakland went over Altamount Pass and the Sunol Grade. In 1878, boats began to ferry S.P. rail cars from Vallejo to Crockett, as the rail line was extended down along the bay littoral through Richmond to Oakland. The East Bay's growth was based on these railroads, and became the region's industrial magnet—a wide arc of shoreline from Oakland stretching north through Berkeley, Richmond, the Carquinez Straits, and the towns of Pittsburg and Antioch. In this new heartland of fire and smoke would be built the Standard Oil Refinery in Richmond, the Hercules Explosive Plant, the C & H Sugar Refinery in Crockett, and eventually the Dow Chemical plant in Pittsburg.

As compared to San Francisco, the slower rate of development coupled with more abundant land led to lower densities, both for the office downtown of Oakland and the residential neighborhoods. Attached row houses are infrequent. Inner-city Oakland lots were 30 ft. wide as compared to the 25 ft. norm in San Francisco. By the twentieth century, most residential lots in the East Bay were at least 40 ft. wide, permitting ample side yards. Front-yard setbacks were also common. Oakland's downtown, however, grew rather large, pulled in different directions: to the west, by the waterfront and rail lines heading toward the Oakland Mole; to the north, by the migration of retail stores up Broadway; and to the east, by the creation of a cultural and civic complex along Lake Merritt. The scale of the downtown led to the emergence of numerous low-intensity and eventually abandoned

24. Oakland Tribune (Foulkes)

sections after the Second World War, as real estate developers moved to the suburbs. After many failed attempts at revitalization, a campaign launched in 1998 by Mayor Jerry Brown has succeeded in the construction of thousands of new residential units.

Early urban development was instigated by rail. The Key System Railway, counterpart to the San Francisco Municipal Railway, was consolidated from smaller companies early in the twentieth century. By the 1940s, 66 miles of track ran through the inner East Bay cities and connected them to San Francisco via ferries (and for a time, the Bay Bridge). The system was dismantled in 1958 after its purchase by a subsidiary of General Motors. Freeways and the BART system spurred the development of southern Alameda County and eastern Contra Costa County. In 1937, the first two bores of the Caldecott Tunnel opened, allowing commuters easy access through the Oakland Hills to Contra Costa County. Highway 24, originally planned to lead to the ill-fated Southern Crossing, and Interstate 580, are the primary routes to the eastern suburbs. By 1972, the BART system ran down the eastern shore of the bay to Fremont and through the hills to Concord. Subsequent extensions carry the line to Pittsburg in the north and Dublin/Pleasanton in the south.

Map 12 Oakland & South Alameda Counties

145

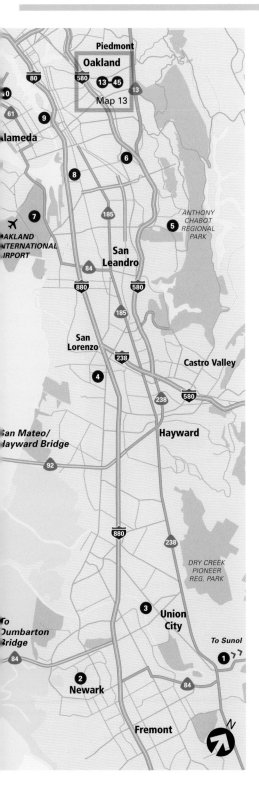

1 Sunol Water Temple (1910)
Willis Polk
Modeled on the Temple of Vesta in Tivioli, where many of the principal waters of Rome came together from the Apennine Mountains, this round temple was built by the Spring Valley Water Company to commemorate the spot at which all the waters of the Alameda watershed meet before continuing on to San Francisco. Twelve Corinthian columns support the conical wood and tile roof. In 1938, in Woodside, the similarly round Pulgas Water Temple (designed by William Merchant) was erected to celebrate the completion of the Hetch Hetchy water project, which brought water 160 miles from the Sierra Nevada to San Francisco. *Calaveras Rd., Sunol*

2 Newark Community Center (1968)
Aaron Green
The building, by a disciple of Frank Lloyd Wright, rises like a faceted mound from the earth, clad in brick walls and covered by a slate roof. Inside, the plan pivots around a brick fireplace, which rises above the roof, and features prow-like overhangs. *35501 Cedar Blvd., Newark*

3 Union City Civic Center & Library (1979)
Aaron Green
A decade later, Green again designed a civic center as a fairly opaque building gently rising from the earth. Here, a six-sided pyramidal roof emerged from the hexagonal plan. *34001 Alvarado Niles Rd., Union City*

4 San Lorenzo Community Church (1944)
Bruce Goff
This church was originally located in Dublin, on the Camp Parks Naval Base, and was constructed from surplus Quonset hut elements. After the base was decommissioned, the pieces were moved and reassembled in San Lorenzo. Two Quonset huts form a 200-foot enclosure for separate sanctuary and classroom spaces; two faceted brick walls, containing entrances, penetrate the long space. *945 Paseo Grande, San Lorenzo*

5 House (1957)
Beverly Thorne
Seven steel-frame members, anchored in a concrete foundation, carry aloft the house and its outdoor terrace. *23 Sequoyah View Dr., Oakland*

6 Mills College.

Across the green from the college's oldest building, the Victorian Mills Hall, the 72-foot tall El Campanil (1904, Julia Morgan) adopts Mission-style details—buttresses, arches, red tiles—alongside new reinforced-concrete construction technology. Subsequently, numerous Spanish Colonial buildings by Walter Ratliff, erected in the 1920s, established the basic character of this bucolic 127-acre campus. One later building, the Science/Mathematics Complex (1971) by Gerald McCue, illustrates the tentative dawn of postmodernism. A grid of tiny holes lends the white stucco surface a utilitarian flavor, while its shed roofs, a clear import from MLTW's Sea Ranch, are covered in pseudo red tiles. The most beautiful building on campus is the Chapel (1967) by Callister & Payne. It is entered through a walled gate reminiscent of Japanese religious compounds. Unpainted and concave redwood strips sheath the nearly round—14-sided—sanctuary. Continuous glass doors around the perimeter and a large glass lantern atop brighten the sacred space. *5000 MacArthur Blvd., Oakland*

7 Oakland International Airport.

In 1960, Welton Becket designed the main two terminals—of which remains the present Terminal One. The more interesting part of the airport lies off Doolittle Drive, where several buildings from the old Oakland Municipal Airport are found. Opened in 1927, the early airfield had five steel and concrete hangers as well as an administration building.

8 Oakland Arena (1966)

Skidmore, Owings & Merrill

The pillbox-shaped arena is one of the best basketball arenas ever built, and the work

12. Giant Shipping Crane at the Port of Oakland

of Chuck Bassett and Myron Goldsmith. Wrapped in a gray-glass curtain wall, thirty-two diagonal columns support the ring from which the roof is suspended. From this ring, 96 steel cables are linked to a steel tension ring in the center of the structure. These support a system of slender concrete ribs, which carry the roof. The 1990s addition of tacky entrance pavilions has partially marred the crystalline, cylindrical geometry. *7000 Coliseum Way, Oakland*

9 Right Away Redy Mix (1989)

Holt, Hinshaw, Pfau, Jones

An amplified concrete and steel structure, featuring climbing steel stair towers and movable external sun-panels, makes this building look like a machine. *401 Kennedy St., Oakland*

9. Right Away Redy Mix (Holt, Hinshaw, Pfau, Jones)

10 Alameda Point.

In 1997, the Naval Air Station Alameda base (founded in 1940) closed, and the 2500-acre site began a transition to civilian uses. The base repaired and maintained aircraft, had two 8,000-foot runways, and was the home to numerous aircraft carriers. There are approximately 300 historic buildings, of which the huge maintenance hangers are most notable.

11 Port of Oakland, Container Handling Complex (1994)

Jordon Woodman Dobson

The maintenance building is connected to the administration building by a truss bridge. The latter, in a design recalling Richard Meier's work, is supported on piers and clad in white porcelain-coated metal.

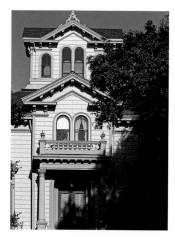

18. Pardee House (Hoagland & Newsom)

12 Middle Harbor Shoreline Park.

Located between the Inner and Outer harbors of the Port of Oakland, this 38-acre park provides an excellent vantage point to view the harbor's giant ships, giant shipping cranes, and gigantic stacks of colorful rectangular containers. George Lucas modeled his Imperial Walkers, or storm trooper carriers, for *The Empire Strikes Back* (1980) after five white cranes erected in 1974. *(See pg 146).* Beginning in 2002, the port installed even more imposing structures,19 super-Panamax cranes, that can unload giant container vessels; with their booms up, they tower 365 feet in height. The park also contains an archaeological recreation of one of the old moles that extended into the bay, providing a terminal for connecting (regional and transcontinental) railways and ferries bound for San Francisco. The site of the Oakland Mole, torn down in 1965, is nearby, near the point where the BART trains emerge from the Bay tunnel. *Middle Harbor Rd., Oakland*

13 Amtrak Station (2000)
VBN
A glass and steel version of a groin vault covers this small passenger rail station. Each of the elevations are faced in glass. *245 Second St., Oakland*

14 The Leviathan (1991)
Ace Architects
The myriad parts of the building are taken from the hurly-burly waterfront landscape, and their collision has been likened to a battle between a sea monster and a navy ship. *330 Second St., Oakland*

15 The Sierra (2003)
Kava Massih
The development of the Jack London Square area into a loft district is epitomized by the largest of the recent projects, a twelve-story block with 220 units. The lively facades feature stucco, corrugated metal, various patterns of glass curtain wall, and even a few bays. *311 Oak St., Oakland*

16 Old Oakland (1870s–1880s)
This ensemble constitutes one of the finest blocks of Victorian commercial buildings on the West Coast, and was the heart of Oakland until the 1920s. *Ninth St. between Broadway and Washington St., Oakland*

17 Lafayette Square (2001)
Walter Hood
A redesign of this original square of Oakland's downtown left a place for the park's longtime users–unemployed men. Sloping lawns and a metal fence create separate mini-parks: a children's playground; tables for chess matches, and a smattering of barbeque pits. *Oakland*

18 Pardee House (1868)
Hoagland & Newsom
The entrance to this ivory Italianate villa is crowned by not one but two split-pediments. The evocative site contains part of the original garden, stables, and water tank. Across 12th Street stands Preservation Park, a collection of five Victorians original to the site and eleven others moved there to create a facsimile of an upper-income residential neighborhood from the nineteenth century. *672 11th St., Oakland*

15. The Sierra (Massih)

Map 13 Downtown Oakland

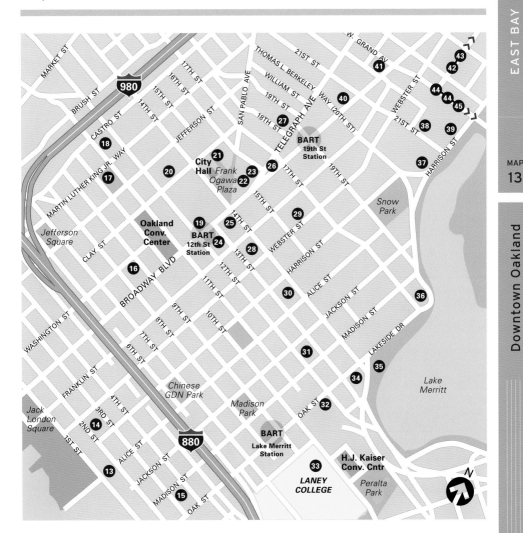

19 Clorox Building (1976)
Cesar Pelli
Along with the neighboring 10-story Wells
Fargo Building, this 24-story tower was the
lynchpin of the City Center redevelopment,
which resulted in the demolition of much of
Oakland's historic core. Shadow-line facing
on the facade creates a sculpted surface for
the polygon-shaped towers. The modern
complex also features a sunken plaza, connected to the BART station. *1221 Broadway,
Oakland*

20 Ronald Dellums Federal Building (1992)
Kaplan, McLaughlin, Diaz
The postmodern complex tries to recapture
the sculpted grace and detailing of 1920s
skyscrapers. Because of far larger floorplates, however, the towers, culminating in

pyramidal roofs, look squat. *1301 Clay St.,
Oakland*

21 Oakland City Hall (1911-14)
Palmer, Hornbostel & Jones
Classical details figured prominently in
the aspirations of California cities as they
built their city halls in the early years of
the twentieth century, even when, as in
Oakland, columns, arches and vaults had
to be fit for the frame of a skyscraper. For
several years, Oakland's third city hall–335
feet—was the tallest building on the West
Coast. The steel-frame building, clad in
granite and sporting terra-cotta accents,
is divided into a monumental base, office-
building shaft, and crowning cupola. *One
Frank Ogawa Plaza, Oakland (See pg 151)*

22 Broadway Building (1907)
Llewellyn Dutton
Renovated in 1998, this flatiron structure
signaled the northward move of Oakland's
downtown after the turn of the century.
150 Frank Ogawa Plaza, Oakland

23 Rotunda Building (1911)
Charles Dickey
This building was once home to Kahn's,
Rhodes, and finally the Liberty House
department stores. The central court is one
of downtown Oakland's grandest interiors,
ringed with a Corinthian colonnade and
capped by a 170-foot high glazed dome.
300 Frank Ogawa Plaza, Oakland

24 Oakland Tribune Tower (1923)
Edward T. Foulkes
The 310-foot tower borrows from many
styles. The narrow tower first breaks out
in a buttressed parapet, of medieval Italian
precedent, and concludes with a copper
French Chateau roof. Later, the red-neon
Tribune sign, covering the parapet, became
Oakland's signature landmark. *401 13th St.,
Oakland*

25 First Western Building (1958)
Stone, Mulloy, Marraccini, & Patterson
The 18-story highrise was the first significant
office building constructed in downtown
Oakland after the Great Depression. The
modernist massing features a projecting
glazed mezzanine, glass-curtain wall slab,
and adjoining elevator core. Between the
rows of plate glass spandrel panels consist
of a thin skin of porcelain enamel iron, colored blue-green, or as the newspapers wrote
at the time, skyazure blue. *1330 Broadway,
Oakland*

26 Cathedral Building (1914)
Benjamin MacDougal
On a triangular gore corner, the twelve-story
building climbs to a crescendo of filigree,
finials, and French Chateaux roof. *1615
Broadway, Oakland*

27 Fox Theater (1928)
Maury Diggs
The impulse to catapult moviegoers faraway
reaches an apogee in this pile of allusions.
A dome, whose shape recalls that of Hindu
temples, rises above the prominent neon
marquee and sign, and is flanked by towers replete with lotus leaves and scalloped
shells. *1807 Telegraph Ave., Oakland*

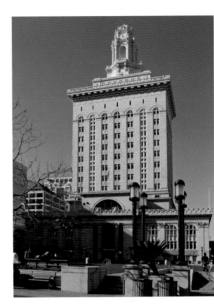

21. Oakland City Hall (Palmer, Hornbostel &
Jones)

28 Financial Center Building (1930)
Reed & Corlett
The city's best art-deco highrise has its
entrance capped by an oak tree incised in
concrete. *401 14th St., Oakland*

29 YWCA (1914)
Julia Morgan
The Italian palazzo exterior matches an
arcaded and colonnaded interior court,
Morgan's take on Bramante's cloister at the
Church of Santa Maria della Pace in Rome.
1515 Webster St., Oakland

30 Hotel Oakland (1912)
Bliss & Faville
In America, the construction of a mammoth
hotel, such as this former 460-room edifice,
has long been a sign that a city had arrived
on the national scene. Correspondingly, its
conversion to a Veterans Administration
Hospital in 1943 signaled the beginning of
downtown Oakland's decline. The Italian
Renaissance-inspired design features an
arcaded courtyard, a Doric loggia, and twin
cupolas. *275 14th St., Oakland*

31 Parking Garage (1962)
Ratcliff & Ratcliff
This exercise in spiraling geometry was
once topped by a heliport. *12th and Madison
Sts., Oakland*

MAP
13

Downtown Oakland

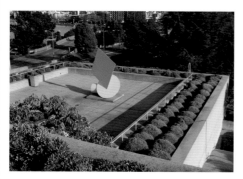

32. Oakland Museum (Roche & Dinkeloo)

32 Oakland Museum (1969)
Kevin Roche & John Dinkeloo
The amalgamation of three separate museums (for art, history, and natural history) looks more like a terraced park, or modern version of the hanging gardens of Babylon, than an art museum. From the surrounding streets, ramps and staircases lead up to a series of platforms that open into the principal galleries or continue onto terraces, pools, and gardens. These outdoor rooms, designed by Dan Kiley, function like indoor galleries; they are picture frames for long views of the city and lake. Throughout the light beige concrete harmonizes with the walnut and oak flooring indoors and rich palette of botanical specimens outside. *1000 Oak St., Oakland*

33 Laney College (1970)
Skidmore, Owings & Merrill
A series of buildings with untreated concrete and brick facades is heightened by a sculptural, triangular tower. *900 Fallon St., Oakland*

34 Alameda County Courthouse (1935)
Will Corlett, James Plachek, Carl Werner, Henry Morton, William Schirmer
Graced by moderne ornament, this W.P.A. monument dominates the southern end of Lake Merritt. The massive concrete structure rises from a 200 x 300 foot base to a somewhat narrower shaft, and concludes in an eagle-perched cupola. *1221 Oak St., Oakland*

35 Camron-Stanford House (1876)
The last of the mansions that once lined Lake Merritt, this Italianate Victorian was the original location of the Oakland Museum. *1426 Lakeside Dr., Oakland*

36 The Essex (2002)
Architecture International
The prominent 20-story condominium tower curves its mass in harmony with Lake Merritt and features bands of blue glass as a further gesture to the waters below. *One Lakeside Dr., Oakland*

37 Kaiser Building (1959)
Welton Beckett
Three characteristics separate this highrise from the downtown pack. The 28-story headquarters of the Kaiser Corporation includes a parking garage atop which is set a garden designed by Ted Osmundson and John Slaley. The facade is covered in a gray-tinted glass curtain wall with gold aluminum alloy spandrel panels set in natural aluminum mullions. Finally, the graceful curve of the highrise and the lower mezzanine play off the undulating shape of Lake Merritt. *300 Lakeside Dr., Oakland (See pg 37)*

38 Ordway Building (1970)
Skidmore Owings & Merrill
Part of the Kaiser Center, this 28-story tower by Chuck Bassett is sheathed in anodized aluminum. The angled spandrels create shadows, and, at the right position of the sun, look to be the color of glistening sterling silver. The H-shaped plan allowed for eight corner offices per floor, instead of the usual four. *One Kaiser Plaza, Oakland*

39 Christ the Light Cathedral (2008)
Skidmore Owings & Merrill
On a 2 ½ acre site facing the lake the Catholic complex includes a cathedral, plaza and parish facilities. Craig Hartman's design for the 1,500-seat sanctuary begins with a plan in the shape of a *vesica pisces*, a pointed ellipse open at both ends. This unusual shape, recalling baroque church plans, embraces geometrical clarity as well as fluid movement and facilitates congregational seating around the alter. The walls of the cathedral consist of a double shell, a wooden frame which is draped in a gown of glass. The inner wooden shell is made up of two spherical segments that lean against one another. Horizontal louvers bridge the bays between the vertical planks of Douglas Fir. Two conical veils of glass are wrapped around the wooden inner shell—separated anywhere from 12 to 20 feet from it. Shaped like a pointed ellipse as well, the roof consists of a sheet of clear glass.

As John King wrote in the *San Francisco Chronicle,* "at certain moments, the inner cathedral will be a shadowy form. At others, the glass exterior will come alive with the flash of captured sunlight. And when the lights gleam inside at night, it's the veil that will disappear, while the wooden inner walls will shine like an etched lantern." *Harrison St. at Grand Ave., Oakland*

40 Paramount Theater (1931)
Miller & Pflueger
Since their introduction at the beginning of the twentieth century, the motion pictures had exposed audiences to ever-more distant visual worlds—jungle journeys, westerns, historical sagas. Likewise, Pflueger's architectural ornament was sufficiently rich with exotic detail to arouse the restless appetites of the mass public. For the Art Deco Paramount Theater, the architect designed screens of cinematographic impressions on almost all built surfaces. The lobby and auditorium are gilded with Aztec figures, floral patterns and streamlined geometries. On the exterior, alongside the giant neon sign, magisterial façade mosaics by Gerald Fitzgerald feature two colossal puppeteers in 70 colors, a commentary perhaps on the new role of the architect as mass entertainer/manipulator. *2025 Broadway, Oakland*

40. Paramount Theater (Miller & Pflueger)

41 Breuner Company Building (1931)
Albert Roller
The former furniture company headquarters is faced in glazed light green terracotta and accented with art deco floral designs. *22nd St. and Broadway, Oakland*

42 First Presbyterian Church (1914)
William Hays
The congregation, who established the first church in the East Bay at 14th and Franklin Streets, later built in the high French Gothic style. *2619 Broadway, Oakland*

43 First Congregational Church (1925)
John Galen Howard
Inspired by the multiple-arched facades of Italian Romanesque churches, such as San Michele in Pavia, and replete with a matching campanile. *2501 Harrison St., Oakland*

44 Bellevue-Staten Apartments (1929)
A.C. Bauman
The red-brick façade is luxuriously accented by cast-concrete carvings with Spanish Baroque references. For the film *Tucker* (1988), largely filmed in Oakland, the base of the building and view of Lake Merritt incongruously stand in for Chicago's Lake Michigan. *492 Staten Ave., Oakland*

44. Bellevue-Staten Apartments (Bauman)

45 Splash Pad Park (2004)
Walter Hood
The landscape architect uses the elevated Interstate 550 as backdrop for the happening weekly farmer's market. Concrete and earthen paths cross the small triangle, while plantings recall the site's history as a wetland. *Oakland*

46 Temple Sinai (1914)
Albert Lansburgh
The buff-brick cladding and terra-cotta moldings, derived from classical sources, are just appetizers for the main course–a raised elliptical dome raised on prominent buttresses, and described at the time of construction as belonging to the "Assyrian style of architecture." *2808 Summit St., Oakland*

47 Moss Cottage (1864)
Heston & Williams
Steeply pitched gables topped by spires and underscored by wavy bargeboards make this picturesque house the best exemplar of the Gothic Revival in California. *Mosswood Park, Oakland*

48 Chapel of the Chimes (1928)
Julia Morgan (1959), Aaron Green
Behind a Romanesque façade, partially screened by cast-concrete Gothic tracery, is one of the most complex interiors in the Bay Area. An off-kilter grid of ascending and descending corridors and stairways leads to a seemingly endless sequence of cloisters, gardens, and chapels. Vaulted ceilings, clerestories and skylights add to the mysterious spatiality and luminosity. *4499 Piedmont Ave., Oakland (See pg 156)*

49 Mountain View Cemetery (1863)
Frederick Law Olmsted
Olmsted's finest landscape in the Bay Area isn't a park, but a park-like cemetery that spills over 200 acres in the Oakland foothills. A straight main mall, punctuated by four circular fountains, bisects the site. From this abstract geometry, sinuous paths of graves and mausoleums meander like tributaries around the brows and canyons of six hills. *5000 Piedmont Ave., Oakland*

50 California College of Arts & Crafts.
The four-acre campus boasts several structures of striking material expression. In 1969, Vernon DeMars added the first two college buildings of substance: a faceted wooden prism as a studio building; and the

50. California College of the Arts Dormitory (Horton)

Corbusian concrete mass of the Founders Hall, whose rich spatial composition for the library is expressed through balconies, alcoves, and a double-height space. In 1993, Jim Jennings designed the glass-block Sculpture Studio. Finally, in 2003, Mark Horton built the Clifton Dormitory, distinguished by its prismatic shape and clear, clouded, and semi-clouded glass walls. *5212 Broadway, Oakland*

51 Chiron Corporation (1999)
Riccardo Legorreta
Bright colors and basic forms, punched by arched windows, are the basis for this multiple-building complex. *4560 Horton St., Emeryville*

52 Emeryville Post Office (1994)
Kava Massih, Ratcliff
This composite corrugated steel, stucco, and concrete building expresses its industrial environs and the process of additions in different materials. *1585 62nd St., Emeryville*

53 Niehaus Residence (c. 1889)
Berkeley's largest and most elaborate Victorian is a two-story Stick Eastlake, topped by a tower that is punctured on all four sides by elaborate dormers. *839 Channing Way, Berkeley*

54 Dwight Way Condominiums (2004)
Leger Wanselja
The standard environmental use of salvaged materials, insulation, and other energy-saving devices is taken to a new level for this hot-rod house. Awnings come from a Porsche hatchback. A gate is made out of Volvo station wagon doors. Discarded street signs are assembled into a fence. *2472-84 Dwight Way, Berkeley*

Map 14 North Alameda & Contra Costa Counties

155

EAST BAY

MAP
14

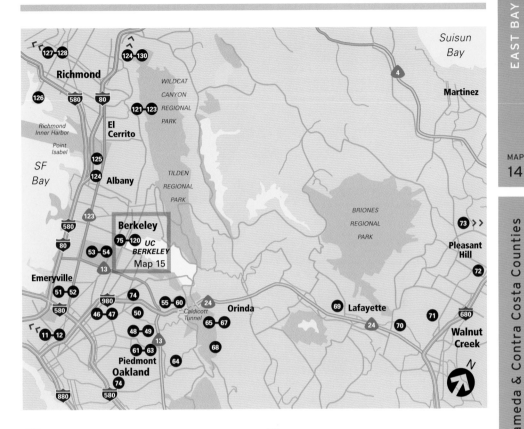

55 House
Jim Jennings

The house is divided into two volumes that grip the steep hillside and connect tenuously via a sheet of etched glass at the street and an elevated deck in the rear. The larger structure, clad in Eterboard cement panels, contains the principal living spaces while the other, sheathed in corrugated aluminum, has space for a studio and parking garage. *119 Strathmoor Rd., Oakland (See pg 159)*

56 Cotton House
Ace Architects

An old saxophone found on the charred ruins is reputedly the inspiration for the two giant horns that visually blare down the hillside. *1985 Tunnel Rd., Oakland*

57 House (2004)
Tom Collum

Atop an arched steel bridge, spanning a creek, floats a perfectly rectangular box for living. The Case Study-influenced house features walls of glass and stucco as well as concrete floors. Steel-mesh decks project from both long sides. *1210 Grandview Dr., Oakland*

58 Drager House (1994)
Franklin Israel

For a house where it is difficult to tell façade from roof, the sloping copper-shingle roof seems more like a mask than a wig. *160 Vicente Rd., Oakland*

57. House (Collum)

59. XYZ House (Banta)

59 XYZ House (2002)
Philip Banta
On the steep site, living spaces are stacked one atop the other, but open out to the far views in curving balconies braced by seismic steel struts. *43 Perth Pl., Oakland*

60 McLane Look House (1995)
Stanley Saitowitz
A curved and sloping roof, supported in part by thin piers, follows the contours of the hills, and illustrates the architect's preoccupation with engaging a site's geology. Similarly, a rock outcrop in the garden reverberates through the interior as a slicing wall dividing the principal living spaces. The exterior is largely clad with a checkerboard of corrugated metal panels. *6131 Ocean View Dr., Oakland*

61 House (1942)
Clarence Mayhew & Serge Chermayeff
Shortly after he immigrated to the United States, Chermayeff designed this wood-frame house, whose two rectangular volumes are connected by a covered, sloped stairway. *330 Hampton Rd., Piedmont*

62 Sawyer House (1963)
Campbell & Wong
A network of steel beams—one of which is 70 feet in height—lifts this house completely above its site on a ravine. An octagonal atrium occupies the center of the cruciform plan, and is topped by a pyramidal steel framework that echoes the lower structural system. Circular skylights complete the masterful play of geometries. *79 Wildwood Gardens, Piedmont*

63 House (1959)
Donald Olsen
From the street one can look straight through the curtain walls of the double-height living room at the panorama of the Bay and Golden Gate. The wood-framed house is faced in white stucco with dark gray trim. *115 Pershing Dr., Oakland*

64 Dave Brubeck House (1954)
Beverly Thorne
Steel beams assertively cantilever the bedrooms over a sharp drop, and create a sense of soaring that corresponds to the jazz pianist's rhythmic flights. These and other I-beams support redwood beams and framing; the infill is of wood cladding, painted red, and white homosote. Expansive eaves and balconies complete the strong planar composition. *6630 Heartwood Dr., Oakland*

65. Moore House (Moore)

65 Moore House (1962)
Charles Moore
Moore designed one of the first post-modern houses before the concept had been coined. The house's shape recalls a variety of historical buildings, ranging from a primitive hut to a Mycenaean Megaron to Louis Kahn's Trenton Bath House. The square plan encloses two aediculas, one for the living area and the other for a sunken bathtub. Each are supported by rustic columns, which also hold up the hipped roof topped by a rectangular projection. *33 Monte Vista Rd., Orinda*

66 Buehler House (1949)
Frank Lloyd Wright
Topped by a copper roof, this brick and red-wood house features the architect's preoccupation with angular planning. In the living room a continuous row of vertical windows looks out onto waterfalls, ponds, bridges and statuary, landscaped by Henry Matsutani. *6 Great Oaks Circle, Orinda*

67. 100 Foot House (Ogrydziak/Prillinger)

67 100 Foot House (2006)
Ogrydziak/Prillinger
Topped by a butterfly roof, this transparent house punctuates its glass walls with Ipe siding, a Brazilian hardwood. *67 Camino Encinas, Orinda*

68 Miramonte High School (1957)
Franklin & Kump
Kump's first major design experiment with space-modules sought to achieve flexibility in classroom size and purpose through standardization. *750 Moraga Way, Orinda*

69 Bentley School (2003)
Kava Massih
A zincalum-clad roof curves and lifts over the building to bridge the two sides of the gymnasium. *1000 Happy Valley Rd., Lafayette*

70 Acalanes High School (1940–1955)
Franklin & Kump
This landmark is the first large school in the United States to demonstrate the theoretical ideas of the 1930s school revolution. Instead of a multi-story masonry block, the one-story school is arranged in what has come to be

known as the finger plan: a grid of classroom blocks flanked by on one side by canopied corridors and on the other side by large metal-sash windows; landscaped courtyards occupy the spaces between the blocks. The design eliminates stairs and heavy foundations, and allows for windows on both sides of a classroom. *1200 Pleasant Hill Rd., Lafayette*

71 Trinity Lutheran Church (1958)
Skidmore, Owings & Merrill, Pietro Belluschi
For this "umbrella of wood," the walls and ceiling are expressed as a single unit. Inside, the stone base walls are set back from the upper covering so as to allow light to emerge from below. *2317 Bjuena Vista Ave., Walnut Creek*

72 City Hall (1990)
Charles Moore
In one of his last commissions, Moore designed a barn-like city hall pierced by windows that overlook a small lake. *100 Gregory Ln., Pleasant Hill*

73 Concord Pavilion (1975)
Frank Gehry
In a crater-shaped bowl, two reinforced concrete piers and a concrete-block sound wall support a massive steel truss roof. *2000 Kirker Pass Rd., Concord*

74 Chick House (1913)
Bernard Maybeck
A broad gable roof turns into a trellised eave at the roof line, contrasting its rectilinear lines with the irregular limbs and branches of surrounding live oaks. *7133 Chabot Rd., Oakland*

69. Bentley School (Massih)

70. Acalanes High School (Franklin & Kump)

75 Julia Morgan Theater (1910)
Julia Morgan
Formerly St. John's Presbyterian Church, the woodsy street façade is marked by the two double-gabled masses of the sanctuary and education wing. The repeating shallow angles of the gables unify the two sides. Clerestory windows under the uppermost gable provide ample light to the auditorium, itself distinguished by a drama of exposed redwood beams and supports. *2640 College Ave, Berkeley (See pg 23)*

76 Feldman House (1974)
Frank Lloyd Wright
This redwood and brick house was completed by the Taliesin Foundation from a design Wright made in 1939 for a site in Los Angeles. A flat roof cantilevers over a terrace and carport. *13 Mosswood Rd., Berkeley*

77 Havens House (1941)
Harwell Hamilton Harris
The architect's major work is a dramatic shelf of three stacked living volumes projecting off the hillside toward the views of San Francisco Bay. Two levels send off cantilevered terraces that wrap around the glazed interior spaces, and seem to float in the sky. Below, piers and three inverted trusses support the weight. The house is best seen from below on Arden Road, where another Harris house from the same year is located. *255 Panoramic Way, Berkeley*

78 House (1952)
Charles Warren Callister
Two massive concrete piers support the front of this L-plan house. The wooden framework of post, beam, and trellis lends a definite Japanese flavor, that also includes shoji screens in most of the windows. *3456 Dwight Way, Berkeley*

77. Havens House (Harris)

80. First Church of Christ Scientist (Maybeck)

79 Newman Hall (1966)
Mario Ciampi
Sheer concrete walls and buttresses enclose the sanctuary and isolate it from the surrounding city. In the chapel, the play of severe abstract masses continues, as an irregular clerestory window separates wall planes of bare cement from a white-coffered ceiling. *2700 Dwight Way, Berkeley*

80 First Church of Christ Scientist (1910)
Bernard Maybeck
Maybeck's masterpiece is a personal synthesis of the dominant architectural ideas of the era: Beaux-Arts planning, flamboyent stylistic languages, Arts & Crafts honesty of structural expression, and experimental construction technologies. The exterior is dominated by shallow, hovering gable roofs with extremely broad eaves. A large window frames Gothic tracery in cast concrete. These gestures to tradition and history, however, are set against utilitarian windows in factory sash and panels of asbestos siding called transite. Similarly, fluted concrete piers blossom Romanesque capitals which, in turn, support the elaborate pergola, a redwood trellis overflowing with Wisteria vines. Red roofing tiles and Byzantine ornament add to the panoply of references. For the sanctuary, cast concrete columns (containing the duct system) hold up a powerful framework of wooden beams, deeply incised with tracery. Maybecks's ability to fuse all these complex maneuvers is testimony to his sculptural approach to architecture. *2619 Dwight Way, Berkeley*

81 Thorsen House (1909)
Greene & Greene
The Pasadena architects' only Bay Area house accommodates the region's wet-

Map 15 Inner Berkeley

161

EAST BAY

MAP
15

Inner Berkeley

ter, foggier climate. There is a steeper roof pitch than in their Southern California houses as well as shallower eaves in order to allow more sunlight to reach the interior. Otherwise, trademark qualities prevail, such as the articulation and softening of timbers, and the use of clinker bricks for the garden wall as a foil to the exterior cladding of split wood shakes. *2307 Piedmont Ave., Berkeley*

82 University of California at Berkeley.
An international competition to design the campus was won by the French architect Emile Bénard in 1898, but later taken over by John Galen Howard, who had placed fourth in the competition. Howard's Beaux-Arts plan consisted of an east-west axis, framed

by symmetrical groupings of buildings that march down the hill toward University Avenue. The view corridor is magnificent, reaching far beyond the city toward the Bay, Golden Gate and Pacific Ocean. Despite the Beaux-Arts geometry, Howard took care to preserve Strawberry Creek and natural glades. Over time, the axis was shortened and a major transverse axis, extending north from Sproul Plaza, was developed. Beginning in the 1960s, the harmony of the plan began to be seriously compromised by taller buildings that often blocked Howard's architectural proportions and treasured long views.

83 Greek Theater (1903)
John Galen Howard
The first structure built as part of the new campus plan creates a Grecian setting for playing out California myths and songs. The 10,000-seat concrete amphitheater opens toward a skene surrounded by an attached Doric colonnade and entablature. *UC Berkeley*

84 Haas School of Business (1992–1995)
Moore, Ruble, Yudell
One of Charles Moore's last buildings is a loose grouping of three distinct wings around a courtyard. Multiple historical references are carried on Roman arches, Arts and Crafts board and batten siding, and restrained postmodernism. *UC Berkeley*

85. Wurster Hall (DeMars, Esherick & Olsen)

85 Wurster Hall (1964)
Vernon DeMars, Joseph Esherick, & Donald Olsen
DeMars comented that "we felt the background for training young architects should be anonymous and utilitarian." This stark and inscrutable building, the campus's unloved exemplar of brutalism, surely met that aim. The overwhelming mass is broken down somewhat into a three-story base and ten-story tower that projects a balcony on its upper floors. Ubiquitous overhanging sunscreens hover above the windows, except on the north face. *UC Berkeley*

86 University Art Museum (1970)
Mario Ciampi
Architecture here works as a gigantic piece of sculpture. A fan-like series of twelve galleries radiates out from the skylit entrance lobby; and galleries are reached by ascending ramps. The strongly cantilevered concrete trays hover on the brink of balance, and, indoors, appear like tiered boxes in a theater

skewed by geological forces. Ironically, steel braces now support many of the cantilevers to resolve, only partially, the building's severe seismic deficiencies. *2630 Bancroft Way (See pg 165)*

87 Hearst Women's Gymnasium (1927)
Bernard Maybeck & Julia Morgan
The reinforced concrete structure is festooned with columns, sculptural groups, and cherub-urns. *UC Berkeley*

88 Music Library (2004)
Scogin Elam
Amber glass and green slate shingles clad this small and elegant structure. The building's slight torque is explained by the fact that the ground floor is aligned to the city grid, while the top floors correspond to Howard's campus axis. *UC Berkeley*

89 Faculty Club (1902)
Bernard Maybeck
Overlooking Strawberry Creek, the whitish plaster building evokes the simplicity and aridity of Mission architecture on its exterior. Inside, the dining hall's open timber framing lends more of a Northern European feel. But here, as elsewhere, Maybeck's personality comes into play through such devices as carved dragon heads on the ends of roof purloins. The steep-pitched redwood interior roof, interestingly, is expressed on the exterior at a gentle angle and clad with red mission tiles. *UC Berkeley*

90 Campanile (1914)
John Galen Howard
Berkeley's landmark 303-foot tower can be seen from across the Bay. This gray-granite version of the Piazza San Marco campanile of Venice features an arched belvedere and tops off in a steep pyramid. *UC Berkeley*

91 Hearst Mining Building (1907)
John Galen Howard
From the outside, the three arched openings of the central volume, flanked by side wings, resemble a train station. The main event, however, lies indoors in the three-story vestibule. Here slender iron columns support open perimeter galleries (at the second and third stories) and resolve into pendentives supporting three domed skylights. Inspired by Henri Labrouste's Biblioteque Nationale in Paris, Hearst Mining is the crowning architectural achievement of the campus. *UC Berkeley*

96. First Unitarian Church (Schweinfurth)

92 East Asian Library (2007)
Tod Williams, Billie Tsien
University design guidelines regrettably
forced the talented New York firm to back off
from their initial experimental design–a case
in point of how the political process of design
guidelines compromises architecture. The
exterior employs light granite cladding and
adds a hipped roof. A bronze screen, used as
a sunscreen and evocative of Asian window
patterns, adds a bit of verve and texture to
three sides of the building. Inside a three-
part stairway system looks like a gigantic
sculpture. *UC Berkeley*

93 Doe Library (1910)
John Galen Howard
Centerpiece to Howard's plan is this Beaux-
Arts block, whose primary façade boasts a
giant-order Corinthian colonnade. The main
reading room, complete with coffered ceiling, stretches 210 feet and accommodates
400 readers. *UC Berkeley*

94 California Hall (1905)
John Galen Howard
This wide, two-story edifice set the tone
for a flurry of other buildings by Howard.
Virtually all are clad in gray Raymond granite
and topped with red-tile roofs set in copper
frames. While most of them restrain their
ornamentation, certain ones asset bolder
classical references, such as Wheeler Hall's
giant-order Ionic gallery–completed in 1917.
UC Berkeley

95 Student Center Complex (1959)
Vernon DeMars and Donald Hardison
These four buildings define the western edge
of Sproul Plaza and provide an additional
sunken plaza. Modern classicism is the rule,
as seen in the King Student Union's stripped
colonnade topped by a trellis or Zellerbach

Hall's symmetrical and columnar exoskeleton. Notable as well is the hyperbolic-
paraboloid roof shells of the adjacent dining
complex. *UC Berkeley*

96 First Unitarian Church (1898)
Albert Schweinfurth
An early Arts and Crafts church features a
rustic, open-beam redwood style and brown-
shingle siding. Likely influenced by McKim,
Mead & White's Low House in Bristol, Rhode
Island, the façade widens into an extra-wide
and shallow gable roof at whose center is
a large round window. The sanctuary also
sports exposed roof beams and vertical redwood wainscoting. *2401 Bancroft Way*

97 Berkeley Women's City Club (1929)
Julia Morgan
Two-story wings, laden with medieval ornamentation, flank a reinforced-concrete tower.
2315 Durant Ave., Berkeley

98 Chamber of Commerce Building (1925-27)
Walter Ratcliff, Jr.
Until the thirteen-story Great Western
Building (1970) was built across the street,
this eleven-story red brick and terra cotta
tower was *the city's tallest building. 2140-44
Shattuck Ave., Berkeley*

99 United States Post Office (1914)
Oscar Wenderoth
This imitation of an early Italian Renaissance
façade is characterized by a row of arches
set upon plain Tuscan columns. *2000 Allston
Way, Berkeley*

100 City Hall (1909)
Bakewell & Brown
An exercise in fourth-order imitation, the architects chose to model the Berkeley City Hall
not on an actual French Renaissance building–
itself harkening back to ancient Rome—but
on Victor Laloux's neo-Renaissance Hotel de
Ville, in Tours, France. For this West Coast
version, the sugary ornamentation is toned
down, but the Gallic slanting roof and cupola
crown are maintained. *2134 Martin Luther
King, Jr. Way, Berkeley*

101 Berkeley Public Library (1930)
James Plachek
The concrete building features a welter of
art-deco ornamentation, including pylons
topped with Mayan-inspired capitals and
chevrons atop the windows. *2090 Kittridge
St., Berkeley*

107. Lawson House (Maybeck)

102 House (1935)
John Dinwiddie
A curving balcony and glass-block windows bring out the qualities of the streamline moderne. *95 Parnassus Rd., Berkeley*

103 House (1957)
Beverly Thorne
Four steel I-beams, mounted on a couple of thin concrete-block walls, support the L-shaped house. The C-shaped driveway is located under the redwood-clad house and behind a curved wall. *1545 Campus Dr., Berkeley*

104 Keeler House (1895)
Bernard Maybeck
Among the architect's earliest works is this house for the Arts and Crafts theorist Charles Keeler. Many prototypical aspects of style are apparent: a steeply pitched roof, redwood plank siding, exposed beams, and a prominent chimney. *1770 Highland Pl., Berkeley*

105 Beta Theta Pi Fraternity House (1893-94)
Ernest Coxhead
One of the first Bay Region designs is this exaggerated asymmetrical composition. Clad in contrasting stucco and shingles, the four steeply gabled sections suggest the appearance of a townscape in a single building. *2607 Hearst Ave., Berkeley*

106 Maurer Studio (1907)
Bernard Maybeck
Varied decorative elements can be discerned, from the Mission Revival, Gothic, Classic, and Japanese. The entrance, framed by a classical column, is also recessed behind a tiled gable roof. *1772 Le Roy Ave., Berkeley*

107 Lawson House (1907)
Bernard Maybeck
For his first reinforced concrete house, Maybeck designed what looks life, from a distance, to be an austere planar composition, relieved only by circular windows and an arched porch. Closer in, however, one sees diamond-shaped patterns and necklaces of stone tiles inset into the concrete. *1515 La Loma Ave., Berkeley*

108 Boke House (1902)
Bernard Maybeck
Except for the absence of heraldic shields, this house possesses the defining qualities of a Swiss chalet - prominent projecting gables, rough-cut lumber, and jig sawn detailing. The rustic wallboards send out numerous projections, including bay windows, porches, balconies, and eaves. *23 Panoramic Way, Berkeley*

109 Greenwood Common (1952)
William Wurster/Lawrence Halprin
A circuit of small houses surround a central park overlooking the bay. The designs are by some of the best architects then working in the Bay Area, including: Donald Olsen (#1), Joseph Esherick (#3), Harwell Hamilton Harris (#4), R.M. Schindler (#7), Henry Hill (#9), and John Funk (#10). All the buildings

109. Greenwood Commons

feature smooth redwood surfaces, crisp corners, asymmetrical massing, and flat or shed roofs. On the Olsen house, four steel columns support a cantilever over a carport; the entrance is reached over a small bridge. The Funk house is divided into two volumes which connect via an entrance corridor; At this point, the downward sloping roofs flatten and transform into a wooden trellis. *Berkeley*

110 Howard House (1912)
John Galen Howard
When it came to domestic living, the Beaux-Arts architect's preferences ran toward a bent L-shaped building whose base is clad in stucco and whose upper floors are pure redwood. *1401 Le Roy Ave., Berkeley*

111 House (1958)
Charles Warren Callister
The architect crafted a Japanese look via stucco spandrels set in wooden frames and a roof pitch that suggests a Shinto shrine. Elsewhere, the walls alternate nicely between vertical redwood boards and horizontal lines of poured concrete. *2637 Rose St., Berkeley*

112 Rowell House (1915)
John Hudson Thomas
On a street lined with redwood trees and redwood homes, this house exemplifies the Arts and Crafts language of woodsy building. Faced in stone, stucco, and redwood, the house exposes timber framing around the entrance, windows and roof, where brackets support the gables. *149 Tamalpais Rd., Berkeley*

113 Mathewson Studio House (1915)
Bernard Maybeck
Two dominant gables are supported by a visible structure of braces and beams articulated in a vaguely Japanese manner. Other nearby Maybecks are: Sack House (1924), *2711 Buena Vista Way;* Tufts House (1931) *2733 Buena Vista Way;* Wallen House (1933) *2751 Buena Vista Way. 2704 Buena Vista Way, Berkeley*

114 Boynton House (1911)
A.R. Monroe, Bernard Maybeck (1924), Clarence & Edna Dakin
The original "Temple of the Wings" was a Greco-Roman Temple without walls; A ring of 32 reinforced-concrete Corinthian columns formed two half-circular porches.

112. Rowell House (Thomas)

After the 1923 Fire, all that remained were the columns, which were incorporated into the present building. *2800 Buena Vista Way, Berkeley*

115 Hume House (1927)
John Hudson Thomas
This irregular grouping of red tile-roofed buildings around a courtyard recalls a Spanish medieval castle, especially given the buttressed walls along the street. *2900 Buena Vista Way, Berkeley*

116 McCue House (1968)
Gerald McCue
The design of this two-story house runs counter to the sprawling rusticity common to the Berkeley hills. Echoing his firm's (McCue, Boone, Tomsick) industrial buildings, sleek colors and right angles lend the house the feeling of a manufactured object. The gray-stained wooden cladding adds to the machine-metallic appeal. *2902 Buena Vista Way, Berkeley*

117 Murphy-Rosenthal House (1997)
Stanley Saitowitz
A fan-shaped lot led to the building's gracious curve. From the street, the row of horizontal windows–with blinders—appears to float atop an open-air parking space and dissolve within the tropical vegetation. *1145 Oxford St., Berkeley*

118 Olsen Residence (1952)
Donald Olsen
This sharp-edged and largely-glazed white house is set atop steel piers and juts out into a grove of laurel trees. The drama of gravity is enhanced as well by a side balcony cantilevered over a creek. *771 San Diego St., Berkeley*

118. Olsen Residence (Olsen)

119 Kip House (1956)
Donald Olsen
Several levels are squeezed into this white box, faced with generous glass curtain walls, a projecting front balcony, and primary-color accents. *775 San Diego St., Berkeley*

120 House (1954)
Joseph Esherick
Atop the Grizzly Peak ridge, Esherick extrudes the landscape contours on the house's gently pitched roofs. Below, over-hanging eaves and pergolas lend a Japanese feeling. *2727 Marin Ave., Berkeley*

121 House (1955)
Donald Olsen
Almost the entire two-story façade is faced in glass. The entry sits upon a concrete plinth covered by an overhang. *1366 Brewster Dr., El Cerrito*

122 House (1948)
Richard Neutra
Facing a golf course, this L-shaped house exhibits one of Neutra's first uses of floor-to-ceiling glass for the garden side picture window—visible from below on Arlington Boulevard. *1411 Atwell Dr., El Cerrito*

123 Mira Vista School (1951)
John Carl Warnecke
The folded roof may have been inspired by a rock outcropping above the school, but is consistent with the architect's interest in sculptural form. *6397 Hazel Ave., Richmond*

124 Rubin House (1960)
George Homsey
The two-story house is clad in shingles and punctured by asymmetrical windows and bays. An enclosed staircase climbs the north side of the structure. *899 Hillside St., Albany*

125 Smith House (1984)
Thomas Gordon Smith
For an otherwise modest tract home, Smith crafts the kind of lavish classical entryway one would expect on a Hollywood back lot. Pairs of mustard-yellow Tuscan columns support a wooden pergola, behind which is a marble and limestone revetment. *5445 Sacramento Ave., Richmond*

126 Ford Motor Company Plant (1931)
Albert Kahn
By the time he designed this factory, Kahn had completed designs for fifty different factories, most of them producing automobiles and most of them contracted by the

Ford Motor Company. Here the two-story, steel-frame structure supports brick curtain walls and industrial window sash. Sawtooth roof trusses provide skylights for the large production floorplate. Operations ceased in 1956 and the building awaits conversion to a historical park. *1414 Harbor Way South, Richmond*

127 Civic Center (1951)
Milton & Timothy Pflueger

After the city's wartime boom, six blocks were combined into a superblock that contains the City Hall, Hall of Justice, Auditorium and Art Center, and Library. The red brick and glass-curtain wall slabs are arranged around a spacious plaza. At the time, the *Architectural Forum* described that even if downtown Richmond was a mile away, the city's dynamic growth would soon swallow up the Civic Center in an expanded business district. Things turned out quite differently for the struggling city. *2540 Barrett Ave, Richmond*

128 Kaun House (1934–1935)
R.M. Schindler

A terrace separates two parts of the L-shaped compound, a garage/studio and the living quarters. The redwood house was one of the first to use sliding glass doors to ease movement toward outdoors and beach. Up the street (at 215 Western Dr.) parts of William Wurster's 1936 concrete-block

129. Al Zampa Memorial Bridge

house are visible, and a look uphill reveals the horizontal strip windows of Donald Olsen's (221 Bishop Dr.) house from 1957. *125 Western Dr., Richmond*

129 Al Zampa Memorial Bridge (2003)

Spanning the Carquinez Straight between Crockett and Vallejo, the westward lanes of traffic on Interstate 80 now cross over one of the few suspension bridges built in the United States since the 1970s. The bridge was named after Al Zampa, the only man to have worked on the first two Carquinez bridges, the Bay Bridge, and the Golden Gate Bridge. The towers are reinforced concrete portal frames with cellular shafts. Eastbound lanes use a steel-truss cantilever bridge, constructed in 1958.

130 Mare Island Naval Shipyard.

In 1854, the first U.S. Naval Base on the West Coast opened on this narrow island in Vallejo. During the Second World War, the 5,500-acre base turned out scores of ships and submarines. The base closed in 1996. The rich trove of architecture includes residences from the Victorian and Spanish-Revival eras, modern barracks housing, and a cornucopia of industrial buildings; most impressive is the waterfront facing the downtown of Vallejo, with its drydocks, cranes, and ship repair and assembly buildings. *Vallejo*

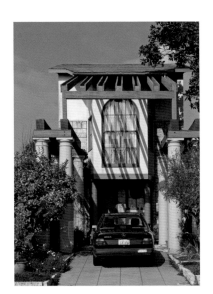

125. Smith House (Smith)

North Bay

The North Bay Counties of Marin, Sonoma, and Napa have long retained a more rural feeling than the rest of the Bay Area. Southern Marin County was developed by a combination of railroads–starting with the North Pacific Coast Railroad in 1875–and extensive ferry links to San Francisco from towns like Sausalito, Belvedere, and Larkspur. Most development, however, has been vehicular, spurred by the opening of the Golden Gate Bridge in 1938 and the Richmond/San Rafael Bridge in 1956. While schemes to run freeways and subdivisions to West Marin were never realized, the corridor along Highway 101 has urbanized intensively. Bedroom communities line the freeway all through Marin and continue in Sonoma County north of Santa Rosa. Napa County, and to an only slightly lesser extent, Sonoma County have also become international tourism destinations. Wineries, gourmet restaurants, spa resorts, and estate homes sprinkle the vine-covered valleys and hillsides.

Marin Civic Center (Wright)

4. Gerhardt Residence (Mack)

1 Headlands Center for the Arts (1907)
In 1987, five artists/architects–Ann Hamilton, David Ireland, Mark Mack, John Randolph & Bruce Tomb–contributed to the renovation of Building 944 of the former army barracks. Among the additions was a steel, unisex latrine. In 1999, artist Leonard Hunter and architect Mark Cavagnero renovated Building 960. *944 Fort Barry, Sausalito*

2 Owens House (1939)
Gardner Dailey
This pioneering glass curtain wall runs two stories and provides sweeping views of the bay. The compact house illustrates Dailey's spatial economy–i.e., short or non-existent hallways. *39 Atwood Ave, Sausalito*

3 Campbell Hall, Christ Episcopal Church (1966)
Henrik Bull
The parish hall overlooks an upper-level terrace and pergola. *Santa Rosa & San Carlos Aves., Sausalito*

4 Gerhardt Residence (1987, 1992)
Batey Mack
This house presents an opaque roadside view, a taut wall interrupted only by a yellow door that looks like Ice Station Zebra. On the view side, by contrast, a glass curtain wall alternates with gray stucco and yellow-stained siding. The shed roof is made from corrugated metal. *8 Wolfback Ridge Rd., Sausalito*

5 Kaplan Residence (1949)
Mario Corbett
The house takes its shape from the fan-shaped ridge. A massive beam slants up to rest on a fin wall, dividing the deck and providing a windbreak. Other later shingled houses by Corbett are located nearby at 17, 19, 23, 27, & 31 Wolfback Ridge Road. *Wolfback Ridge Terrace, Sausalito*

6 House (1953)
Charles Warren Callister
The final stretch of Currey Lane contains a series of superb mid-century houses, characterized by: rectangular volumes, smooth

Map 16 Marin County

171

NORTH BAY

MAP
16

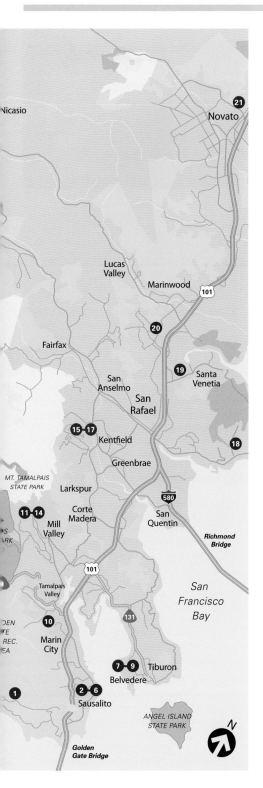

redwood siding, flat or angled roofs, clear or smoked-glass clerestories on the street side, large plate-glass windows facing the bay. A fine example is Henrik Bull design at 290 Currey Lane, viewed best from down below on Toyon Lane. Callister came up with the gem on the block; here, an angular roof, overhanging eaves, decks, and projecting glass windows all contribute to a sublime crystalline geometry. *250 Currey Ln., Sausalito*

7 First Church of Christ Scientist (1952)
Charles Warren Callister
This diamond-shaped church, crowned by a thin spire, offers one of the most pleasing harmonies of concrete and wood anywhere, as evidenced especially by the adjacent grains of weathered concrete and redwood. Likewise, much of the exterior consists of concrete (and occasionally) redwood piers that frame redwood and leaded-glass bays. Inside the light effects from skylights, clerestories, and the clear/colored-glass bays are ethereal. *San Rafael Ave. at Laurel St., Belvedere*

8 Rey House (1893)
Willis Polk
The pseudo-Mediterranean estate rises from its commanding site as a picturesque mass, clad in stucco, projecting a dramatic wooden porch, and covered with a red tile roof. The hillside promontory site is one of the most dramatic in the entire Bay Area. *428 Golden Gate Ave., Belvedere*

7. First Church of Christ Scientist (Callister)

9 McLeod House (1962)
Joseph Esherick

As Charles Moore wrote in *Architectural Forum* (April 1965), "there is the sense that the architect plunged down the steep hill past the oak to the marine view, gobbled it all up and brought forth the house in chunks of light and outlook." Esherick himself felt the rooms of the house were like the carriages of a train, each offering changing perspectives. *11 Crest Rd., Belvedere*

10 Fernwood Cemetery (1973)
Skidmore Owings & Merrill

Two long concrete walls, 20 feet high and completely solid, enclose a corridor of spaces lit by parallel tracks of skylights. At one end, the chapel's wood-coffered ceiling forms a particularly effective contrast to the stout walls. *301 Tennessee Valley Rd., Mill Valley*

10. Fernwood Cemetery (SOM)

11 Outdoor Art Club (1905)
Bernard Maybeck

Ingeniously, Maybeck extended the internal structure of posts and roof beams outside of the interior volume so that they function as a decorative framework atop the façade. Along with the façade the supports are clad in redwood shingles. The interior truss-roof framework is particularly noteworthy. *One W. Blithedale Ave., Mill Valley*

12 Mill Valley Library (1969)
Wurster, Bernardi & Emmons

Set along a creek in a redwood grove, Wurster crafted an homage to Maybeck's nearby Art Club. The gable-roofed structure covers a much larger area and adds concrete as a principal constructional and cladding member. Steel-sash windows project through the roof as glazed dormers, creating a vertical rhythm on the exterior. *375 Throckmorton Ave., Mill Valley*

13. Cary House (Esherick)

13 Cary House (1960)
Joseph Esherick

A fairly simple box covered by a shed roof is enlivened by several projecting trellises and decks as well as window and door frames painted deep orange. The projecting saddle-bag window, which not only offered a view out but also modulated the lighting of the house, was quite influential. *One Rider Ln., Mill Valley*

14 Pence House (1962)
Marquis & Stoller

Four hip-roofed pavilions cast a striking profile along a ridge below Mount Tamalpais. The Japanese feeling is enhanced by translucent fiberglass partitions that enclose a small courtyard. *4 Walden Ln, Mill Valley (See pg 4)*

15 Stebbins House (1959)
Jack Hillmer

In this tour-de-force house, roof beams expand from a fireplace to form a triangular grid. The lapped board railing of the balcony extends to the living room. Steel-supported cantilevers carry the bedroom balcony over the carport. *75 Upland Rd., Kentfield*

16 Hall House (1947)
Hillmer & Callister

The living room extends as a deck on a floating cantilever. Inverted triangular braces support the carport roof. *405 Goodhill Rd., Kentfield*

17 Sky Arc House (2004)
Will Bruder

Clad in pewter-gray zinc, translucent fiberglass awnings provide protection from the sun. The main sitting room expands to a cantilevered wood deck framed by perforated metal railings. *One Ravine Way, Kentfield*

19. Marin County Civic Center (Wright)

18 Harrison House (1960)
Beverly Thorne

This Marin dwelling is the only representative (#26) of John Entenza's celebrated Case Study House movement built in the Bay Area. Setting a precedent for building on steep downward slopes, the main house volume lies under the carport and its steel angular roof. This roof hovers over the double-height living room, where light is admitted through abundant clerestory windows and sliding glass doors. Below, nine steel piers, resting in concrete caissons, hold up this "ranch in the sky," from whose open deck are afforded panoramic views. *177 San Marino Drive, San Rafael (See pg 174)*

14. Pence House (Marquis & Stoller)

19 Marin County Civic Center (1957–1972)
Frank Lloyd Wright

For his last major commission, Wright designed a complex that could both invigorate and ameliorate the new vehicular age. Bringing together all county offices and agencies in a single complex, the ¼ mile long building takes its model from the Roman aqueduct. Here rectangular masses bridge the site's rolling topography, spanning three valleys, under which run roads. As seen commonly from Highway 101, the sweeping arches translate the mobility of suburbia into a mobile form of architecture. The complex gives us a taste of what Broadacre City—Wright's vision for the multi-centered, low-density, auto-oriented suburb—could have been. The two great wings meet at a circular library, from which rises a pylon. Each wing is bisected by an atrium that ends in a sliced semi-dome. The roof is a lightweight concrete shell, decorated with circular motifs. Originally intended to be gold, Wright settled on a blue, rubber-based polymer paint sprayed on the surface. The blue roof atop the earth-toned stucco building perfectly complements the surrounding landscape in the long California dry season. *3501 Civic Center Dr., San Rafael*

Map 17 Napa & Sonoma Counties

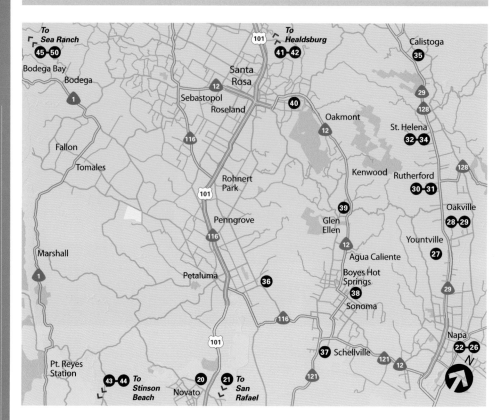

20 Christ Presbyterian Church (1959)
Campbell & Wong
An octagonal plan is covered by a folded roof and faced with plate glass windows. *620 Del Ganado Rd., San Rafael*

21 Buck Institute for Age Research (1999)
Pei, Cobb, Freed
Modernism's austerity and abstraction are appropriate for this attempt to explore the merciless paradox of life. Five buildings cluster around a hexagonal courtyard landscaped by Dan Kiley. Travertine stone shrouds the complex of sliced cylinders and rectangles. *8001 Redwood Blvd., Novato*

22 E. Wiler Churchill House (1892)
Ernest Coxhead
A picturesque silhouette is created by a huge barn-like roof, cut into by dormers and a giant cylindrical bay, and clad in herringbone brick panels and shingles. *486 Coombs St., Napa*

23 Copia: The American Center for Wine, Food and the Arts (2001)
James Polshek
Long stone and concrete walls provide a backdrop for the exhibition of wine and cuisine, and complement a working kitchen garden designed by Peter Walker. *500 First St., Napa*

24 Oxbow School (2003)
Stanley Saitowitz
Along the Napa River, the arts high school is set atop a five-foot plinth, just above flood stage. The long mass is broken up into discrete boxes separated by landscaped voids.

18. Harrison House (Thorne)

On the street side, the steel-framed boxes create a checkerboard of rectangular surfaces - some flush, others recessed, some clad in horizontal wood panels, others in vertical, some in small-pane glazing, others in expanses of plate glass. On the river's edge, the studio buildings are almost completely glazed. At ground level, their rollup glass doors open onto a continuous outdoor terrace that works as an outdoor room. The studios are filled with light and air and feature long views of the river and surrounding mountains. *530 Third St., Napa*

25 Kirlin House (1980)
Batey Mack
Surrounded by vineyards, the house is designed around an H-plan. Aside from the two courtyard entrances, the warm stucco walls appear fortress-like. *2456 Third Ave. Napa*

26 Munger House (1950)
Jack Hillmer
At the front, clerestory windows float between concrete-block walls and an origami-like roof. The garden side features glass walls set between wooden posts. *1111 Hilton Ave., Napa*

27 Napa Valley Museum (1998)
Fernau & Hartman
A rectilinear volume is clad in a variety of materials that differentiate the different functions of the museum: off-white cement panels for the galleries; a rust-colored Korten steel elevator; a lobby and store clad in wood; and a projecting balcony framed in red and orange steel. *55 Presidents Circle, Yountville.*

27. Napa Valley Museum (Fernau & Harman)

24. Oxbow School (Saitowitz)

28 Cakebread Cellars (1980)
William Turnbull

This large wooden composition was inspired by the scale and shape of barns in the valley. Beneath the gentle swells of the mountains, the built silhouette bursts skyward in out-croppings of gables, dormers, and turrets. *83 St. Helena Highway, Oakville*

29 Opus One Winery (1991)
Johnson, Fain & Pereira

Approached through a commanding entry drive lined with olive trees, the building rises out of the vineyard fields atop an earthen berm, takes on the forms of classical French architecture, and resolves as a redwood per-gola. This transition from earth to rusticated limestone (laden with arches, keystones, and engaged columns) elegantly ends in the cylindrical trellises, which recall the textures of the fields. *7900 St. Helena Highway, Oakville*

30 Dominus Winery (1998)
Herzog & de Meuron

The architects appropriate elements from the site to connect the straight geometries of the vineyards and the jagged shapes of the coastal ranges. The building consists of a long and low (two-story) box, bisected by two covered openings, that continues the horizontal line of the fields. A structure of concrete columns, beams, and tilt-up walls is covered in a remarkable skin of galvanized steel gabions (commonly used in river and highway engineering as retain-ing structures) filled with loose basalt rocks from the area. The caged stone provides a rain screen as well as thermal insulation. Although the cages are uniformly sized, three grades of mesh and three grades of stone size modulate their texture and the quality of light filtered through to the inte-rior. From a distance the stone-like struc-ture appears to rise out of the bare earth as an architectural plateau. *2570 Napanook Rd., Rutherford*

31 Berggruen House (1989)
Fernau & Hartman

This house looks like a rustic village of small vernacular structures. The L-shaped com-plex, inspired by California's ramshackle farmworker's housing, sports myriad materi-als—corrugated metal, both horizontal and vertical wood siding—, bright primary colors, and frequent projecting bays and gable roofs. *Bella Oaks Ln., Rutherford*

33. Lodi Bunkhouse (Ranieri)

32 Goldman House (1979)
Batey Mack

Nestled in the brow of a hill, this simple rectangle is clad in concrete block and industrial-sash windows and doors. A vine-threaded portico shields the entire front. *1065 Greenfield Rd., St. Helena*

33 Lodi Partnership Bunkhouse (2003)
Kuth Ranieri

For this conversion of a long industrial shed into residences the architects draped an exo-skeleton of fiberglass panels atop the exist-ing frame. *1085 Lodi Lane, St. Helena*

34 Zakin House (2005)
Stanley Saitowitz

Atop a podium, one hovering L-shaped bar rests its ends upon another grounded L-shaped bar, while several concrete piers sup-port the hovering volume. The right angles, rhythmic columns, and gravity-defying shapes work together to give measure to the irregular backdrop of the surrounding nature. *291 Crystal Springs North, St. Helena*

35 Clos Pegase Winery (1987)
Michael Graves

Graves won a 1984 competition, spon-sored by the San Francisco Museum of Modern Art, to design a winery, sculpture, garden, and hilltop residence. The winery is a postmodern extravaganza, powdered with blank rectangular niches, giant eyelid openings, warm colors, and a welter of regular geometries—squares, cylinders, cones, triangles. Irony abounds, such as the entrance portico split by a giant Tuscan column or the two chimneys at opposite ends that serve as fireplaces for the owner's office and dining room. On the production side of the building, a giant pediment is supported by squat columns and dominated by an over-scaled portico. *1060 Dunaweal Ln, Calistoga*

36 Petaluma Adobe State Park (1834-38)
The small site is all that remains of a vast tract of land, one of the largest ranchos in California history, once belonging to General Mariano Vallejo. The half-quadrangular structure is encircled by wooden verandas to protect the adobe bricks from moisture, and was constructed largely by Indian labor. *3325 Old Adobe Rd., Petaluma*

37 Cornerstone Festival of Gardens (2004)
The nine-acre site features a gallery of landscape garden designs, including: Martha Schwartz's mini-golf links narrating the history of landscape design; Claude Cormier's swathing of a tree with 70,000 sky-blue Christmas balls; and Tom Leader's straw bale enclosure of worn screen doors. *23570 Highway 21, Sonoma*

38 Meyer House (1990)
Stanley Saitowitz
This razor-sharp house reshapes both its site and its inhabitants. A ravine separates the master bedroom suite, atop a hill, from the main living area, on a separate promontory. The bridge that joins them, tartly expressed by red steel trusses, connects discrete realms of landscape and occupants. The house, understood as a machine of construction and experience, thus inscribes the divisions of domesticity in the ground and sky. *3880 Langtry Dr., Sonoma*

39 Knipshild Residence (1985)
Batey Mack
A cylinder with two wings encloses an entry courtyard. The severe, symmetrical cube

43. McDonald House (Saitowitz)

recalls the Euclidian formalism of Aldo Rossi. The postmodern feel continues in blank walls, deep-set windows, false fronts, and colors ranging from orange to purple to aquamarine. *880 Avora Ln., Glen Ellen*

40 Spring Lake Park Visitors Center (1993)
Obie Bowman
A glass and wood pyramid pops out of a forest of oaks and buckeyes. This experiment in green architecture rests on concrete retaining walls set below grade to reduce the building's profile and conserve energy. The steel frame supports insulated glass walls that can be covered by wooden louvers. Solar panels clad the south-east side. *391 Violetti Dr., Santa Rosa*

41 Frediani House (1955)
Mario Corbett
The entry pavilion, rotated at a 45-degree angle, brings an intriguing tension to this bar-shaped house. *Fitch Mountain Rd, Healdsburg*

42 Conrad-Shah Residence (2006)
Cary Bernstein
The shape of this simple ranch-type house is a response to the ridge upon which it sits. The plan twists around the ridge and the roof wriggles up and down with the land's undulations. *5555 Chemise Rd., Healdsburg*

43 McDonald House (1992)
Stanley Saitowitz
The roof on this vacation home resembles a crashing wave. Indeed, maritime motifs abound, such as the overall shape of the building into a ship's hull and prow, or the weathering of the redwood boards to a condition that looks like driftwood. *51 Dipsea Rd., Stinson Beach (Marin County)*

40. Spring Lake Park Visitors Center (Bowman)

44 **Wright Violich House** (2004)
Peter Pfau
Characteristic of the architect's residential work—as seen as well in 2001's Outside-In House in San Anselmo—is the design of living spaces as extension of the outdoors. For this small beach house, thin redwood walls and glass walls open up to the sea and surf. *Two Sonoma Patio, Stinson Beach (Marin County)*

45 **Condominium I** (1964)
Moore, Lyndon, Turnbull, Whittaker
The first demonstration project at Sea Ranch groups ten units tightly together in a windswept, dramatic meadow. It was constructed out of heavy timber posts and beams, and sheathed in vertical redwood boards that weathered over time to blend in with the rocks of the coast and the trunks of Monterey Cypress and Bishop Pine trees. Inhabitants view the marvelous scenery through varied architectural lenses, which include: large plate-glass windows, saddle-bag (or bay) windows, walled courts, and greenhouses. The form is both revolutionary and evolutionary. In one sense, the building can be understood as the shipwreck of Modernism, a convulsion of wind-washed boards and glass shards cast onto a meadow beyond the churning ocean. At the same time, Condominium I refracts the old barns and sheds on the site, and evokes images of traditional villages dug into sea cliffs or hillsides. As William Turnbull described Sea Ranch: "We took our clue from the simplicity and appropriateness of the (nearby) barn. Condominium 1 was formed around two courtyards: one to shelter the inhabitants and one to corral the cars." Despite its possession by the landscape, the smooth and angular forms rise to the level of artistic mastery. *Sea Ranch*

46 **Hedgerow Houses** (1966)
Joseph Esherick
As a counterpart to Condominium 1, Esherick sited these six demonstration houses closer to the protective wind barrier of the hedgerows. Instead of smooth, vertical redwood boards, the houses are clad in shingles, and several feature sod roofs. The roofs are angled to create wind-protected places, and their volumes are shaped to provide views in all directions. *Sea Ranch*

47 **Moonraker Athletic Club** (1966)
Moore, Lyndon, Turnbull, Whittaker
Three earthen berms and a north-facing wall block the wind from the sunken swimming pool. Held up by angled buttresses, the wall contains shed-roofed projections for changing rooms. Inside, the supergraphic shapes and letters were done by Barbara Stauffacher. In 1971, the Ohlsen Recreation Center replicated many of these features with a more sculptural diving structure. *Sea Ranch*

47. **Moonraker Athletic Club (Moore, Lyndon, Turnbull, Whittaker)**

48 **Hines House** (1968)
Moore, Lyndon, Turnbull, Whittaker
MLTW took advantage of a pitched site to carve a vertical patio between two blocks, a space that is both courtyard and stairway. Inside, the linear axis of circulation is expanded by projections (or saddlebags) for living areas. *Sea Ranch*

49 **Brunsell Residence** (1982)
Obie Bowman
Covered by a sod roof, this house integrates, Zen-like, with the ground of the flat meadow. A south-facing solarium affords passive solar energy. *Sea Ranch*

50 **Sterns Residence** (1993)
Obie Bowman
By placing bender boards beneath 1" x 12" redwood planks, the wood wraps gracefully over time and acquires the monumental appearance of the area's old barns. The house also featured Sea Ranch's first corrugated sheetmetal roof. *Sea Ranch*

Photo Credits

PRIMARY PHOTOGRAPHERS:
Pad McLaughlin
pages 4, 6, 10, 11, 13, 16, 23, 32, 35, 37, 39, 41, 42, 43, 47, 51, 80, 114 (bottom), 124, 126, 129 (right), 130, 132, 134, 136, 137 (top), 138, 139, 140 (top + bottom), 141 (bottom), 142 (bottom, left + right), 143 (top + bottom), 146 (top + bottom), 148 (top), 150, 151, 152, 153 (top + bottom), 154, 155, 156, 157 (bottom), 158 (bottom, right), 160 (top + bottom), 162, 164, 165, 166 (top + bottom), 167, 168, 169 (top + bottom), 170 (top + bottom), 171, 172 (top + bottom), 173, 174.

John Santoro
pages 8, 9 (top), 14, 15, 17, 18, 19 (top + bottom), 25 (left + right), 28, 29 (top + bottom), 38, 53, 55 (bottom), 62, 63, 64, ,67 (bottom), 68, 69, 72, 73, 74 (top + bottom), 75 (top + bottom), 76 (bottom), 77 (top), 79, 82, 83 (bottom), 84 (left + right), 85 (top), 86 (top + bottom), 87 (top), 88 (left + right), 90, 91, 92 (top + bottom), 93 (top), 94 (left + right), 95 (top + bottom), 100 (top + bottom), 102 (top + bottom), 103, 105 (top), 107, 108, 109, 110 (top), 111 (left + right), 112, 113 (top), 118 (left), 119 (top + bottom),122 (top),123 (top + bottom).

SUPPLEMENTAL PHOTOGRAPHERS:
Morley Baer
pages 44, 45, 178, 179.

Philip Banta
page 157 (top).

Obie Bowman
pages 45, 177 (bottom).

Lis Evans
pages 98, 105 (bottom).

Thom Faulders
page 59.

Fernau + Hartman
page 49, 175 (top).

Anne Fougeron
pages 104, 137 (bottom).

Santiago Giraldo-Tobón
pages 120, 125.

Tim Griffith
pages 56 (bottom), 129.

Tim Hursley
pages 78, 96, 118 (right), 129 (left), 142 (top).

Jim Jennings
pages 55 (top), 97, 159.

Jaime Kripke
page 116.

Kuth-Ranieri
pages 88 (bottom), 176.

Leddy Maytum, Stacey
pages 85 (bottom) ,93.

Nick Lehoux
page 83 (top).

Jane Lidz
pages 76 (top), 128.

David Duncan Livingston
page 56 (top).

Kava Massih
pages 148 (bottom), 158 (bottom, left).

Mathew Millman
page 115.

Ogrydziak/Prillinger
pages 57, 158 (top).

Michael Riordan
page 77 (bottom).

Stanley Saitowitz
pages 99 (left + right) 122 (bottom), 131, 175 (bottom), 177 (top).

Mitchell Schwarzer
pages 9 (bottom), 24 (bottom), 36, 147.

Craig Steely
page 117.

Ezra Stoller/Esto
page 66.

Studios Architecture
page 135 (top + bottom).

Sherman Takata
page 141 (top).

Bruce Tomb
page 127.

Marc Treib
page 31 (top + bottom).

UC Berkeley CED Environmental Design Archives
pages 20, 163.

ILLUSTRATIONS:
John Ellis Drawings
pages 24 (top), 26, 27, 65, 67 (top), 87 (bottom), 89 (bottom), 110 (bottom), 144.

Index

Notes